Understanding Digital Troubleshooting

Third Edition

Written by: Don L. Cannon, Ph.D.
Assoc. Prof of Electrical Engineering
University of Texas at Arlington

*With
contributions by:* Gerald Luecke, MSEE
Charles W. Battle
Ken M. Krone
Les Mansir
Pete Sanborn

SAMS

A Division of Macmillan Computer Publishing
11711 North College. Carmel. Indiana 46032 USA

This book was developed by:
The Staff of the Texas Instruments Information Publishing Center

Appreciation is expressed to:
Mike Henderson for his valuable contributions on isolating system faults using hardware and software techniques. Tektronix, Inc., Simpson Electric Co., John Fluke Mfg. Co., and Hewlett Packard Co. for supplying equipment photographs.

International Standard Book Number: 0-672-27337-3
Library of Congress Catalog Card Number: 91-60987

Trademarks

Table of Contents

Preface

As new systems emerge and older systems are being redesigned using digital techniques, there is an increasing need for individuals familiar with finding and repairing faults in digital systems. Such experience is valuable in servicing such systems in terms of both repair and preventative maintenance.

This book has been created for the reader who wants or needs to understand the techniques used in this fast emerging service related activity. It is directed at the person who may want to do repair on personal equipment as a hobby as well as at the person who may be considering entering the field as a career occupation. It will also be useful to persons designing digital systems to increase their awareness of how to make their designs more testable and repairable.

In order to accomplish these objectives the reader must understand basic engineering concepts and electronic fundamentals. The book is designed to provide this understanding using simple mathematics (addition, subtraction, multiplication, and division) and with no extensive background in circuit theory or engineering practice required. This information is provided in the first two chapters of the book.

Using the background information provided in Chapters 1 and 2, the basic approaches and techniques of troubleshooting are introduced in Chapter 3 for simple digital systems using simple and inexpensive test equipment. This information is specifically applied to the two main types of digital systems in Chapters 4 and 5. Chapter 4 covers troubleshooting combinational logic systems whose outputs are only a function of the present inputs to the system. Chapter 5 covers troubleshooting more complicated digital systems known as sequential systems whose outputs are a function of the present as well as past inputs to the system.

With the troubleshooting fundamentals covered in Chapters 3 through 5, the next three chapters deal specifically with troubleshooting subsystems found in computer systems. Chapter 6 considers problems that can occur in computer memories and how these problems can be detected. Chapter 7 deals with the techniques of troubleshooting problems in the input and output circuits of digital systems and computers. Chapter 8 considers problems that are due to signals arriving too early or too late to cause the proper system operation. These timing problems require specialized techniques and test equipment to properly identify problems and their cause and correction.

Chapter 9 deals with complex digital systems and troubleshooting techniques and equipment used with such systems. These techniques use some of the most sophisticated equipment available to analyze the behavior of complex systems such as powerful personal computers and their components. As more and more of such systems are placed in fewer integrated circuits, such circuits become very difficult to test. Chapter 10 shows how these very complex devices can be designed for testability and how these test structures can be used to determine if such components are faulty and need to be replaced. These topics are at the very forefront of modern system design and testing and will provide the reader with modern state of the art information on the techniques of digital system testing and troubleshooting.

It is hoped that the information presented in this book will be easily grasped by its readers and that these ideas will increase their appreciation of the operation and repair of modern digital systems. For owners of electronic systems (personal computers, televisions, etc.) this information should help them be aware of the problems associated with repairing or replacing parts of such systems. For designers of such systems, this information should help make them more aware of the need to make their designs testable and repairable.

D.L.C.

Digital System Fundamentals

ABOUT THIS BOOK

Even though semiconductor technology and integrated circuits have contributed to a much higher reliability for digital systems, there are still occasions when digital systems do not operate properly. When a digital system fails to operate properly, it is said to have a bug or a failure. The process of locating the fault is called troubleshooting or "debugging". In order to detect a trouble, bug, or failure in a digital system, the operation of digital systems must be understood. In order to understand the system operation, the operation of the components that make up the system must be known.

This book has been written to help understand digital systems and digital system component operation and to help locate faulty parts when a digital system fails. Its express purpose is to relate faulty system operation to faulty operation of the system part that caused the problem. Since the isolation of a system failure to a specific subsystem, component or part usually requires electrical measurements to be made at various points in the system, much of the component and system operation will be presented from a measurement viewpoint. The measurement information combined with techniques of isolation and elimination by logical reasoning provide the reader with the tools required to troubleshoot and repair modern digital systems. In addition, because basic digital system operation must be understood, the book provides an excellent review of digital systems for the reader.

ABOUT THIS CHAPTER

Digital system operation uses basic properties of electrical signals as digital system components are coupled together to form the system. This chapter is on digital system fundamentals. It not only reviews the basic properties of electrical signals, but also the basic operation of many digital components as well.

ELECTRICAL SIGNALS

Analog and digital are common types of electrical signals. Analog signals vary continuously in a smooth motion over time. Digital signals vary sharply between discrete voltage levels.

Most readers are aware of the fact that there are two general types of electrical signals; analog and digital. Signals that have continuously and smoothly varying amplitude or frequency are called analog signals. An analog signal may consist of variations in direct current (dc) or alternating current (ac). The digital signal is usually at one voltage level or another with only occasional and rapid changes or transitions between these two levels.

In most systems, the variations of the signal values or levels with time for either type of signal is related to system information. In fact, the principal use of electrical signals is to transfer information from one part of a system to another part or from one system to another system.

DC CIRCUITS

Measurement instruments used in testing circuits indicate readings by: changes in needle position over a scale (analog readings) or by discrete numbers on a digital display (digital readings).

A simple dc circuit is shown in *Figure 1-1a*. This circuit consists of only two resistors in series and a voltage source. Also shown are two basic measurement instruments that will be used in examples throughout the book. The ammeter indicates the measured electrical current value by the position of a needle on a calibrated current scale. This is an analog ammeter. The voltmeter indicates the measured electrical voltage value as a number on a digital display. This is a digital voltmeter. Both analog and digital meters are used in testing electrical circuits. This circuit and these instruments provide a basis for a review of the basic properties of electrical circuits.

The voltage source acts as a source of electrical power and provides the currents and the resultant voltage drops that appear throughout the circuit. Electrical voltage is the force that causes current to flow in an electrical circuit. Current flow is the flow of the negatively charged electrons in a material. Metallic conductors such as gold, silver, and copper have many free electrons so they have little resistance to the flow of current. Carbon has fewer free electrons and has a higher resistance; thus, many resistors such as those in *Figure 1-1a* are made from carbon.

Ohm's Law

Ohm's Law defines that the voltage drop across a resistor is proportional to the current through the resistor.

The basic relationship between the current that flows through a resistor and the voltage drop across the resistor is shown in *Figure 1-1b*. This relationship, where the voltage is equal to the current times the resistance value, is called Ohm's law. The resistance is expressed in units of ohms, the current is expressed in units of amperes, and the voltage drop is expressed in units of volts. The voltage drop across a resistor is directly proportional to the current through the resistor. The resistor consumes power by converting electrical power to heat. The amount of power consumed (dissipated) in a resistor can be calculated by any of the following where voltage is in volts, current is in amperes, and resistance is in ohms:

1. The voltage across the resistor multiplied by the current through the resistor,
2. The resistance of the resistor multiplied by the square of the current through the resistor, and
3. The square of the voltage across the resistor divided by the resistance of the resistor.

In the circuit of *Figure 1-1a*, E, the source voltage, is a constant value; therefore, the current flow is constant. Since the values are constant, a plot of the circuit voltages and currents versus time are straight horizontal lines as shown in *Figure 1-1c*. Such dc voltages and currents are important in verifying circuit operation even in high-speed digital systems.

Figure 1-1.
DC Circuit Fundamentals

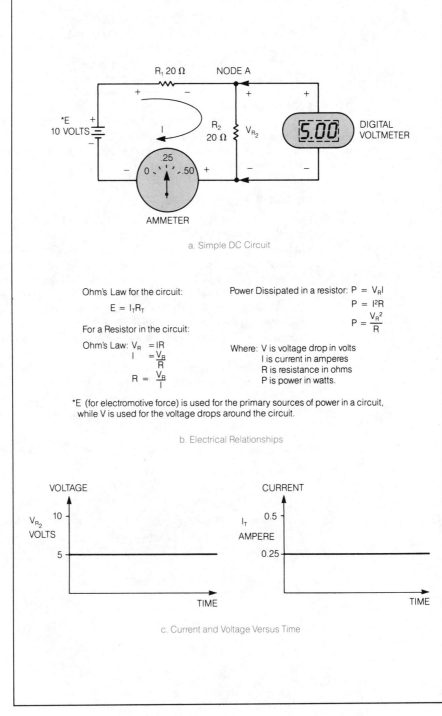

a. Simple DC Circuit

Ohm's Law for the circuit:

$$E = I_T R_T$$

For a Resistor in the circuit:

Ohm's Law: $V_R = IR$
$I = \dfrac{V_R}{R}$
$R = \dfrac{V_R}{I}$

Power Dissipated in a resistor: $P = V_R I$
$P = I^2 R$
$P = \dfrac{V_R{}^2}{R}$

Where: V is voltage drop in volts
I is current in amperes
R is resistance in ohms
P is power in watts.

*E (for electromotive force) is used for the primary sources of power in a circuit, while V is used for the voltage drops around the circuit.

b. Electrical Relationships

c. Current and Voltage Versus Time

Kirchhoff's Law

The current flowing out of a circuit node must equal the current flowing into it (Kirchoff's current law). Also, in a closed circuit, the sum of the voltage drops across all components in the circuit must be equal to the source voltage(s) (Kirchoff's voltage law).

In order to determine the current and voltage values in the circuit of *Figure 1-1a*, certain fundamental rules of circuit operation must be understood. The first of these rules is that the currents flowing into a connection of two or more wires or components must be equal to the currents flowing out of the connection. The connection point is known as a circuit node. The rule is known as Kirchhoff's current law after the man, Gustav R. Kirchhoff, who first stated the law.

Kirchhoff's voltage law is a similar rule that applies to electrical voltages. It requires that the sum of the voltages across all the components in a closed path around the circuit must be zero. Put another way, the source voltage applied to a circuit path must be equal to the sum of the voltage drops across the components in that path.

Calculations

The same current flows through all components in a series circuit. Multiplying this current by the total resistance in a resistive series circuit equals the total circuit voltage drop.

In *Figure 1-1a*, the closed path consists of the source voltage E and the resistors R_1 and R_2. The sum of the voltage drops across R_1 and R_2, indicated as V_{R_1} and V_{R_2}, must equal the value of the source E. Further, if the current through the voltmeter is assumed to be zero, the current flowing into node A from R_1 will flow out of the node into R_2 and back through the ammeter to the source E. In other words, the same current flows through the series circuit comprised of E, R_1, and R_2, as long as no current is flowing through the voltmeter. If this current is called I, the voltage across R_1 is IR_1 and the voltage across R_2 is IR_2; thus, the total voltage drop across R_1 and R_2 is $IR_1 + IR_2$. Said another way, the voltage drop across R_1 and R_2 is $I(R_1 + R_2)$; that is, I times the sum of R_1 and R_2. This voltage must equal the source voltage E; thus, $E = I(R_1 + R_2)$. Since $I = E/R_T$, the current in the circuit is found by:

$$I = 10/(20 + 20)$$
$$I = 10/40$$
$$I = 0.25 \text{ ampere}$$

Once this current is known, the voltage across R_2 can be computed by:

$$V = IR_2$$
$$V = 0.25 \times 20$$
$$V = 5 \text{ volts}$$

The voltmeter indicates 5 volts because it is measuring the voltage drop across R_2. Also, since R_1 is 20 ohms, the voltage drop across it is 5 volts, and the sum of the voltage drops equals the source voltage.

AC CIRCUITS

AC circuits have currents and voltages that change in polarity (whether they are plus or minus) with time. A common ac voltage is that available from the household power outlet. This voltage has a waveform as shown in *Figure 1-2b*. It is a sinusoid and is often called a sine wave. The circuit used in *Figure 1-1a* is repeated in *Figure 1-2a*, but now has a sinusoidal voltage source and ac measuring instruments. Meters that measure dc voltage will not measure ac voltage properly. AC meters must be used to measure ac voltage and currents.

Voltage

A sinusoidal voltage and current may be measured by either of the three values shown in *Figure 1-2b*. The peak value is measured from the zero reference to either the positive or negative peak. The peak-to-peak value is measured from the positive peak to the negative peak. For sinusoidal waveforms, the most commonly measured value is the root-mean-square (rms) value, which is the value that produces the same power dissipation in a resistor as a dc voltage of the same value.

The rms (root-mean-squared) value is just that — the square root of the average (mean) of a number of squared instantaneous values of a waveform.

The rms value is a calculated value. As shown in *Figure 1-2c*, the instantaneous values at several equally spaced points on the positive alternation are measured. Each of these values is squared and the squared values are added together. The sum of the squares is divided by the number of measurements to obtain the mean value. Finally, the square root of the mean is taken and the result is the rms value. For a sinusoid, the rms value is equal to 0.707 times the peak value. Conversely, the peak value is 1.414 times the rms value. The relationship between the rms value and the peak value is illustrated in *Figure 1-2b*.

Cycle

Two properties of an alternating repetitive waveform such as a sine wave are cycle and frequency. When a point on a waveform repeats itself, the waveform has gone through one cycle. Frequency is the number of cycles per second, now called hertz.

Another important property of the sinusoid is its cycle. The sinusoid cycle repeats a given number of times in a second. This is the frequency of the sinusoid, and is expressed in the unit hertz, where 1 hertz (Hz) equals 1 cycle per second. The time between similar points on the waveform is called the period, indicated in *Figure 1-2b* as T. The period is the reciprocal of the frequency; that is, 1 divided by the frequency. Thus, a sinusoid that repeats its cycle at 100 times per second has a frequency of 100 hertz and a period of 1/100 or 0.01 second. This period is more conveniently indicated as 10 thousandths of a second or 10 milliseconds.

Phase

The horizontal axis of the plot of a sinusoidal waveform also can be in electrical degrees. One cycle occurs in 360 degrees. With the horizontal axis in degrees, the phase of a waveform can be compared to a given reference point.

Comparisons of the way sinusoidal waveforms vary when plotted vs. time will provide a means of measuring the phase of the waveforms.

While the peak-to-peak, peak or rms current or voltage values can be used to compute circuit values, care must be taken to use the same units throughout any calculation.

Also, an input waveform can be compared to the output waveform resulting from that input and the phase delay between them can be measured. In *Figure 1-2d*, waveform B is delayed 90 degrees from waveform A. (The frequency of each waveform must be exactly the same in order to compare phases.)

Ohm's Law for AC

Since the circuit of *Figure 1-2a* contains only resistance, Ohm's law can be used for the computations of the currents and voltages. Either the peak value, the peak-to-peak value, or the rms value can be used for calculations, but the same unit must be used throughout. Most ac voltmeters and ac ammeters are calibrated in rms values. For the circuit in *Figure 1-2a*;

$$I_T = E / R_T \qquad\qquad V_{R2} = IR_2$$
$$= 10/40 \qquad\qquad = 0.25 \times 20$$
$$= 0.25 \text{ ampere rms} \qquad = 5 \text{ volts rms}$$

Thus, the ammeter indicates 0.25 ampere and the voltmeter indicates 5 volts. Again, it is assumed that no current flows through the voltmeter.

Figure 1-2.
AC Circuit Fundamentals

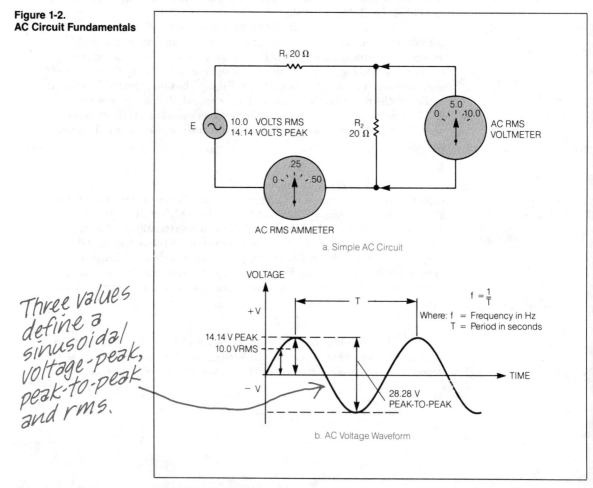

a. Simple AC Circuit

Three values define a sinusoidal voltage-peak, peak-to-peak and rms.

b. AC Voltage Waveform

Figure 1-2.
AC Circuit Fundamentals
(cont.)

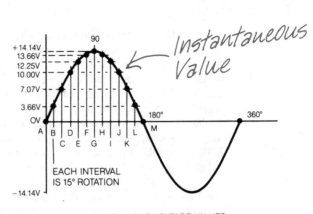

Instantaneous Value

EACH INTERVAL
IS 15° ROTATION

INSTANTANEOUS VOLTAGE VALUES
OF A VOLTAGE SINE WAVE

Degrees Rotation	Point	Instantaneous Voltage Value (Volts)	Square of Instantaneous Voltage (Volts²)
0	A	0.0	0.0
15	B	3.66	13.396
30	C	7.07	49.985
45	D	10.00	100.000
60	E	12.25	150.063
75	F	13.66	186.596
90	G	14.14	199.939
105	H	13.66	186.596
120	I	12.25	150.063
135	J	10.00	100.000
150	K	7.07	49.985
165	L	3.66	13.396
180	M	0.0	0.0

TOTAL = 1200.009

MEAN = $\dfrac{1200}{12}$ = 100

$V_{RMS} = \sqrt{100} = 10V$

$10\ V_{RMS} \div 14.14 V_{PEAK} = 0.707$

c. RMS Calculation

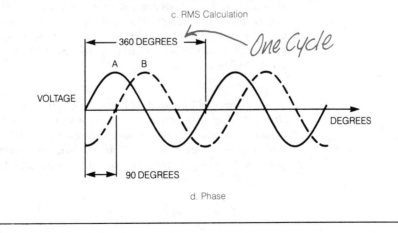

One Cycle

360 DEGREES

A   B

VOLTAGE

DEGREES

90 DEGREES

d. Phase

COMPLEX SIGNALS

Analog Signals

An analog signal can be a combination of several different sinusoidal waveshapes.

In order for either dc or ac voltage to carry information, some part of the signal must be related to the information. For example, ten different values of dc voltage could represent ten different numbers. Ten different frequencies of sinusoidal voltage could be used for the same purpose. Similarly, a large number of sinusoids of different frequencies and voltage amplitudes could be added together to produce any desired signal waveshape. The waveform shown in *Figure 1-3* represents such a signal. This is an analog signal in that the signal amplitude varies continuously from one value to another with respect to time. Different combinations of the component sinusoids cause different waveshapes. When the many different sinusoids produced by the instruments and voices of an orchestra and choral group are picked up by microphones and converted to electrical signals which are added together, the resulting waveform has a very complicated shape and is continually varying. Such signals can be sent over long distances using telephone lines or radio signals and reproduced as sound at the receiving point.

Digital Signals

Digital signals represent information in a coded form using voltage levels to represent the binary values of 0 or 1, in different combinations. The transition between voltage levels is ignored when identifying the 0 or 1 states.

The same information also can be represented by digital signals if some coding method is used. (Digital codes will be discussed later.) A digital signal also varies with time, but the signal levels occur within one of two voltage ranges to represent the binary values 0 or 1, as shown in *Figure 1-4a*. When the signal is at the voltage or current level that represents the 1 value, a logic 1 occurs, and when the signal is at the voltage level that represents the 0 value, a logic 0 occurs. Of course, transitions (changes) must occur between 0 and 1 levels, but the digital system must be designed so that the voltage level is ignored during transitions from a 0 to a 1 or vice versa. The level of voltage that represents a logic 0 or 1 depends on the type of devices used in the digital circuits. This will be explained a little later.

MEASURING COMPLEX SIGNALS

Usually the variations in the voltage levels of digital and non-sinusoidal analog signals occur at a very high speed so that it is not possible to determine the characteristics of the signal with simple voltmeters and ammeters. In order to examine and measure these rapidly varying signals and complex waveforms, special test instruments must be used. One of these is the oscilloscope.

Oscilloscope

The oscilloscope displays the plot of the signal amplitude versus time as the signal is actually occurring, even if the signal only lasts for a few millionths or billionths of a second. It is connected to the circuit in much the same way as a voltmeter and can be used to measure amplitude, period, and phasing. The measurements of interest are made from the plots displayed on

**Figure 1-3.
Non-sinusoidal Analog
Signal**

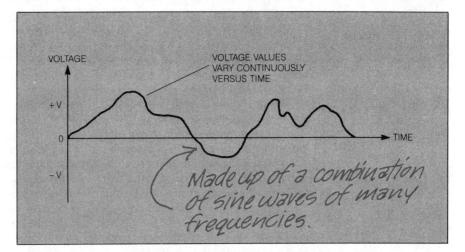

**Figure 1-4.
Digital Signal**

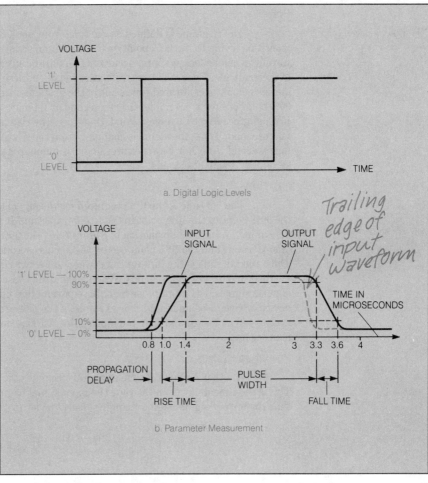

The oscilloscope is a special test instrument for viewing digital and analog signals. Time variation details of these electrical signals are displayed on a CRT, enabling signal parameters such as amplitude, period, and phase to be measured.

the screen or face of the oscilloscope cathode-ray tube (CRT) rather than reading the position of a needle on an analog meter or the numbers displayed on a digital voltmeter. A grid, called a graticule, over the screen in combination with calibrated controls permits accurate measurements. The oscilloscope works much like a home television receiver except it displays plots of electrical signals instead of pictures.

By properly adjusting the oscilloscope controls, very fine details of electrical signals can be examined. For example, by making the time scale small enough, the first pulse shown in *Figure 1-4a* will look like the one shown in *Figure 1-4b*. In fact, all digital signals exhibit the features shown in *Figure 1-4b* when the time scale has been reduced enough so that the time required to actually change the voltage from a 0 to a 1 level and back can be determined. One important measure of a digital circuit is how fast it can respond to a signal input that forces it to change from a logic 0 to a logic 1 or vice versa. These times are shown in *Figure 1-4b* as the rise and fall time, respectively. The rise and fall time measurements can be made easily once the digital waveform is shown as indicated in *Figure 1-4b*.

Rise Time

The time required to go from the 10% point to the 90% point on a waveform's 0 to 1 transition is the rise time.

The rise time is defined as the time from the 10% point on the transition swing to the 90% point on the transition swing. These points on the waveform can be located fairly accurately on the amplitude calibration lines of the graticule. Then, the time difference between these two points can be measured on the calibrated time scale of the graticule. In *Figure 1-4b*, the 90% point occurs at 1.4 millionths of a second or 1.4 microseconds and the 10% point occurs at 1.0 microsecond; therefore, the rise time is 1.4 - 1.0 or 0.4 microsecond. Thus, the signal is changing from the 0 level to the 1 level in 0.4 microsecond. Another way of expressing this number is as 400 billionths of a second, or 400 nanoseconds.

Fall Time

The fall time of a waveform is the time from the 90% to the 10% point on the 1-to-0 transition.

The fall time is the time required for the signal level to fall from the 90% point to the 10% point in the 1-to-0 transition. It also can be easily determined from the information in *Figure 1-4b*. The 90% point occurs at 3.3 microseconds and the 10% point occurs at 3.6 microseconds on the time scale. Thus, the fall time is the difference between these two times, which is 0.3 microsecond or 300 nanoseconds. When measuring these and other parameters of pulse signals, the input pulse must have parameters better than those of the device or circuit being tested. For example, if the device under test has a rise time of 400 nanoseconds, then the input pulse rise time must be less than 400 nanoseconds.

Propagation Delay

Another important time in digital circuits is the propagation delay. This is the time delay from the time the input signal begins changing until the time the output signal begins changing. Each device in a circuit as well as

Digital circuits have propagation delay — the time
it takes for a signal change
to travel from input to output. Such delays accumu-
late as the signal passes
from circuit to circuit.

the wiring between them has some propagation delay. Since the delay of each device adds to the delay of every other device as the signal passes through several devices, the total delay can be significant in circuits that have critical timing. This will be discussed in detail in a later chapter.

Propagation delay is measured from the 10% point on the input pulse to the 10% point on the output pulse as shown in *Figure 1-4b*. In this example, the propagation delay is 1.0 - 0.8 = 0.2 microsecond or 200 nanoseconds.

Transfer Characteristic

The transition (change) time between logic levels and the threshold voltage for the logic levels are important. The transition can be plotted as a function of time to show how fast or slow the circuit is in making this change. The change can be described on a graph as shown in *Figure 1-5* for a given circuit type where the output voltage is plotted as a function of the input voltage. This plot is called the transfer characteristic of the device.

The transition between
the 0 and 1 logic levels determines the speed of op-
eration of the circuit.

Ideally, for digital operation, the voltage curve should show a sudden change from one level to another at some point, called the logic threshold, halfway between the 0 and 1 logic levels. Practically, there is some small amount of slope in the curve in the transition region. Generally, an input or output level is considered to be at the logic 0 level if it is below the level that begins the entry into the sloping part of the transfer curve. In *Figure 1-5*, this is any input voltage less than 0.8 volt, with a typical value being 0.4 volt. Similarly, a logic 1 input occurs when the input voltage is above (to the right of) the sloping part of the transfer curve. In *Figure 1-5*, a 1 is shown to be above 2.0 volts, with a typical level of 2.4 volts. The center point of the slope in the transition region is considered to be the logic threshold. In this example, it is 1.4 volts.

**Figure 1-5.
Typical Transfer
Characteristics**

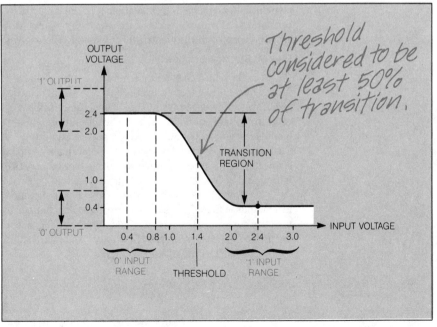

Device Families

The values given above are the typical values associated with the popular TTL (Transistor Transistor Logic) family of devices. However, the voltage levels for logic 1 and 0 vary considerably from one logic family to another and the levels for the three important logic families are shown in *Figure 1-6*. The TTL levels, repeated from *Figure 1-5*, show that both logic levels are represented by positive voltages. In contrast, the ECL (Emitter Coupled Logic) family has a threshold of 0 volts. A 1 level is represented by any voltage greater than 0.2 volt with a nominal 1 level of 0.4 volt. A 0 is represented by any voltage more negative than -0.2 volt, with a nominal level of -0.4 volt.

The CMOS (Complementary Metal Oxide Semiconductor) family is much different from the ECL family. CMOS inverters and gates have an almost ideal (square) transfer characteristic (sudden change in voltage in the transition region) with the logic levels being a function of the power supply voltage used. Generally, the threshold is one-half the power supply voltage. In *Figure 1-6*, the values shown are for a CMOS inverter or gate operating with a power supply of 5 volts. The threshold is 2.5 volts, the 1 range is from 3.5 volts up to 5 volts, and the 0 range is from 0 to 1.5 volts.

Signal Distortion

Real digital signals in operating circuits rarely have the perfect rectangular shape as shown in *Figure 1-4a*. A waveform more likely to be found in real circuits is shown in *Figure 1-7a*. Notice that the signal goes through the transition region, but overshoots the desired 1 or 0 level. It then returns toward the desired level, but again overshoots in the other direction. This oscillation around the desired value, called ringing, continues until the signal finally settles down to the desired value. Ringing is caused by energy storage elements (inductance and capacitance) in the circuits. In fact, the rise and fall time effects of *Figure 1-4b* also are caused by energy storage elements in circuit wiring or in the electrical components themselves.

Energy Storage Elements

Capacitance in a device or circuit stores energy in an electrostatic field. This stored energy resists change in voltage and tries to hold the voltage level constant at the stored value. Capacitance is what causes the gradual rise or fall in voltage levels at any node or measurement point within the circuit. A manufactured component called a capacitor sometimes is used in circuits for the purpose of storing energy; however, even if a component capacitor is not connected in the circuit, some capacitive storage exists in the interconnecting wiring and between elements of devices such as transistors.

The interconnecting wiring also has inductance which stores energy in a magnetic field. This stored energy resists changes in current and tries to hold the current in the wire at a constant level. Thus, the energy stored in the magnetic field causes current flow to continue for a short time after the controlling current has stopped.

**Figure 1-6.
Signal Levels of Three
Logic Families**

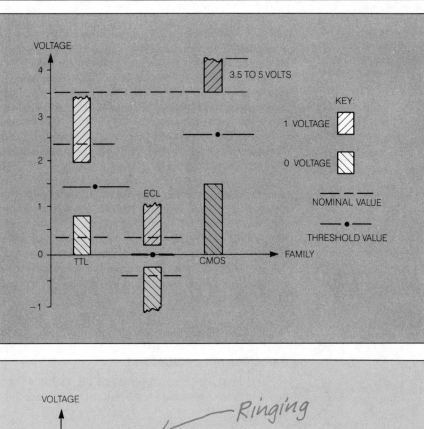

**Figure 1-7.
Undesirable Digital
Signals**

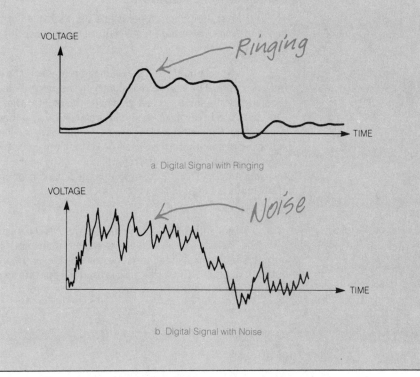

a. Digital Signal with Ringing

b. Digital Signal with Noise

Noise

Noise signals riding on
digital levels can cause a
system to respond in er-
ror, disrupting the sys-
tem's operation.

The waveform in *Figure 1-7b* shows noise (voltage that has a random magnitude) added to the desired digital signal. In a circuit containing transistors capable of switching very fast, each of the large up and down swings might cross the logic threshold and be interpreted as a separate 0 or 1 signal value. Thus, the system would think the signal had changed several times instead of only once, which of course, would upset system operation. To insure reliable system operation, either the circuits must be made so that they do not respond to the noise portion of the signal, or the noise must be minimized, or both. These factors will receive considerable attention in the later chapters of this book.

How a circuit responds to a ringing or noisy signal depends a great deal on the type of devices used. As discussed earlier, there are several different types of digital circuits or logic families currently used in digital systems. The key differences between device types are related to the components they use and the operating voltage levels. These factors affect the rise time, the fall time, the propagation delay, the voltage range for logic 0, the voltage range for logic 1, the immunity of the device to noise voltages, and the currents that flow into and out of the devices under 0 and 1 signal conditions. These properties and the basic features of the common logic families will be examined in detail in Chapter 3. Regardless of which logic family is used in a digital system, certain basic digital operations are available in each. These operations will be considered next.

BASIC DIGITAL OPERATIONS

Most digital logic operations are performed by combinations of four logic functions: Inversion, AND, OR, and Exclusive OR.

Inverter

An inverter's output logic level is always opposite the input logic level. If the input is 1, the output is 0, and vice versa.

The schematic or logic diagram symbol for the inverter is shown in *Figure 1-8a*. The small circle shown on the output indicates inversion. (Sometimes the small circle is shown on the input rather than the output.) The operation in terms of logic values of 0 or 1 also is shown in the truth table in *Figure 1-8a*. The truth table is used to summarize the logic functions of digital gates and elements. It describes the state of the output for any combination of input states. As can be seen from this table, the operation of the inverter is as its name implies; that is, the output is the inversion or opposite of the input. If the input is a logic 0, the output is a logic 1.

AND Gate

The output of an AND gate will only be a logic 1 if *both* inputs are logic 1, any other inputs will result in logic 0 outputs.

The truth table and symbol for the AND gate are shown in *Figure 1-8b*. The basic operation of the gate can be summarized by saying that a 1 output will occur only if all inputs are at the 1 level. If any input is at a 0, the output will be a 0. Thus, this gate is used to generate an output only if all required input conditions are met.

Figure 1-8.
Basic Digital Operations

INPUTS	OUTPUT
0	1
1	0

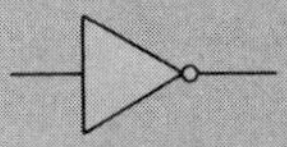

a. Inverter Truth Table and Symbol

INPUTS		OUTPUT
A	B	C
0	0	0
0	1	0
1	0	0
1	1	1

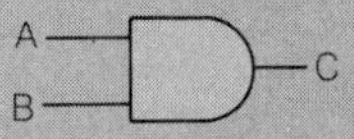

b. AND Gate Truth Table and Symbol

INPUTS		OUTPUT
A	B	C
0	0	1
0	1	1
1	0	1
1	1	0

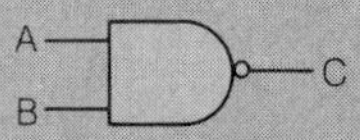

c. NAND Gate Truth Table and Symbol

INPUTS		OUTPUT
A	B	C
0	0	0
0	1	1
1	0	1
1	1	1

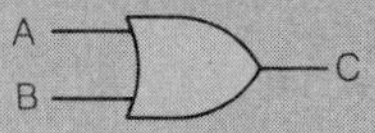

d. OR Gate Truth Table and Symbol

INPUTS		OUTPUT
A	B	C
0	0	1
0	1	0
1	0	0
1	1	0

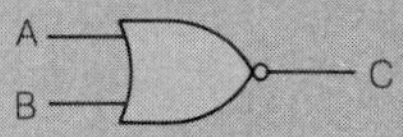

e. NOR Gate Truth Table and Symbol

INPUTS		OUTPUT
A	B	C
0	0	0
0	1	1
1	0	1
1	1	0

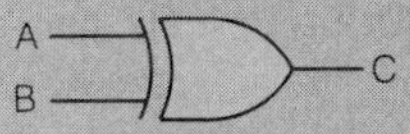

f. Exclusive — OR Gate (XOR Gate)

An AND gate with an inverter on its output is a NAND gate. *Any* input of a 0 level will result in a 1 output.

A related gate is shown in *Figure 1-8c*. This is the NAND gate which operates as an AND gate with an inverter on its output. Thus, if any input of a NAND gate is at the 0 level, the output will be at a 1. Only if all NAND inputs are at the 1 level will the output be a 0. The NAND gate can be used in the same way as an AND gate when the desired output condition is a 0 instead of a 1.

OR Gate

Any input of a 1 will give an output of 1 in an OR gate. The related NOR gate will have an output of 1 only when all inputs are 0.

Another fundamental digital operation is that of the OR gate, shown in *Figure 1-8d*, and its related function, the NOR gate, shown in *Figure 1-8e*. The OR gate has an output of 1 if any of the inputs are 1. It will have an output of 0 only if all inputs are 0. The NOR, which can be considered to be an OR followed by an inverter, operates exactly opposite. If any input is a 1, the output of the NOR gate will be a 0. Only if all inputs of the NOR are at 0 will the output be at 1.

Notice that the OR performs the same operation for 1 inputs that the NAND performs for 0 inputs; that is, if any input reaches the desired condition, the gate output will be a 1. Similarly, the NOR performs the same function for 1 inputs that the AND performs for 0 inputs; that is, if any input reaches the desired value, the output will be a 0. Since the gates are logically equivalent, any digital system can be constructed using only NAND gates or NOR gates.

Exclusive OR Gate

A device used in binary adder circuits, an exclusive-OR (XOR) gate will output a 1 only if the inputs are different.

An often used digital operation is that of the eXclusive-OR (XOR) gate shown in *Figure 1-8f*. In this device, the output will be a 1 only if the inputs are different. If the inputs are both the same (both 0 or both 1), the output will be 0. The XOR gate is useful for comparing one digital signal to another. It is also used in binary adder circuits.

All the devices shown in *Figure 1-8* are of the class known as combinational logic circuits. These circuits provide an output that is a function of the present input values. There is no storage of information in such devices. However, information storage is necessary for many digital operations and several ways have been developed to accomplish this function. The basic one-bit storage function is discussed next.

STORAGE OF DIGITAL INFORMATION

Asynchronous Flip-Flop

Combinational gates can be interconnected to form an R-S flip-flop, a basic digital storage circuit.

Combinational devices can be interconnected in such a way as to provide the storage of digital information as shown in *Figure 1-9*. The basic connection is shown in *Figure 1-9a*. (R stands for Reset and S stands for Set. The bar over the signal is read as "not"; thus $\overline{R}$ is read as "R not".) In this circuit, if it is assumed that both the $\overline{S}$ and $\overline{R}$ inputs are at the 1 level, the gates simply act as inverters. Thus, if the Q output is at the 0 level, it forces the $\overline{Q}$ output to the 1 level. (The bar over the signal name indicates its logic level is the opposite (inversion or complement) of the signal name without the bar.)

Figure 1-9.
Simple Asynchronous
Storage Devices

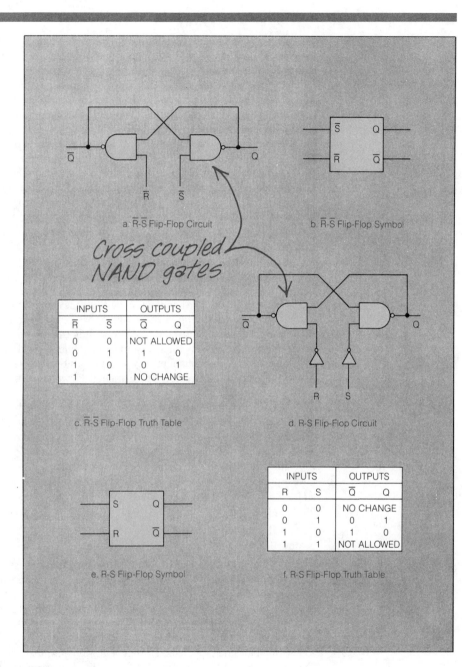

a. $\overline{R}$-$\overline{S}$ Flip-Flop Circuit

b. $\overline{R}$-$\overline{S}$ Flip-Flop Symbol

Cross coupled
NAND gates

INPUTS		OUTPUTS	
$\overline{R}$	$\overline{S}$	$\overline{Q}$	Q
0	0	NOT ALLOWED	
0	1	1	0
1	0	0	1
1	1	NO CHANGE	

c. $\overline{R}$-$\overline{S}$ Flip-Flop Truth Table

d. R-S Flip-Flop Circuit

INPUTS		OUTPUTS	
R	S	$\overline{Q}$	Q
0	0	NO CHANGE	
0	1	0	1
1	0	1	0
1	1	NOT ALLOWED	

e. R-S Flip-Flop Symbol

f. R-S Flip-Flop Truth Table

This places 1's on both inputs of the right gate, which maintains the Q output at a 0 level. Thus, the circuit is storing a 0 on the Q terminal, and its complement, a 1, at the $\overline{Q}$ terminal.

In this and all circuits, if an input symbol has a bar over it, the signal is inactive when the input is at 1 and active when the input is at 0. In *Figure 1-9a*, if a 0 is placed on the $\overline{S}$ input, the Q output is forced to a 1 and the $\overline{Q}$ output is forced to a 0. The outputs will remain in this state even after the $\overline{S}$ input returns to a 1; therefore, the output is stored. The $\overline{S}$ input is referred to as an active low input since a low (0) on this input causes the circuit to respond to the input. In this case, the response is to store a 1 into the circuit at the Q terminal (and a 0 at the $\overline{Q}$ terminal). Thus the $\overline{S}$ input is a Set-Not input that will set the circuit to store a 1 when it is brought low or to a 0. Similarly, bringing $\overline{R}$ low will reset the circuit so that Q is brought to a 0 and stores a 0 on its terminal (while $\overline{Q}$ stores a 1 level). This circuit performs the basic operation of storing a single binary digit (bit).

The circuit is called a flip-flop because of the way the outputs flip and flop to maintain the complement of each other. The particular circuit shown in *Figure 1-9a* is called a Set-Not/Reset-Not flip-flop because the inputs are active with a 0 input. The symbol for the circuit is shown in *Figure 1-9b* and its truth table is shown in *Figure 1-9c*. Notice that $\overline{R}$ and $\overline{S}$ cannot both be at 0 at the same time, since that would be commanding the flip-flop to store both a 0 and a 1 at the same time, which it cannot do. If both $\overline{S}$ and $\overline{R}$ inputs are 1's, the flip-flop outputs do not change; they simply maintain their storage on Q and $\overline{Q}$. A low on $\overline{S}$ causes the circuit to store a 1 and a low on $\overline{R}$ causes the circuit to reset and to store a 0 on the Q output terminal.

If a flip-flop is needed that responds to active high signals (1 on the input lines) instead of active low signals, the circuit of *Figure 1-9a* could be changed to do this by adding inverters on the inputs as shown in *Figure 1-9d*. The logic symbol is shown in *Figure 1-9e* and the truth table is shown in *Figure 1-9f*. This flip-flop is a Set-Reset flip-flop which maintains storage as long as both inputs are at the 0 level. A 1 on the S input will cause the flip-flop to store a 1 on the Q terminal and a 1 on the R input will cause a flip-flop to store a 0 on the $\overline{Q}$ terminal. Again, both R and S cannot be active (at a 1 level) at the same time.

Synchronous Flip-Flop

The type of storage shown in *Figure 1-9* is known as asynchronous storage since the output of the flip-flop changes immediately (except for propagation delay) when an active signal is applied on either the R or S input. Another type of flip-flop provides a control terminal for determining when the device stores the input information. The control terminal is called a strobe, clock, or latch input and the flip-flop is called a clocked or synchronous flip-flop. The symbol for one type, called a D-type flip-flop, is illustrated in *Figure 1-10*. The input terminal is indicated by a D and the clock terminal is indicated by a triangle. The relationship between the input and output signals is shown in

**Figure 1-10.
D-Type
Flip-Flops**

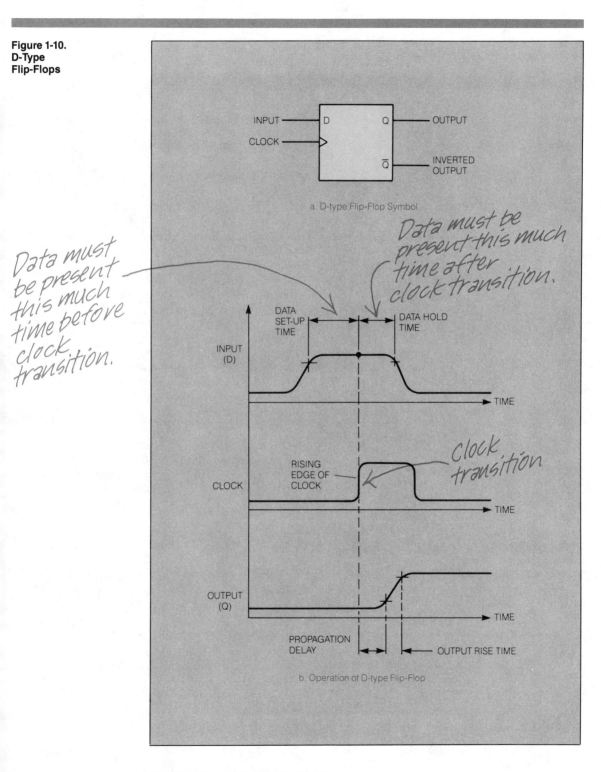

a. D-type Flip-Flop Symbol

Data must be present this much time before clock transition.

Data must be present this much time after clock transition.

Clock transition

b. Operation of D-type Flip-Flop

**Figure 1-11.
Asynchronous
Flip-Flops**

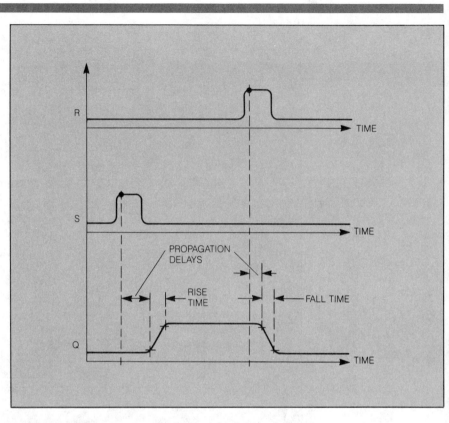

Figure 1-10b. The input on the D terminal may change, but the Q output does not change until the clock signal makes a transition from a 0 level to a 1 level. At that time, the Q output takes on the value that D had when the transition on the clock signal occurred. The transition on the clock waveform from a 1 to a 0 or further changes on the D input have no further effect on the data stored on the Q output of the flip-flop.

A leading-edge triggered flip-flop stores data when the clock goes through a 0 to 1 transition.

Since the data is stored when the clock input makes a transition from low to high, this is called a leading or rising edge-triggered flip-flop. There are also flip-flops that store when the clock makes a high-to-low transition and these are called trailing or falling edge-triggered flip-flops. They have the same logic symbol except a small circle is placed on the clock terminal.

The time relationships between the clock and input signals and the output signal *(Figure 1-10b)* include the circuit parameters of rise time, fall time, propagation delay, set-up time, and hold time. The rise and fall times and propagation delay were defined in *Figure 1-4b.* The set-up and hold times refer to how long the input data must be stable before and after the clock transition.

Figure 1-11 shows the timing for the asynchronous R-S flip-flop. There are still rise and fall time and propagation delay considerations, but since there is no clock signal, there is no set-up or hold requirement. The output simply responds to the S and R inputs immediately (except for propagation delay) whenever a change occurs.

SERIAL AND PARALLEL DIGITAL DATA

Digital data that moves from point to point on a single wire over a period of time is called serial data. If a given set of 1's and 0's represents some system information and it is to be sent in serial form from one part of the system to another, the transfer requires only a single line and a single set of transmission and receiving circuits as shown in *Figure 1-12a*. In serial transmission, the least significant (right-most) bit, D_0, is sent first and the most significant (left-most) bit, d_7, is sent last.

Serial data transmission is the least expensive way to handle digital information, but it also is the slowest way since each 0 and 1 in the sequence takes a certain amount of time. The total time to send the information depends upon the number of bits and the period of each bit. If each bit takes 10 nanoseconds and eight bits are transmitted, then 80 nanoseconds are required for serial transmission.

If these same eight bits are transmitted in parallel (all eight at the same time), only the time of one bit, 10 nanoseconds, is required. In parallel data transmission, a separate line, transmitting circuit, and receiving circuit are used for each bit. This is shown in *Figure 1-12b*. Of course, parallel transmission circuits are more expensive because of the extra hardware. The method chosen at any particular point in a system usually depends on whether operating speed or hardware cost is more important, or on the requirements of the interface to another system.

Serial data transmission sends all of the bits of data over a single wire, sequentially. It is inexpensive, but slow.

Parallel data transmission uses one wire for each separate bit, sending all bits at the same time. It is faster, but more expensive than serial data transmission.

DIGITAL CODES

Since digital circuits use only the 0 and 1 levels of voltage, codes made up of various combinations of bits must be used to represent information. What information a given code represents depends upon its use within a digital system. It could represent some numerical value, a command or an instruction, an alphabetical character, or some on-off control pattern. The meaning of the code in these applications is assigned by some reference table or the way the system circuits are connected.

The number of different things a code can represent depends upon how many bits are in the code. Some possibilities are illustrated in *Figure 1-13*. If only a single bit is used, as shown in *Figure 1-13a*, only two different actions or numbers, such as 0 and 1, No and Yes, or ON and OFF can be represented. By using a 2-bit code, four different numbers or commands, as shown in *Figure 1-13b*, can be used since there are four different bit patterns with the two bits. With a 3-bit code, as shown in *Figure 1-13c*, 8 different numbers or instructions can be represented. In all cases, the number of different patterns of 0's and 1's available for an n-bit code is equal to 2^n. Thus, a two-bit code is 2^2, or 4 different 0 and 1 assignments. Similarly, the 3-bit code is 2^3 or 8 different combinations of 0 and 1. An 8-bit code can represent 256 combinations and a 16-bit code can represent 65,536 combinations.

Digital codes using multiple bits with 1 or 0 values can represent many different types of information.

Figure 1-12.
Digital Data
Transmission

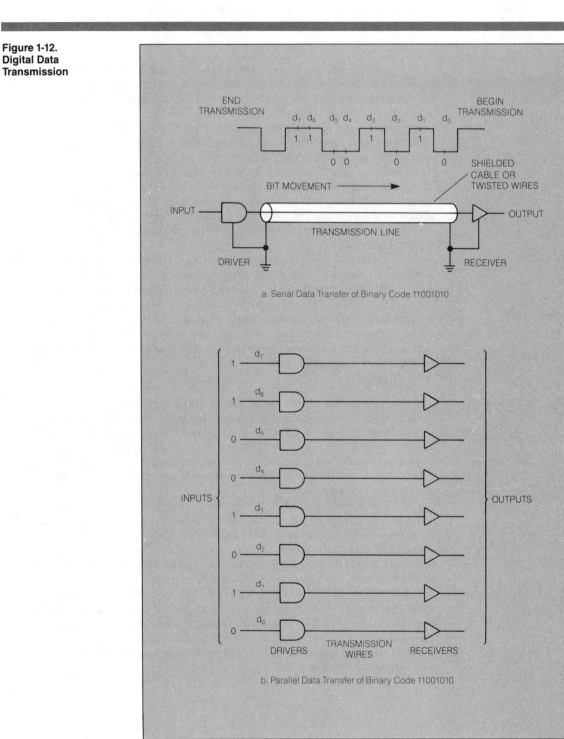

a. Serial Data Transfer of Binary Code 11001010

b. Parallel Data Transfer of Binary Code 11001010

Figure 1-13.
Simple Binary Codes

Bit Values	Possible Meanings	
d_0	Number	Instruction
0	0	OFF
1	1	ON

a. 1-Bit Code

Bit Values		Possible Meanings	
d_1	d_0	Decimal Numbers	Commands
0	0	0	STOP
0	1	1	GO STRAIGHT
1	0	2	GO RIGHT
1	1	3	GO LEFT

b. 2-Bit Code

Bit Values			Decimal Number	Instruction
d_2	d_1	d_0		
0	0	0	0	ADD
0	0	1	1	SUBTRACT
0	1	0	2	MULTIPLY
0	1	1	3	DIVIDE
1	0	0	4	ABSOLUTE
1	0	1	5	NEGATE
1	1	0	6	INCREMENT
1	1	1	7	DECREMENT

c. 3-Bit Code

BCD

BCD uses a 4-bit code to represent the decimal digits 0 through 9. It is easy to use, but is inefficient because only 10 of the 16 possible 4-bit combinations are used.

One commonly used digital code is the 4-bit code of *Figure 1-14*, which can represent the numbers 0 through 15 in the decimal (base 10) number system or the alphanumerics 0 thru 9 and A thru F in a hexadecimal (base 16) number system. If a four-bit code is limited to the patterns 0000 through 1001, the hexadecimal and decimal numbers are limited to the numbers 0 through 9. Thus, one simple way to represent decimal numbers in a binary code is to use only the first ten combinations of *Figure 1-14* and replace each digit in the number with its 4-bit code. Then, whenever a 4-bit code is received, it can be decoded by reversing the process and replacing the 4-bit code with its corresponding decimal digit. This method of representing decimal numbers with equivalent 4-bit binary codes is called the BCD (Binary Coded Decimal) code. This code is simple, but inefficient, because it only uses 10 of the possible 16 combinations of a 4-bit code.

DIGITAL SYSTEM
FUNDAMENTALS

**Figure 1-14.
Hexadecimal (Base 16)
Digits and Binary
Equivalents**

Binary Code	Hexadecimal Digit	Binary Code	Hexadecimal Digit
0000	0	1000	8
0001	1	1001	9
0010	2	1010	A
0011	3	1011	B
0100	4	1100	C
0101	5	1101	D
0110	6	1110	E
0111	7	1111	F

**Figure 1-15.
Binary-to-Decimal
Conversion**

Bit Position								
n	7	6	5	4	3	2	1	0
2^n	128	64	32	16	8	4	2	1
BINARY NUMBER	0	1	0	1	0	0	1	1
BIT VALUE $\times 2^n$	0	64	0	16	0	0	2	1

SUM OF PRODUCTS = 64 + 16 + 2 + 1 = 83
THEREFORE: $01010011_2 = 83_{10}$
(SUBSCRIPT INDICATES BASE OF NUMBER)

**Figure 1-16.
Binary-to-Hexadecimal-
to-Decimal Conversion**

HEXADECIMAL DIGIT POSITION n	1	0
BINARY NUMBER	0 1 0 1	0 0 1 1
HEXADECIMAL EQUIVALENT DIGITS	5	3
16^n	16	1
HEXADECIMAL DIGIT VALUE $\times 16^n$	80	3

SUM OF PRODUCTS = 80 + 3 = 83
THEREFORE: $01010011_2 = 53_{16} = 83_{10}$

Binary Numbers

Numbers represented in binary code are used directly by microprocessors and other digital systems.

To avoid this and other problems with the BCD code, many digital systems, particularly those using microprocessors, use the binary code directly to represent numbers. The binary code can represent a binary (base 2) number just as the decimal code represents decimal (base 10) numbers. It is a simple matter to convert from base 10 to base 2 numbers and back so the full value of a binary code can be utilized. When working with more than one number system at a time, the base of a particular number, if not identified by words, is indicated by a subscript immediately after the last digit; e.g., 1001_2 or 9_{10}.

Binary-to-Decimal Conversion

In binary-to-decimal conversion, the value of each binary digit is multiplied by 2^N. The value of N depends on the position of the digit in the code. The sum of these products is the decimal number.

The conversion from a binary number to a decimal number is illustrated in *Figure 1-15* for the 8-bit binary number 01010011. The binary digit positions are identified as bits 0 through 7 starting from the right-most bit. Bit 0 is the least significant bit and bit 7 is the most significant bit. Each binary digit value (0 or 1) is multiplied by 2^n where n is the bit position. These products are added and their sum is the decimal number. In the example of *Figure 1-15*, only bits 0, 1, 4, and 6 have the 1 value; therefore, 1 is multiplied by the power of 2 for each digit (1, 2, 16, and 64) and these products are added to produce the result of 83. Thus, 83 is the decimal equivalent of the binary number 01010011.

Binary-to-Hexadecimal Conversion

Binary numbers with more than eight digits generally use hexadecimal numbers as an intermediate step. The conversion is simple.

This procedure can be used for any binary number with any number of digits, as long as the appropriate powers of 2 are known or can be calculated. However, for binary numbers with more than eight digits, it is more convenient to use a procedure which uses the hexadecimal (base 16) numbers as an intermediate result. The hexadecimal equivalent of a binary number is determined by replacing each group of 4 binary digits, beginning with the right-most four bits, by their corresponding hexadecimal digit. For the binary number 0000 0000 0101 0011, the base 16 number is 0053 which can be written as 53_{16}. Then a process similar to that of *Figure 1-15* can be used, but using powers of 16 (instead of powers of 2 since each digit is a base 16 digit) as shown in *Figure 1-16*. Now the position 0 digit is a 3, the position 1 digit is a 5, and all the other digits are 0. For position 0, $16^0 = 1$ and 1 times 3 is 3. Similarly, for position 1, $16^1 = 16$ and 16 times 5 is 80. Then 80 plus the previously determined 3 is the decimal equivalent 83. This is much easier than working with the individual binary bits, particularly for binary numbers with more bits.

If the procedures of *Figure 1-15* and *Figure 1-16* are carried out for 8-bit binary codes, the binary numbers ranging from 0000 0000 to 1111 1111 represent the hexadecimal numbers ranging from 00 to FF which represents 256 decimal numbers from 0 to 255. This is the case for an unsigned (all numbers positive) binary number code.

Negative Numbers

The left-most bit of a signed binary number is used as the sign bit; 1 indicates a negative number, 0 a positive.

It is also possible to represent negative decimal numbers with a binary code by using the left-most bit of the binary number as the sign bit. If the sign bit is 0, the number is positive. If the sign bit is 1, the number is negative. There are still 256 numbers possible with an 8-bit code, but now the numbers range from -128 to $+127$. (0 is a positive number.) The simplest procedure for converting one type of signed number code, the 2's complement number code, to its decimal equivalent is as follows:

If the sign bit is 0, use the procedure of *Figure 1-15* or *Figure 1-16* and affix a plus sign in front of the decimal number.

If the sign bit is 1, convert the binary code to hexadecimal using *Figure 1-16*, subtract the hexadecimal code from FF and add 1. Convert this hexadecimal code to its decimal equivalent and affix a minus sign.

The process is illustrated for both positive and negative number codes in *Figure 1-17*. The binary code 0111 0100 is equal to 74_{16} and is a positive number. The decimal equivalent of the number is found by $(7 \times 16) + 4$ which is $+116$.

The conversion of the binary number 11000010 is somewhat more complicated since the left-most 1 indicates it is a negative number. First the binary number is converted to its hexadecimal equivalent C2. Then C2 is subtracted from FF to yield 3D and 1 is added to 3D to yield 3E. The decimal equivalent of the hexadecimal number 3E is $(3 \times 16) + 14 = 62$. Thus, the decimal equivalent of the hexadecimal number C2 is -62 if the C2 represents a signed (2's complement) binary code. With this code, the binary numbers 0000 0000 to 0111 1111 (hexadecimal numbers 00 through 7F) represent the decimal numbers 0 to $+127$, respectively. The binary numbers 1000 0000 through 1111 1111 (hexadecimal numbers 80 to FF) represent the decimal numbers -128 to -1, respectively.

Decimal-to-Hexadecimal Conversion

The conversion from decimal to hexadecimal is done best by following a set procedure.

The reverse of the process in *Figure 1-16* can be used to convert a decimal number to its hexadecimal equivalent and then to its binary equivalent. The process is illustrated in *Figure 1-18*. The decimal number is first divided by the largest number that is a power of 16 that will give a quotient of 1 or larger. That quotient is the most significant (left-most) hexadecimal digit. The remainder is divided by the largest power of 16 and the quotient is the next significant hexadecimal digit. When the last quotient is zero, the preceding remainder or quotient is the least significant hexadecimal digit. A similar process would be used for negative decimal numbers. The conversion can be checked by using the process of *Figure 1-16* to convert the hexadecimal result back to decimal.

Alphanumeric Code

The ASCII code is a 7-bit binary code that allows 128 different alphanumeric characters and commands to be represented in binary form.

Of course, numerical values are not the only information needed in a digital system. The system may need to represent alphabetical and numeric characters in a communication situation or it may need to represent some control command in a system. For alphanumeric information, many systems use the American Standard Code for Information Interchange (ASCII, pronounced "as key"). The ASCII code is a 7-bit binary code which can represent 128 different characters and control operations. This code is presented in *Figure 1-19* with the binary code represented by hexadecimal numbers. Thus, the code for the characters *ASCII CODE* is the sequence of hexadecimal numbers 41 53 43 49 49 20 (for space) 43 4F 44 45. The ASCII code for the number 39 is the hexadecimal digits 33 39.

Figure 1-17.
Signed Binary
(2's Complement) Code
to Decimal Conversion

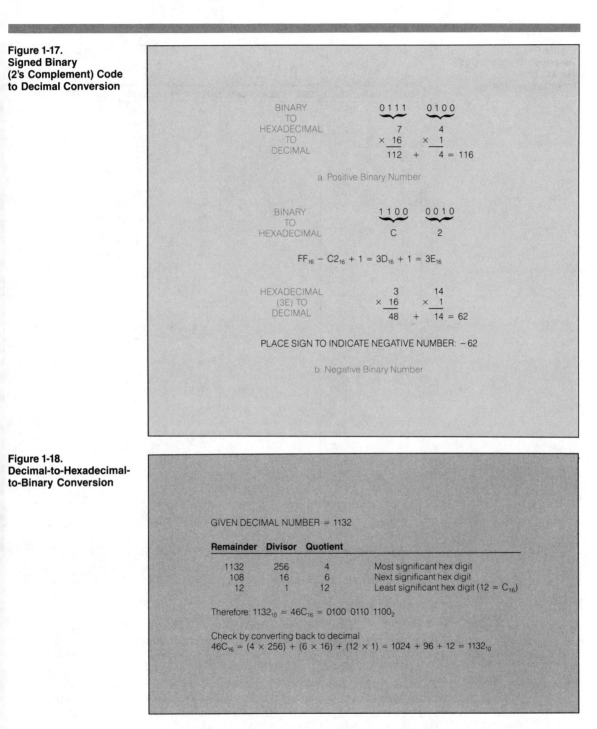

BINARY
TO
HEXADECIMAL
TO
DECIMAL

0 1 1 1   0 1 0 0

7   4

$\times\ 16$ $\times\ 1$

112 + 4 = 116

a. Positive Binary Number

BINARY
TO
HEXADECIMAL

1 1 0 0   0 0 1 0

C   2

$FF_{16} - C2_{16} + 1 = 3D_{16} + 1 = 3E_{16}$

HEXADECIMAL
(3E) TO
DECIMAL

3   14

$\times\ 16$ $\times\ 1$

48 + 14 = 62

PLACE SIGN TO INDICATE NEGATIVE NUMBER: -62

b. Negative Binary Number

Figure 1-18.
Decimal-to-Hexadecimal-
to-Binary Conversion

GIVEN DECIMAL NUMBER = 1132

Remainder	Divisor	Quotient	
1132	256	4	Most significant hex digit
108	16	6	Next significant hex digit
12	1	12	Least significant hex digit (12 = C_{16})

Therefore: $1132_{10} = 46C_{16} = 0100\ 0110\ 1100_2$

Check by converting back to decimal
$46C_{16} = (4 \times 256) + (6 \times 16) + (12 \times 1) = 1024 + 96 + 12 = 1132_{10}$

Figure 1-19.
American Standard Code
For Information
Interchange (ASCII)

DEC	HEX	CHR	DEC	HEX	CHR	DEC	HEX	CHR	DEC	HEX	CHR
0	0	NUL	32	20	SP	64	40	@	96	60	
1	1	SOH	33	21	!	65	41	A	97	61	a
2	2	STX	34	22	"	66	42	B	98	62	b
3	3	ETX	35	23	#	67	43	C	99	63	c
4	4	EOT	36	24	$	68	44	D	100	64	d
5	5	ENQ	37	25	%	69	45	E	101	65	e
6	6	ACK	38	26	&	70	46	F	102	66	f
7	7	BEL	39	27	'	71	47	G	103	67	g
8	8	BS	40	28	(	72	48	H	104	68	h
9	9	HT	41	29	)	73	49	I	105	69	i
10	A	LF	42	2A	*	74	4A	J	106	6A	j
11	B	VT	43	2B	+	75	4B	K	107	6B	k
12	C	FF	44	2C	,	76	4C	L	108	6C	l
13	D	CR	45	2D	–	77	4D	M	109	6D	m
14	E	S0	46	2E	.	78	4E	N	110	6E	n
15	F	S1	47	2F	/	79	4F	O	111	6F	o
16	10	DLE	48	30	0	80	50	P	112	70	p
17	11	DC1	49	31	1	81	51	Q	113	71	q
18	12	DC2	50	32	2	82	52	R	114	72	r
19	13	DC3	51	33	3	83	53	S	115	73	s
20	14	DC4	52	34	4	84	54	T	116	74	5
21	15	NAK	53	35	5	85	55	U	117	75	u
22	16	SYN	54	36	6	86	56	V	118	76	v
23	17	ETB	55	37	7	87	57	W	119	77	w
24	18	CAN	56	38	8	88	58	X	120	78	x
25	19	EM	57	39	9	89	59	Y	121	79	y
26	1A	SUB	58	3A	:	90	5A	Z	122	7A	z
27	1B	ESC	59	3B	;	91	5B	[	123	7B	{
28	1C	FS	60	3C	<	92	5C	~	124	7C	¦
29	1D	GS	61	3D	=	93	5D	]	125	7D	}
30	1E	RS	62	3E	>	94	5E	^	126	7E	~
31	1F	US	63	3F	?	95	5F	–	127	7F	DEL

NOTES:

(1) Column Heads; DEC = Decimal, HEX = Hexadecimal, CHR = Character.
(2) Characters For HEX 0 through 1F are control functions.

SIGNAL CONVERSION

Analog signals must be converted to digital signals to be handled by digital systems.

It was stated earlier that analog signals can be coded into digital signals so they can be processed by digital circuits. Basically, the encoding is accomplished by assigning numerical values to represent the voltage levels of the signal. These numerical values are not necessarily the actual voltage levels. The analog signal is measured (sampled) by the encoding circuit at periodic time intervals and the equivalent binary number for the voltage level is output as a digital signal. The circuit that does this is appropriately called an analog-to-digital (A/D) converter. Its complement, the digital-to-analog (D/A) converter, is used to convert the digital code back to an analog signal.

The concept of A/D and D/A conversion is built around a principle called Nyquist's Sampling Theorem:

> If an analog signal is uniformly sampled at a rate at least twice its highest frequency content, then the original signal can be reconstructed from the samples.

The theorem can be described by the equation:

$$f_s \geq 2BW$$

The sampling frequency is f_s and the bandwidth of the signal (which defines the highest frequency) is BW.

Sampling an Analog Signal

Figure 1-20 shows how an analog signal varies with time. The times at which the waveform is sampled are superimposed on the figure and, as shown, the amplitude of the signal does not change very much in the short time interval between samples. As a result, the sample at the sample time is a close representation of the signal for a short time on either side of the sampling point.

Obviously, more samples in the time T would reproduce the waveform more accurately, but as stated by Nyquist's theorem, if the signal is sampled at a rate which is greater than twice the highest frequency contained in the signal, the samples will contain all the information contained in the original signal. If the maximum frequency of signals that are present in a control system is 100 hertz, then sampling for A/D conversion must be at least 200 times per second.

Nyquist's theorem states that a sample of a signal taken at a rate that is at least twice the highest frequency of the signal will contain all the information of the original signal.

**Figure 1-20.
Sampling an Analog
Signal**
*(Source: N. M. Schmitt and
R. F. Farwell,* Understanding
Electronic Control of
Automation Systems, *Texas
Instruments Incorporated,
Copyright © 1983)*

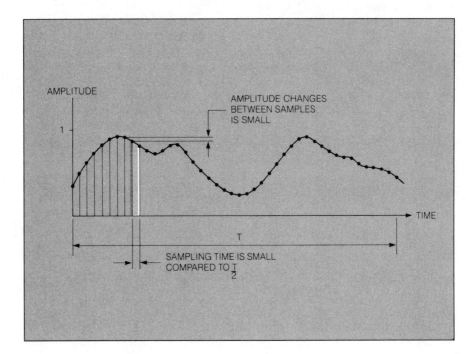

Analog to Digital

An A-to-D converter converts samples of an analog input, taken at specified time intervals, to unique digital codes representing the input levels.

The basic principles of an A/D converter are shown in *Figure 1-21a*. The input is a continuously varying signal that is sampled at specific times determined by the sampling rate. The sampled voltage value is converted to a unique digital code for that value. In *Figure 1-21a*, an 8-bit code is used. All bits of the code come out of the converter at the same time (in parallel) each time the input is sampled and the code represents the input signal value at the sample time. The codes are sent to other digital circuits in the system in parallel (each bit over a separate wire) or they are sent out one bit after the other in time over a single pair of wires (serially). It should be apparent that if the code is an n-bit code and it is sampled at a rate of s times per second, then the bit rate in bits per second is n × s when the signal is sent serially down a line.

Digital to Analog

The D-to-A converter uses a digital code representing an analog output to reconstruct the analog signal.

At the D/A converter, the input is the same or similar parallel code that was output from the A/D converter. (If the code is in serial form, it must be converted to parallel form for use by the D/A converter.) The D/A converter outputs a voltage level corresponding to the input code as shown in *Figure 1-21b*. During the sample period, the voltage level remains constant; therefore, the output has stepped voltage levels. The output is restored very nearly to its original continuously changing shape by passing the signal through an amplifier and filter as shown. The more A/D samples taken, the more closely the filtered D/A signal matches the original.

Figure 1-21. Signal Conversions
(Source: J. L. Fike and G. E. Friend, Understanding Telephone Electronics, *Texas Instruments Incorporated, Copyright © 1983)*

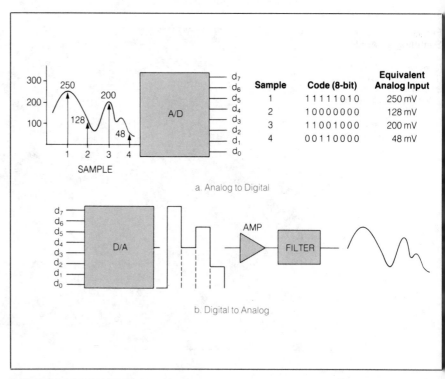

Sample	Code (8-bit)	Equivalent Analog Input
1	1 1 1 1 1 0 1 0	250 mV
2	1 0 0 0 0 0 0 0	128 mV
3	1 1 0 0 1 0 0 0	200 mV
4	0 0 1 1 0 0 0 0	48 mV

a. Analog to Digital

b. Digital to Analog

WHAT HAVE WE LEARNED?

1. The basic components of digital systems are inverters, combinational gates (AND, OR, NAND, NOR, and XOR) and single-bit storage elements called flip-flops.
2. Flip-flops can be classified as asynchronous (no clock input) or synchronous (storage occurs only when the clock signal makes a level transition).
3. The binary signals 0 and 1 can be used as the single output of a single gate or they may occur in combinations called binary codes.
4. Binary codes may be sent in serial or parallel from one part of a system to another part, or from one system to another system.
5. Binary codes may represent numerical values (signed or unsigned), alphanumeric characters, or system commands and instructions.
6. The hexadecimal code is often used by humans when working with binary digital systems because it is easier and the human is less likely to make an error.

Quiz for Chapter 1

1. If in the circuit of *Figure 1-1a*, the values for R_1 and R_2 are changed to 10 and 30 ohms respectively, what will be the voltmeter indication?
  a. 2.50
  b. 5.00
  c. 7.50
  d. 8.00

2. In the case of problem 1, what will be the ammeter indication?
  a. 0.25
  b. 0.50
  c. 0.75

3. If a sinusoidal voltage has a peak value of 173.2 volts, what is its rms value?
  a. 100
  b. 122.45
  c. 127.15
  d. 173.20

4. If the sinusoid of problem 3 has a period of 2.5 milliseconds, what is its frequency in hertz?
  a. 2500
  b. 400
  c. 250
  d. 100

5. If an exclusive-OR gate has inputs of 0 and 1, what will be the output?
  a. 0
  b. 1

6. If a binary code of 10100110 represents an unsigned decimal number, what decimal number is equivalent to the code?
  a. 140
  b. 106
  c. 156
  d. 166

7. What is the binary equivalent of the decimal number 102?
  a. 10010011
  b. 01100011
  c. 01101001
  d. 01100110

8. What is the decimal equivalent of the hexadecimal number 3E8?
  a. 576
  b. 1000
  c. 1025
  d. 8350

9. What decimal number does the signed binary (2's complement) code 10100100 represent?
  a. -92
  b. -166
  c. 92
  d. 166

10. Convert the decimal number 1000 to its binary equivalent.
  a. 001111101000
  b. 000100000000
  c. 000000001000
  d. 100011100011

11. Convert the decimal number -32 to its binary equivalent (2's complement form).
  a. 00010000
  b. 10010000
  c. 00110010
  d. 11100000

12. Find the decimal equivalent of the following BCD code: 01100111
  a. -67
  b. 103
  c. 67
  d. 76

13. Write the decimal number 80 as a BCD code.
  a. 01010000
  b. 1000000
  c. 10000000
  d. 00000101

14. If a resistor of 10 ohms has a sinusoidal current of 14.14 amperes peak flowing through it, how much power in watts is dissipated in the resistor?
  a. 100
  b. 141.4
  c. 1000
  d. 2000

Digital System Functions

ABOUT THIS CHAPTER

In the last chapter, some of the basic digital components and signals were reviewed. Individual digital signals, digital codes, and digital components are of little use unless they are combined in some unique way to provide a needed operation. A particular arrangement of basic digital gates and storage elements to perform desired tasks make up a digital system.

The overall function of a digital system is the main concern of the system designer, the system user, and the system troubleshooter. The proper operation of the system must be understood in order to troubleshoot to find the cause of a system failure. Fortunately, all digital systems share some basic and common functions that can be easily understood. These will be considered in this chapter.

GENERAL DIGITAL FUNCTIONS

All digital systems contain the basic functions of input, output and processing as shown in *Figure 2-1*. Memory is used in many, but not all, digital systems.

Input

The input function provides a means for humans or other systems to input information and commands into a digital system.

The input function provides the way to get commands and information into the system. The information needed by a system depends on the purpose of the system. The information may come from human operators (commands) or it may come from sensors that convert physical quantities such as temperature, position, and speed to electrical signals that can be processed. The purpose of the input function is to provide the proper interface between the outside world and the processing function. The interface may contain signal conditioning, temporary storage, and/or gating.

Processing

The processing function performs operations on the system inputs to produce new outputs.

The processing function is the main reason that a particular system exists. In its simplest form, the processing function simply acts as a switch or routing device between input and output. However, most of the time, the processing function performs actions on the inputs to produce new outputs.

For example, a hand-held calculator accepts numbers and commands that are input by an operator through the keypad. The processing function operates on the numbers according to the command. For instance, if the + key is pressed, it commands the processor to add the numbers and pass the results to the output function for display to the operator.

Figure 2-1.
Basic Digital Functions

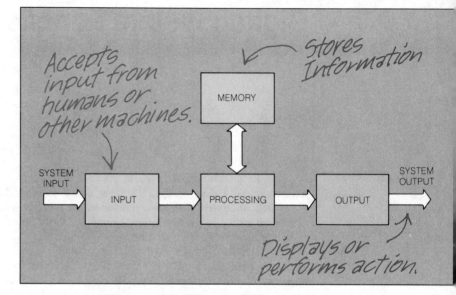

There are as many examples of the processing function as there are types of digital systems. Generally, all of the system decision-making and basic operational features are designed into the circuits that make up the processing function. In some types of system structures, the processing function may be distributed throughout the system. If the structure is that of a computer, there will be a centralized circuit or group of circuits that is called the processor.

Output

The system output function displays the system results for humans and/or performs some operation or controls some action.

After the information has been processed, the output function delivers the results to the outside world. Like the input function, it may contain signal conditioning, temporary storage, and/or gating. The output results usually are either displayed for human operators or are used to control external physical devices. Thus, the control signals could turn on a motor or light, adjust the motor speed or light brightness, and turn off the motor or light.

Memory

The memory function is not necessary in all systems, but it is used in most complex systems. Memory is necessary when the processing function needs to remember information for use at a later time.

Memory is the storage of information, data or instructions by the system for initial or later use as the processing proceeds.

For example, an elevator control system must know where the elevator car is relative to a requested floor to determine whether to send the car up or down. A memory circuit keeps track of the car's position at all times. Thus, the processor can obtain the floor position from memory and the present floor request command from the input function, then calculate which direction and how far the car must move. The results of the calculation go through the output function to control the hoist motor's direction and speed.

In a computer system, the memory function is required to store information or data during processing as well as to store the sequence of operations (instructions or program) that is to be performed on the information. Basically, storage is required in all systems whose present behavior depends on its past behavior. Whether or not memory is used in a given system determines what type of system it is. The basic types of systems will be considered in the next section.

TYPES OF DIGITAL SYSTEMS

Digital systems can be classified into two general types; combinational and sequential, depending on the use of memory.

Combinational Systems

Systems that do not require information storage or memory are called combinational digital systems. Such a system is shown in block diagram form in *Figure 2-2a*. In a combinational logic system, once the inputs are present, the outputs can be determined without referring to past input conditions. In other words, the system outputs are a function only of current input conditions.

**Figure 2-2.
Combinational Logic
System**

*Present inputs
determine
outputs.*

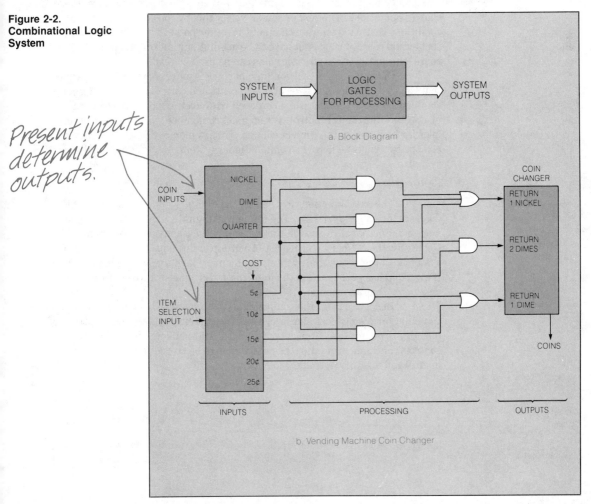

a. Block Diagram

b. Vending Machine Coin Changer

Simple Coin Changer

The example combinational digital system shown in *Figure 2-2b*
consists only of AND and OR gates which provide the logic for a simple coin
changer. One set of inputs indicates the denomination of the coin inserted into a
vending machine and the other set of inputs indicates the cost of the item
purchased. For simplicity, it is assumed that only one coin (either a nickel,
dime, or quarter) can be inserted for a purchase, and the cost of any available
item is either 5, 10, 15, 20 or 25 cents. Obviously, change is not required if a
nickel is used for a 5 cent purchase, a dime for a 10 cent purchase, or a quarter
for a 25 cent purchase.

A nickel change must be generated when a dime is entered to
purchase an item costing a nickel OR when a quarter is entered for items
costing either 10 or 20 cents. A dime change is generated when a quarter is
entered to buy an item costing either 10 or 15 cents. If a quarter is entered to
buy a 5 cent item, two dimes in change must be returned. The simple set of
AND and OR gates shown in *Figure 2-2b* provides the logic to perform these
change operations. The reader should verify this by considering all the
conditions that will generate change. One other point that should be noted is
that actual coin values do not have to be used. A suitable digital code
representing the three possible coins can be used instead.

Of course, an actual vending machine is more complex, considering
that the cost of an item may be above 25 cents and considering the different
combinations of coins that can be entered. However, if more than one coin can
be entered, the digital control system must remember what has been entered
in order to generate the correct change. Thus, a memory function is required
and the system is no longer a combinational system, but a sequential digital
system.

Sequential Systems

The basic functions in a sequential digital system are shown in block
diagram form in *Figure 2-3a*. The sequential digital system consists of one or
more combinational subsystems and a sequential (memory) subsystem.
Generally, the memory will consist of a group of flip-flops for non-computer
systems. In the sequential system, the memory keeps track of what operations
the system has performed in the immediate past since future operations
depend on that knowledge.

In *Figure 2-3a*, the components of the sequential system include a
combinational logic block that processes the current inputs and the outputs of
memory to generate system output signals. Another combinational logic block
controls the memory inputs (the next values to be stored from the current
inputs) and memory outputs.

**Figure 2-3.
Sequential Logic System**

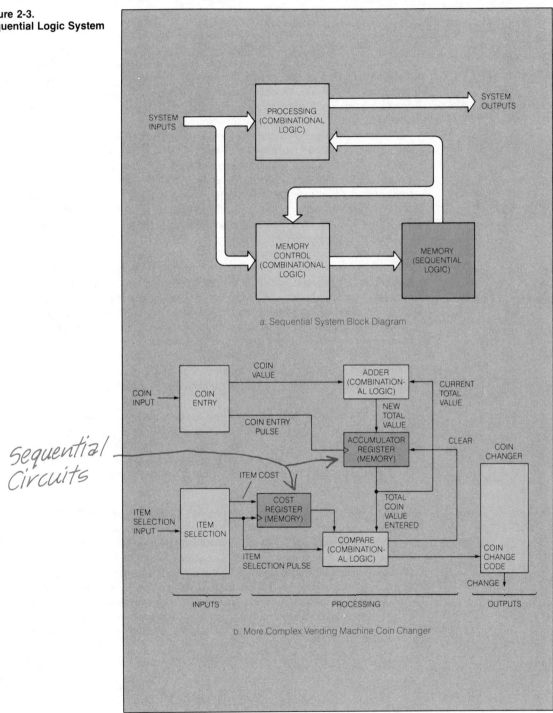

a. Sequential System Block Diagram

Sequential Circuits

b. More Complex Vending Machine Coin Changer

More Complex Coin Changer

Complex digital systems
contain both combinational
and sequential circuits.

Figure 2-3b shows an example of a sequential system. It is based on the example of *Figure 2-2*, but this time the actual logic gate configuration is not shown. The various blocks contain several gates. In this example, the machine is capable of receiving more than just one coin and the cost of available items ranges from 5 to 100 cents in 5 cent increments. The memory circuits must keep track of how much money is received, then the cost of the item must be subtracted from this amount to determine the change to be returned to the customer. Memory also may be required to keep track of how many of each coin denomination has been returned when more than one coin is returned.

The coin entry detector senses which denomination coin has been entered and sends the value in digital code to one of the adder inputs. Each coin entered also causes the detector to generate a pulse which loads the value from the accumulator register (which is initially zero) to the other adder input. The adder adds the two values together and stores the sum in the accumulator register. This process repeats for every coin entered. (The register is a memory function. It will be explained later.)

When the item selection is made, the item selection pulse enters the cost of the item into the cost register. The item selection pulse also causes the compare logic to subtract the cost from the total amount of money received. If the amount received is greater than the cost, the compare logic determines the combination of coin denominations required for change and its outputs indicate the number of nickels, dimes and quarters that must be returned. These number codes are sent to the coin changer mechanism which, in turn, outputs the required number of each coin denomination to the change return cup. A signal from the compare logic then clears (sets to all zeros) the accumulator register to prepare for the next selection.

The changer mechanism as well as the coin input mechanism may be combinational or sequential logic digital systems. In this example, though, they are considered to be components just as registers, AND, and OR gates are components. The sequential system of *Figure 2-3* is more complicated than the combinational system of *Figure 2-2*, but it can do much more.

Structures

Complex digital systems
can be just one integrated
circuit (an example is a microprocessor or microcom-
puter) or they can be
constructed of a mixture of
SSI, MSI and LSI
functions.

Since only the simplest systems can be made using just combinational logic (gates), most systems also have sequential logic (memory). There are several different types of sequential system structures. The one illustrated in *Figure 2-3b* would use gates in a small scale integration (SSI) IC and registers in a medium scale integration (MSI) IC. Some systems include memories in a large scale integration (LSI) IC and others consist only of SSI components such as gates and flip-flops. Complex sequential systems are available in single circuit form in a very large scale integration (VLSI) IC. These complex types of sequential systems generally are made using a computer structure and are called microcomputers. They are used in various control applications and they are the heart of the personal computer and small business computer. By adding to the capability and speed of such systems, they become minicomputers and even large general-purpose computers. Since the computer structure will be the most common in the future, the rest of this chapter and a large portion of this book is devoted to this type of digital system.

COMPUTER FUNCTIONS

A computer is a complex
sequential digital system
that contains memory, in-
put, processing and output
functions.

A computer is a complex sequential digital system that includes all the basic functions shown in *Figure 2-1;* however, the functions are interconnected as shown in *Figure 2-4.* These functions can exist as four or more different integrated circuits (IC's). If the processor is a separate IC, it is called a microprocessor. If all four functions are placed in a single IC, it is called a microcomputer.

**Figure 2-4.
Computer System
Structure**

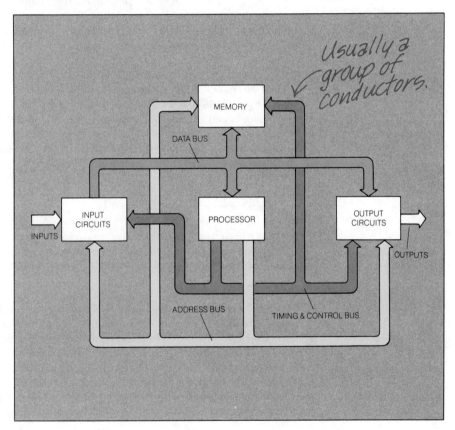

Integrated Circuit

A digital integrated circuit is a complete electronic circuit in a physically small package. It performs at high speed, is low cost and highly reliable.

An integrated circuit is a circuit of one or more complete functions fabricated on a single piece (called a chip) of solid-state material and sealed in a small plastic, metal, or ceramic package with metal leads for connection to the outside world. Some analog circuits such as operational amplifiers and nearly all digital circuits are available in IC form. These circuits are highly reliable, low cost, have low power consumption, and are small which simplifies the design, construction and testing of modern electronic systems.

Buses

Normally, a bus is a group of wires or printed circuit conductors carrying parallel digital data. The buses used to connect a computer system are: data bus, timing and control bus, and address bus.

The three types of buses that interconnect the functional parts are shown in *Figure 2-4*. Although a bus can be a single conductor such as a ground bus, the term usually refers to a group of printed circuit conductors or wires over which parallel digital data is sent. In microcomputers, the bus usually has 8 or 16 conductors and the bus is said to be 8 (or 16) bits wide because the conductors are placed side-by-side. The flat and wide conductor assembly made up of insulated wires is referred to as ribbon cable.

Data Bus

The data bus allows transfer of data (the system numerical and character information) between the processor and the other functions; memory, input and output. The data bus is two-way so that information can flow to or from the processor, but in only one direction at a time. The processor controls when and which function can use the data bus. These timing and control signals are sent from the processor on the one-way timing and control bus.

Timing and Control Bus

The signals on this bus determine when the memory, input, or output devices are permitted to transfer data to or from the processor. A transfer to the processor from the input or memory is called a read operation. A transfer from the processor to the output or memory is called a write operation.

Address Bus

The one-way address bus is used to send location codes from the processor to the other functions. The address indicates which location in the input, output, or memory subsystem is to send data to or receive data from the processor. The processor generates an address or obtains it from an instruction and places the address on the address bus. The processor then sends timing and control signals on the timing and control bus to turn on either the input, output, or memory subsystem and cause either a read operation from the addressed location or a write operation to the addressed location.

The signals on the three buses exist only for a brief period of time. Typically, the address and timing and control signals are placed on the buses for about 250 to 500 nanoseconds. The data transfer between the processor and the selected subsystem must occur during this time interval. Special test equipment is required to observe the occurrence of such fast action events and to detect if the appropriate signal patterns have occurred at the appropriate time. Such test equipment will be discussed in later chapters.

Instructions

The computer program stored in memory is a step-by-step sequence of instructions that define the operations the system must perform to accomplish a given task.

In addition to storing data, the memory in the computer stores instruction codes for reference by the processor. The instruction codes must be binary codes that are included in the instruction set for the particular processor used. The instruction set is fixed by design; thus, only instructions in the set will be recognized by the processor as one of the instructions or operations it is capable of performing. Reading and executing these instructions is the role of the processor in the computer system.

The instructions give the step-by-step operations the system must perform to accomplish a particular task. These instructions are the program for the computer and they define the overall function of the system. Normally, the instructions are stored in system memory in sequential locations; that is, in one location after another. When the system is first turned on, the processor starts at a predefined location to fetch the first instruction in the program from memory and temporarily stores it in the instruction register inside the processor. The instruction is decoded by combinational circuits to determine which instruction it is and the instruction is executed. Then the next instruction is fetched from memory and placed in the instruction register, and so on. The sequential circuits in the processor generate address, data, and timing signal sequences to control the fetching, decoding and execution of the instruction.

MORE DIGITAL COMPONENTS

In Chapter 1, the basic digital components were discussed, but as digital systems become more complex, they involve more than just gates and flip-flops as components. This is particularly true in computers where each component may contain thousands of gates and flip-flops in a single integrated circuit. Some of these components such as the register have already been mentioned, but now let's examine them in more detail.

Registers

Temporary memory inside a microcomputer system that usually stores from 8 to 16 bits is provided by a group of flip-flops called a register.

A register is a group of flip-flops that provide a memory function for a particular processing function such as an input register, an output register, an accumulator register and an instruction register. Registers in microcomputers usually can store either 8 or 16 bits. Since each flip-flop can store one bit, either 8 or 16 flip-flops are grouped to form one byte (or word) in a register.

Usually, the flip-flops operate all at the same time so that all bits are transferred into or out of the register at the same time for parallel data operation. However, some registers are designed to receive data in parallel form and output the data in serial form. Others work just the opposite; they receive data in serial form and output it in parallel form. For now, let's consider the parallel in/parallel out register.

Registers send and receive parallel data, convert parallel inputs to serial outputs or vice versa, or provide a simple timed gating function.

The operation of each individual flip-flop is similar to that of the D-type flip-flop shown in *Figure 1-12*. The structure for a 4-bit register is shown in *Figure 2-5*. The clock terminals of four D-type flip-flops are connected together and this common connection is the external clock terminal. Then, when the external clock signal changes from a 0 to a 1 level, whatever is on the input to the register will be stored in the 4 flip-flops. The information will appear within a short time on the output terminals of the flip-flops. Registers are typically sold as 4-bit or 8-bit versions. If a 16-bit register is required, two 8-bit registers are connected together. The register shown in *Figure 2-5* can provide temporary storage for a 4-bit code. Later, it can act as an output device to output the stored 4-bit code. Or the register may not be used for storage, but simply as a method to gate information from the processor to an output device. All that is required to make the register output its contents is to provide a clock signal to the clock terminal whenever the processor is ready to output data. However, since there are many registers within a computer, there must be a circuit that examines the timing signals and the address signals from the processor and makes sure that the data goes to the correct register at the correct time.

Selecting a Register

Selecting the proper register to send or receive data is accomplished by sending an address that selects the register, along with the proper control and timing signals.

The basic structure is shown in *Figure 2-6*, with the circuit that distributes the clock signal to the output registers indicated as an address decoder. The details of the decoder circuit will be considered shortly. For now, let's just say that when the processor wants to output data to one of the output registers, it puts the address for that output register on the address bus. In the example of *Figure 2-6*, an 8-bit address, which can select one of 256 different output registers, is shown. (The number 8 with the / across the line indicates that the single line represents an 8-line bus.) The figure also shows that the register and the data bus can handle 8 bits of parallel digital data. Since the data bus bit width is usually the same as the processors internal registers, this processor is assumed to be an 8-bit processor. Also, it is assumed that the processor produces a 0 signal, called $\overline{\text{IOW}}$ (abbreviation for Input Output Write Not), of a few hundred nanoseconds duration to indicate when data is on the lines for the output subsystem. The data should be clocked into the register at the end of this 0 period; that is, when it makes the 0-to-1 transition. The purpose of the decoder is to decode the address when the $\overline{\text{IOW}}$ signal is active and send a pulse to the appropriate output register clock terminal. Now let's learn how the decoder operates.

**Figure 2-5.
4-Bit Register**

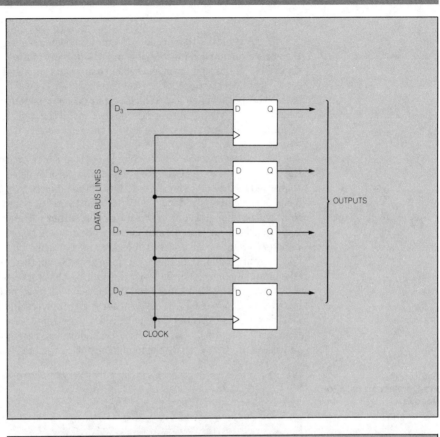

**Figure 2-6.
Processor Output
Register Structure**

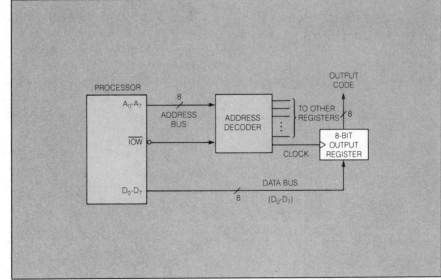

Decoders

An example 3-to-8-line decoder shows how a 3-bit selection address activates the clock of 1 of 8 output registers to select the desired register.

A typical 3-to-8 decoder circuit is shown in *Figure 2-7*. The signal on the enable terminal $\overline{E}$ must be low in order for any of the outputs to go to a 0 regardless of the signals on the select code inputs A, B and C. If $\overline{E}$ is held at a 1, all outputs of the decoder are held at a 1. When $\overline{E}$ goes low, one and only one of the 8 outputs will go low. Which output goes low is determined by the 3-bit binary select code input to the decoder. Thus, if the 3-bit code of 000 is input while $\overline{E}$ is at 0, output 0 will be at 0. If the 3-bit code is 111 while $\overline{E}$ is at 0, output 7 will be at 0.

Now refer to *Figure 2-8* and note that $\overline{E}$ will go low when $\overline{IOW}$ and all the other inputs to the OR gate are low. The decoder select inputs are connected to the least significant 3 bits of the address bus. The most significant 5 bits of the address code and $\overline{IOW}$ are sent to an OR gate whose output is sent to $\overline{E}$. Output line 0 is sent to the clock of an output register. Output from the register will occur (and data from the processor will be latched into the register) whenever all address lines are at 0 and while $\overline{IOW}$ is low. This is true because only if all inputs to the OR gate are at 0 will the output of the OR gate (the input signal to $\overline{E}$) be 0. Thus, the address that corresponds to the register shown will be the 8-bit binary code 0000 0000 which can be expressed as a hexadecimal code of 00_{16}. If seven other registers were added to the system and the outputs 1 through 7 of the decoder were sent to the clock terminals of registers 1 through 7, respectively, these additional registers would respond to addresses 01_{16} through 07_{16} during an output-to-register instruction.

**Figure 2-7.
Pin Connection for 3-to-8
Decoder.**

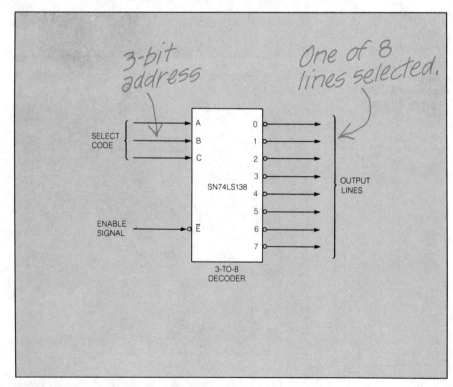

**Figure 2-8.
Computer Output
System**

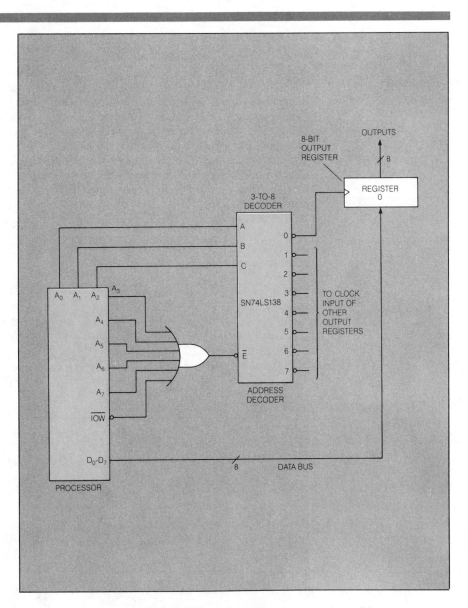

Input registers function basically like output registers; however, they require a different control signal and a three-state buffer on their output.

By using combinations of 3-to-8 decoders, it would be possible to develop clock signals for up to 256 output registers (addresses 00_{16} through FF_{16}). Of course, each decoder (32 would be required) would have to respond to its own unique bit pattern on address lines A_3 through A_7. A similar structure would be used on input registers with two modifications. Some signal such as an $\overline{IOR}$ (Input Output Read Not) would be used instead of an $\overline{IOW}$, and the output circuitry of the register would have to include a three-state buffer. In fact, all microcomputer devices that are allowed to send information to the data bus must have a three-state buffer.

Three-State Buffers

The three-state buffer not only has the two 1 and 0 states of a logic gate but also a third high impedance state. The third state acts like an open circuit to isolate the register from the data bus.

The three-state buffer, as its name suggests, has three states. Two of them are like any other digital device, either low (0) or high (1). The third state is a high impedance state that is essentially an open circuit; thus, in this state, it looks like an open switch to signals on its input. This allows the buffer to connect or disconnect signals to a data line. This is shown in *Figure 2-9* in conjunction with a 4-bit register comprised of four flip-flops. The usual common clock signal and the 4 parallel data lines are inputs to the register. There are 4 parallel data output lines that connect to the data bus, but these will be connected to the outputs of the register only if the three-state buffer is enabled. The signal that enables the output buffer is indicated as $\overline{OE}$ (for Output Enable Not). It must be at 0 for the buffer to connect the register outputs to the data lines. If $\overline{OE}$ is a 1, the buffer is in the high impedance state. In this state, the flip-flops are not placing a voltage on the lines; therefore, they are not drawing or sending current into the data lines. Thus, the three-state buffer isolates the register from the data line.

**Figure 2-9.
Register With Three-
State Output Buffer**

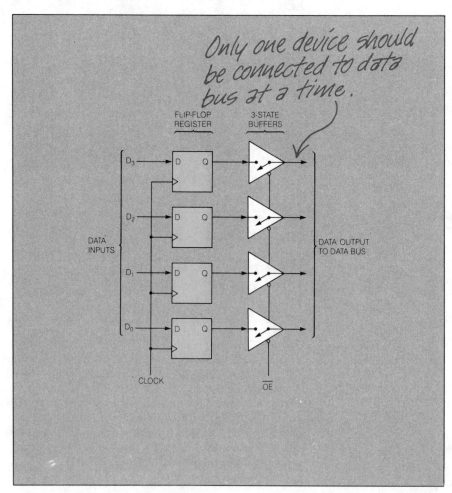

UNDERSTANDING DIGITAL TROUBLESHOOTING

A control signal to a three-state buffer insures that only one device at a time is connected to the data bus.

This feature is important in microcomputers since many components can send information onto the data bus, but it is important that only one device be connected to the data bus at any given time. If two or more devices were allowed to place 1's and 0's on the lines at the same time, the output circuits of the devices could be damaged and the data values would be totally uncertain. The microprocessor can control which device is connected to the data bus by sending an output enable to the three-state buffer only for the device chosen. Thus, an addressing scheme must be used so the microprocessor can be sure that the correct device is enabled.

Figure 2-10 illustrates how this can be done for input registers. The same decoder structure and addressing scheme is used as shown in *Figure 2-8*, except the decoder is enabled when $\overline{\text{IOR}}$ (Input Output Read Not) is low (instead of $\overline{\text{IOW}}$). Since only one decoder output (as determined by the address) is low at any given time, only the $\overline{\text{OE}}$ for one input register is a 0 at any given time so only one register can send its data to the processor.

Notice that the same address can be used in *Figure 2-10* for an input register as can be used in *Figure 2-8* for an output register. However, both input and output registers won't be enabled at the same time because the $\overline{\text{IOW}}$ and $\overline{\text{IOR}}$ signals control the decoder enable.

**Figure 2-10.
Computer Input System**

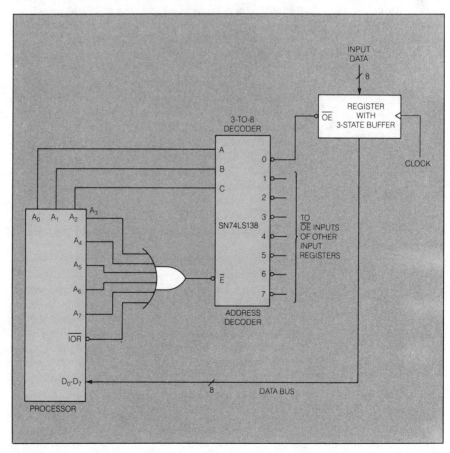

Memories

Registers are only one form of storage that exists in a computer structure. Also needed are storage devices that can store a large quantity of n-bit codes (typically 8-bit codes) to hold the program instruction codes, the system data, and system constants. These devices are referred to as memory. They typically have a quantity of locations that is a power of 2 with either 1, 4, or 8 bits stored in each location. The quantity of locations is often referred to in terms of K bits or K bytes where 1K equals 1,024 which is 2^{10}. Memory devices are available in single package ICs from 1K up to 256K bits.

Read-Write Memory

RAM is used for longer term storage of program instructions, data and constants. It consists of a matrix of storage cells for a given number of words times the number of bits per word. It can be written into and read from. An address code applied to the memory locates the specific word.

The organization of a 2,048 (2^{11}) location (8 bits per location) memory is indicated in *Figure 2-11*. This memory is a random access read-write memory, more commonly referred to only as random access memory (RAM). The control signals for the memory operation include the output enable ($\overline{OE}$), write enable ($\overline{WE}$) and a chip select ($\overline{CS}$). The 11-to-2,048 decoder is part of the memory device. If $\overline{CS}$ is not at a 0, the decoder is not enabled and no location can be read from or written into. If $\overline{CS}$ is at a 0, the memory can be read from or written into, depending on the state of $\overline{WE}$ and $\overline{OE}$. To read from the memory, $\overline{WE}$ must be at a 1 and $\overline{OE}$ must be at its active 0. The opposite is true for a write operation; that is, $\overline{WE}$ must be a 0 and $\overline{OE}$ must be a 1. Many memory circuits do not have the $\overline{OE}$ input, so $\overline{CS}$ and $\overline{WE}$ also control the read operation. In this case, $\overline{WE}$ stays at a 1 (for read) unless a specific write command is given to change $\overline{WE}$ to a 0.

The other input to the memory device is an 11-bit address code to select any one of the 2,048 locations. The memory can be thought of as consisting of 2,048 input registers as previously discussed, which also can be connected as output registers. The 11-to-2048 decoder that generates the latch for input or output enable for each of these internal registers (or memory locations), is simply a greatly expanded version of the 3-to-8 decoders discussed in *Figures 2-8* and *2-10*. Once the address is decoded, the memory location is selected. Then the location either receives data (write operation) from the processor (if $\overline{CS}$ is 0 and $\overline{WE}$ is 0) or it sends data (read operation) to the processor (if $\overline{CS}$ is a 0 and $\overline{OE}$ is a 0). The flip-flops that make up each memory location usually are not the clocked type of flip-flop, but are more like the R-S flip-flop discussed in Chapter 1.

Memory Addressing

Since the memory is essentially an expanded set of input/output registers, it is connected to the processor using a method very similar to the structures of *Figures 2-8* and *2-10*. The connection of two memories of the type shown in *Figure 2-11* to a processor is illustrated in *Figure 2-12*. There are 8 positions available but only 2 are shown for simplicity. Each block labeled M is a 2,048 location memory with an integral 11-to-2048 address decoder like that shown in *Figure 2-11*. The 11 least significant address bits go to each memory to

Figure 2-11.
Memory Circuit Structure

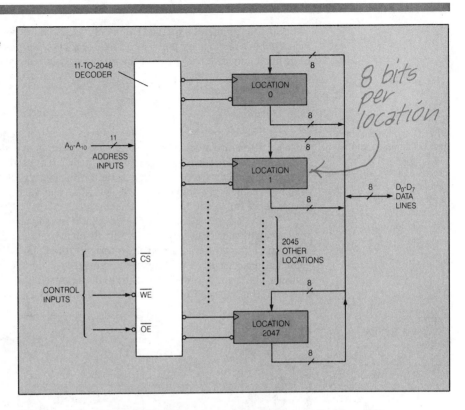

indicate which of the 2,048 locations is requested. The next 3 address bits (A_{11}-A_{13}) go to the select inputs of the 3-8 memory select decoder to determine which of the 8 possible memories is enabled. The most significant two address bits (A_{14}-A_{15}) go to a NAND gate along with a signal called MEMEN (Memory Enable) to determine when the 3-to-8 decoder is enabled to decode an address to generate a 0 output on one of its lines. This is similar to the method used in *Figures 2-8* and *2-10*.

The Processor (CPU) outputs a control signal (MEMEN) to indicate to the external circuits that a memory operation is to occur. WE and DBIN control whether the operation is a write or a read.

The processor uses MEMEN to indicate to the external circuits when a memory operation is to occur. It also outputs a $\overline{WE}$ and a DBIN (Data Bus In) to control the read or write operation of the memory. Since this processor makes DBIN a 1 for a read operation, an inverter is inserted in the line so that the required 0 appears at the $\overline{OE}$ input of the memory. With all the connections of *Figure 2-12* in place, any one of the 16,384 locations shown (2,048 × 8 = 16,384) can be individually and randomly addressed by the processor. Memory M0 is turned on when the most significant five bits (A_{11}-A_{15}) of the address are 11000. Memory M1 is turned on when A_{11}-A_{15} are 11001. Thus, the address range for the 2,048 locations in M0 is from 1100 0000 0000 0000$_2$ (C000$_{16}$) to 1100 0111 1111 1111$_2$ (C7FF$_{16}$). Similarly, M1 will respond to addresses in the range from 1100 1000 0000 0000$_2$ (C800$_{16}$) to 1100 1111 1111 1111$_2$ (CFFF$_{16}$). With the other memory circuits added which are controlled by the other six outputs of the 3-to-8 decoder, memory locations with addresses from 1101 0000 0000 0000$_2$ (D000$_{16}$) to 1111 1111 1111 1111$_2$ (FFFF$_{16}$) can be addressed.

This indicates a method commonly used to allow memory to be increased in a microcomputer. The addressing scheme is designed for some large maximum, but only a few of the memory ICs are installed. Later, all that has to be done to increase memory capacity is to plug in (assuming sockets are provided) more memory ICs.

Read-Only Memory

ROM (Read-Only Memory) is addressed and read the same as RAM. You cannot write into it. Its information is stored permanently when it is manufactured; thus, it is non-volatile.

The example of *Figure 2-12* concerns the use of memory devices that can be written into or read from. Another type of memory commonly found in microcomputers is the read-only memory (ROM). It is used to store program instructions and data that remain constant. The memory addressing and reading scheme is the same as that discussed for the read-write memory, except there is no need for a write enable signal.

The advantage of using ROM is that it is non-volatile while most read-write memories are volatile. A volatile memory loses all its information when operating power is turned off. Internally, the ROM is a large-scale combinational circuit, consisting of the same n-to-2^n decoder for both the address inputs and three-state output buffers controlled by $\overline{CS}$ and $\overline{OE}$. However, the "storage" consists of a fixed wiring pattern that connects the

**Figure 2-12.
Computer Memory
System**

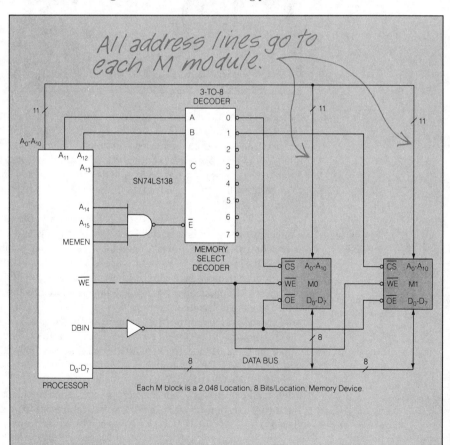

PROMs are ROMs that can be programmed after manufacture; EPROMs are ROMs that can be re-programmed after being erased.

outputs of the 2^n AND gates of the decoder combinational logic to the output OR gates whose output is in turn sent through the three-state buffers. For the ROM, the wiring pattern is fixed during the manufacturing process and cannot be altered. The PROM (Programmable ROM) can be programmed after manufacture, but only for one time. It is then like the ROM. The EPROM (Erasable PROM) is electrically programmed for permanent storage (read-only storage), but the storage patterns can be erased by exposure to a sufficient amount of ultraviolet radiation. The memory then can be programmed again. Both the PROM and EPROM require a special hardware device to do the programming.

Processors

The central control component in a computer structure is the processor. A processor on a single chip IC is called a microprocessor. The four general sections of this very complex device are illustrated in *Figure 2-13*. Each of these sections plays a certain role in the processor fetch and execute cycle activity mentioned earlier.

**Figure 2-13.
Processor Simplified
Block Diagram**

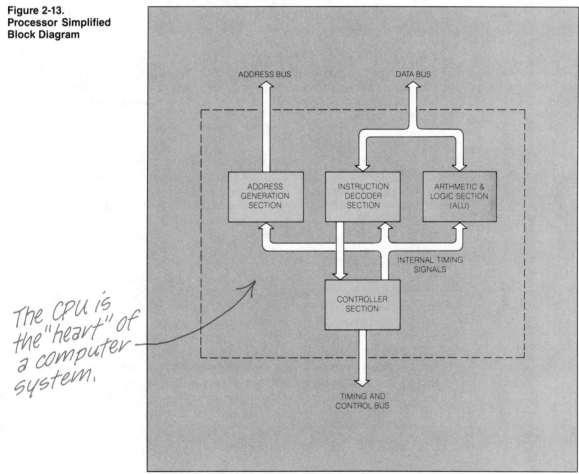

The CPU is the "heart" of a computer system.

Controller

The controller is a sequential digital system that provides the central control function for the processor subsystem. It does this by fetching and executing instructions, as directed by the instruction decoder.

The controller section is the central control unit for the processor. The controller is a sequential digital system that fetches and executes instructions. It performs the fetch cycle by outputting the address of the instruction to be fetched on the address bus and outputting memory read control signals on the timing and control bus. It places the processor data bus in an input mode and latches the instruction code coming from memory into the instruction register. This may complete the fetching of a simple instruction. However, some instructions may require two or three memory locations to be read to get the complete instruction information. The controller keeps track of these requirements and continues reading memory at successive locations until the complete instruction is in the instruction register. The instruction decoder informs the controller which instruction is to be executed. If the instruction is a memory or input/output read or write, the controller generates the memory address or input/output address and the appropriate control signals to read or write the information required by the instruction. If the instruction involves an arithmetic or logic operation, the controller activates the appropriate section of the arithmetic-logic unit (ALU). These sequences of activities are built into the design of the sequential logic that makes up the controller section.

Instruction Decoder Section

The instruction decoder section has an instruction register for temporary storage of the instruction code obtained from memory. It also contains a combinational logic decoder that interprets this code for the controller section.

Address Generation Section

The program counter is a special register that holds the address of the present or next instruction of the program depending on where the computer is in its operation cycle.

The address generation section has one or more registers to keep track of data locations involved in the instruction execution and a special register called a program counter that keeps the current address of the next instruction to be fetched. As each location in memory is accessed during the instruction fetch, one is added to the contents of the program counter so it will contain the address of the next memory location in the program sequence. The program counter is a special type of register called a counter. Not only can it store an address code just as an ordinary register can, but also it can add one to the value (increment the value) stored. In other words, it counts by 1. This is all that's needed to keep track of the instruction location since the instructions normally follow one after another in the part of memory used for program instructions. Sometimes the instruction fetched requires that the next instruction fetch be from a location somewhere in memory out of this sequence. If so, the instruction will contain the address of the out-of-sequence location and its address is loaded into the program counter. The instruction fetch then goes to the new program counter location, and fetches instructions in sequence until it is told to return to the original sequence or go to a new sequence.

Arithmetic-Logic Unit

An ALU contains circuits such as adders and logic gates to do the arithmetic and logical operations required of the processor.

The ALU is somewhat more complex than the instruction decoder and address generator sections. It contains adders, subtractors, logic gates, and other devices to perform such operations as addition, subtraction, absolute value, multiplication, OR, NOT, AND, and so on. The ALU also provides a set of registers for internal storage of data codes within the processor for fast access and reference.

Usually, the internal circuitry of the processor is of little interest to designers and users of microcomputer systems since it is just a component. As long as the designer knows how to connect the processor in a system with other components (as in *Figures 2-8, 2-10, and 2-12*), what goes on inside the processor is of little concern. Even programmers only have to know what internal storage locations are available for program operations in order to successfully write programs for a given system.

There are many digital components that are used in computer and other digital systems that have not been covered in these first two chapters. However, the most common devices have been introduced, so that it is now possible to consider techniques for finding faults in digital systems. The basic techniques for troubleshooting simple digital systems will be presented in the next chapter.

WHAT HAVE WE LEARNED?

1. The basic types of digital systems have been studied. They consist of combinational logic systems (no memory) and sequential logic systems (with memory).
2. Both combinational and sequential circuits are used in most complex systems.
3. The system structure that is becoming more and more common is the computer structure.
4. The basic functions of all computers are the memory, input, output, and processor.
5. Parallel in/parallel out registers are made up of flip-flops with a common clock.
6. A three-state buffer acts as a switch to disconnect or connect signals to a bus.
7. A ROM stores information permanently so it won't be lost when power is removed.
8. A RAM can be written into as well as read from and is used to store changeable information.
9. Each location in a RAM and ROM memory has a different address so it can be randomly and individually accessed by the processor.
10. The processor's main job is to fetch and execute instructions.

Quiz for Chapter 2

1. The purpose of the processing function in a system is:
   a. to store information that is needed later.
   b. to generate outputs on the basis of present and past inputs.
   c. to get information into, act on it, and output it from the system.

2. Memory is required in a system if:
   a. the outputs are a function of inputs.
   b. the system must store system constants or data.
   c. the outputs are a function of past inputs.
   d. the outputs are a function of past inputs or events that have already been implemented.
   e. all of the above.
   f. b, c, and d above.

3. The processor in a computer performs:
   a. the function of main system memory.
   b. involves transfer of data only from memory to processor or back.
   c. provides only arithmetic or logic operations.
   d. is the central control element of the system.

4. The purpose of the fetch cycle in a computer is to:
   a. obtain input data.
   b. obtain memory data.
   c. obtain an instruction.
   d. implement a specific operation.

5. When a processor is in its execution cycle:
   a. no memory read operation is involved.
   b. the instruction code is in the instruction register.
   c. only ALU operations are being performed.
   d. the program counter is not involved in the cycle

6. A memory circuit that has 9 address inputs has how many storage locations?
   a. 256
   b. 512
   c. 1024
   d. not determined by this set of inputs.

7. If, in *Figure 2-12*, an OR gate were used instead of the NAND gate and an inverter were used in the MEMEN line, what would be the first address in hexadecimal of the first location of the MO memory circuit?
   a. 0
   b. 1000
   c. C000
   d. F000

8. In question 12, what would be the last address in hexadecimal of the last location of the M1 memory circuit?
   a. 0FFF
   b. 3FFF
   c. CFFF
   d. FFFF

9. If a memory circuit provides 8,192 locations with 1 bit per location, how many such circuits would be needed to provide a memory of 16,384 locations with 8 bits per location?
   a. 2
   b. 8
   c. 16
   d. 32

10. If a processor is used in *Figure 2-12* that does not output $\overline{MEMEN}$ but does output signals $\overline{MEMR}$ (0 for a memory read operation) and $\overline{MEMW}$ (0 for a memory write operation), what logic gate could be used with $\overline{MEMR}$ and $\overline{MEMW}$ as inputs to generate MEMEN?
    a. OR
    b. NOR
    c. AND
    d. NAND
    e. Exclusive OR

Troubleshooting Fundamentals

ABOUT THIS CHAPTER

In the last two chapters, the basic principles of operation of electrical circuits, digital components, and digital systems were reviewed. With this background information, it is possible to begin looking at the basic techniques for finding faults in digital systems and repairing them.

The approach to troubleshooting electronic systems is much like that used by a detective. It involves gathering evidence (making measurements) and reasoning through the evidence to pinpoint the guilty component, wire or connection in the system. Fortunately, it is a process that can be learned easily.

Even in very complicated systems, failures almost always are caused by some simple fault which can be found with relatively inexpensive and simple test equipment. The basic faults that will be considered in this chapter are short circuit, open circuit, improper voltage level, and component failure.

SHORT CIRCUIT

A short circuit, usually just called a short, is an electrical connection that is not supposed to be in the system. It has the same effect as deliberately connecting a wire from one point to another.

Short in a DC Circuit

A short in a circuit is simply an electrical connection that is not supposed to be there. It bypasses current from an intended path causing some components to receive no current and possibly overloading others.

The effect of a short in a direct current circuit can be seen by examining the simple circuit of *Figure 3-1*. The circuit in *Figure 3-1a* is like the one used to introduce the concepts of voltage, current, resistance, and power in Chapter 1.

Since the two resistors are connected in series to a power supply, the same current will flow through each. Also, since they are of equal value (1,000 ohms each), the same voltage drop will appear across each. In *Figure 3-1a*, the voltage of 5 volts from the power supply is applied across a total circuit resistance of 2,000 ohms so that a current of 0.0025 ampere or 2.5 milliamperes flows through the resistors. This causes 2.5 volts to be dropped across each resistor.

In *Figure 3-1b*, the circuit is changed slightly by placing a short across R2. Since a short is like a wire connection and since a wire offers very little resistance to current flow, all of the current from the power supply flows through R1 and the short. No current flows through R2 so that the voltage across R2 is 0 volts. Further, since the full 5 volts from the power supply now

**Figure 3-1.
Effect of a Short in a
Simple DC Circuit**

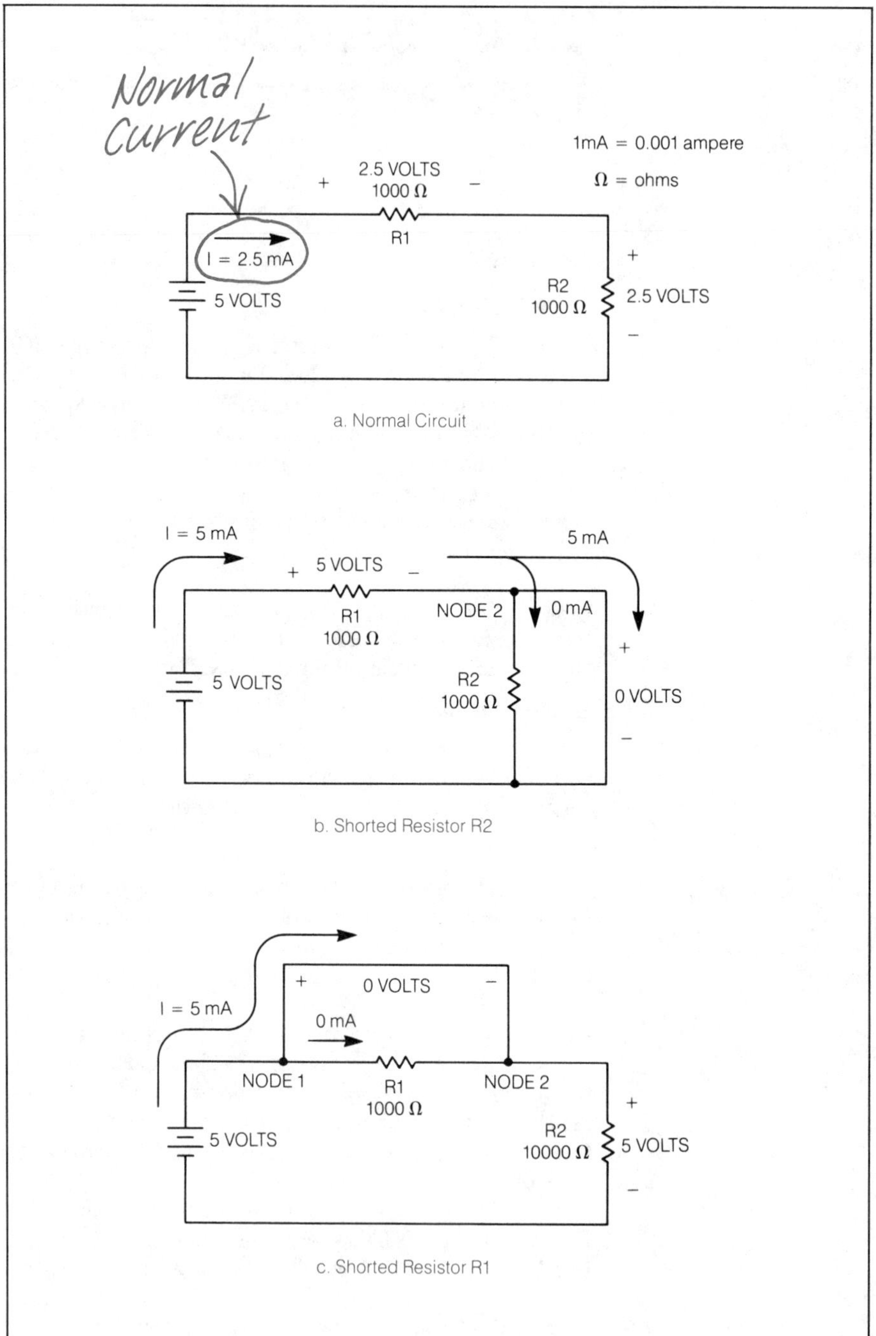

a. Normal Circuit

b. Shorted Resistor R2

c. Shorted Resistor R1

appears across R1 alone, the current flowing through R1 and the short is 5 mA. This is another factor to consider in restoring the circuit; that is, excessive current through R1 due to the short could damage R1. Thus, the value of R1 should be measured to verify that it is good.

A short in a dc circuit can be detected by measuring significant changes in node voltages, circuit or branch current(s), or circuit resistance.

Notice that there are three general ways to detect that the short has occurred. First, the voltage across R2 has changed from 2.5 volts to 0 volts. Thus, measuring the voltage from node 2 to ground would indicate a short from that node to ground. (Recall from Chapter 1 that a circuit node is the point of connection of two or more paths.) The second indication of the presence of a short is that the current from the supply has doubled, which indicates that the resistance in the circuit has been halved which, in turn, indicates that one of the two resistors has been shorted out of the circuit. The current indication is not as good a measurement as the voltage indication since it does not pinpoint which resistor has been shorted. The third way to detect the short is to disconnect the power supply and measure the resistance from node 2 to ground. If the resistance is 0 ohms instead of 1,000 ohms, there must be a short from node 2 to ground. However, this measurement is not as simple as the voltage measurement since it requires disconnection of part of the circuit, the power supply, before the measurement can be made.

Another example of a short in the circuit of *Figure 3-1a* is shown in *Figure 3-1c*. In this case, there is a short between nodes 1 and 2 across R1. The same type of measurements as outlined above can be used to indicate and isolate the short. Although the short is indicated in *Figures 3-1b* and *3-1c* as an external short, the effects and measurements would be the same if the resistor developed a short internally.

Another possible place for a short to occur in this circuit is from node 1 to ground across the power supply. However, the results of this short probably would isolate it because either the short would be blown into an open condition or the power supply would be damaged. In either case, the power supply would provide a momentary large pulse of current with a very low output voltage.

Short in a Logic Circuit

A short in a digital logic circuit results in a permanent logic state being applied to one or more gates regardless of any other logic inputs.

A simple digital logic circuit without a short is shown in *Figure 3-2a*. In *Figure 3-2b*, a short to ground is shown to occur somewhere along the line from the output of gate 2 to the B input of gate 3. The effect of the short is to permanently apply a logic 0 to the B input of gate 3. (In these discussions, ground or zero volts is a logic 0 and +5V is a logic 1.) Thus, the output of gate 3 and the circuit depends only on the conditions of the signals X and Y and not on the conditions of W and Z. In the normal circuit *(Figure 3-2a)*, the output of the circuit will be a 1 if either X AND Y both are 1 OR if W AND Z both are 1. In the faulty circuit, the output does not depend upon the levels on W and Z and becomes 1 only if X AND Y both are 1.

Figure 3-2.
Effect of a Short in a
Logic Circuit

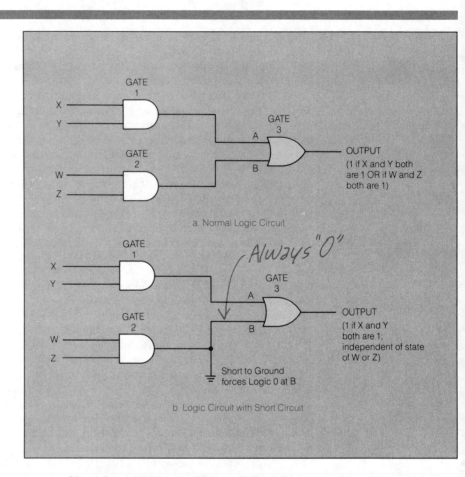

a. Normal Logic Circuit

Always "0"

b. Logic Circuit with Short Circuit

With reasoning, the general location of a short in a logic circuit can be pinpointed. Actual measurements will isolate the problem.

Upon observing that conditions of W and Z have no effect on the system output, one could reason that there is a 0 on the output line of gate 2. If the output of gate 2 were permanently stuck at a 1 level, the output of the circuit also would be permanently stuck at the 1 level, but this is not observed. If one of the inputs to gate 2 were stuck at 1, the other input would still have an effect on the output; the circuit output would become 1 whenever the active input became 1. This also is not observed. The only way the circuit output could be independent of both W and Z and not be a 1 at all times is if there is a short to ground on the W input line, the Z input line, or on the line between the gate 2 output and the gate 3 input B. It would only take three voltage measurements to determine which of the three lines is shorted to ground. Even without the reasoning process, seven voltage measurements (measurement at each gate input and output) would determine the existence of any shorts in the circuit. Once such shorts are detected, the troubleshooter must take the next step of determining the actual cause of the short; that is, is gate 2 defective, is gate 3 defective, or is the short in the wiring? This will be covered a little later, but now let's discuss the opposite condition of a short — the open.

OPEN CIRCUIT

The open circuit, usually just called an open, is a break in the wiring or a component. The main clue to an open is that current cannot flow. The effects of an open on the circuits of *Figure 3-1* and *3-2* are shown in *Figure 3-3*.

Open in a DC Circuit

An open is a physical break in a circuit's wiring or one of the circuit's components. A very high circuit resistance is one indicator. Current cannot flow in a circuit where an open occurs.

In *Figure 3-3a*, the open occurs between the two resistors so that the current flow from the power supply and through the two resistors is zero; therefore, the voltage across each of the two resistors is zero. Thus, if a current meter is placed in the circuit, it will indicate 0 mA. If a voltmeter is placed from node 2 to ground, it will indicate 0 volts (as it did in the case of *Figure 3-1b*). If the voltmeter is placed on the right end of R1, before the break, it will indicate 5 volts (which would not be the case in the circuit of *Figure 3-1b*). If a resistance check is made from node 1 to ground with the power supply disconnected, the meter will indicate infinity ohms, which is the resistance of an open circuit. If the ohmmeter is placed at node 2 to ground, it will indicate 1,000 ohms (instead of 0 ohms as in the case of *Figure 3-1b*). Thus, it is possible to determine if the fault is caused by an open or short if enough measurements are made. The basic features of the open are the zero current flow in the circuit, the unusual ohmmeter reading (in some cases infinity), and the unusual voltage readings at various points in the circuit.

Figure 3-3.
Effect of Open Circuit

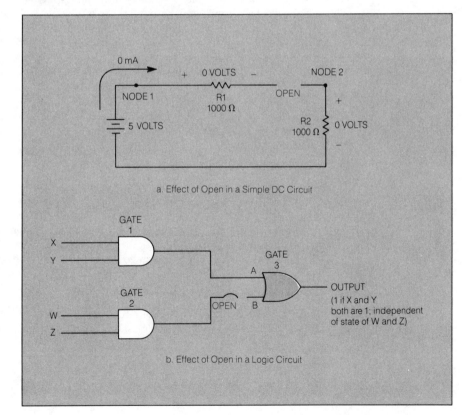

a. Effect of Open in a Simple DC Circuit

b. Effect of Open in a Logic Circuit

Open in a Logic Circuit

If the open circuit appears in a digital circuit of the type shown in *Figure 3-2*, the circuit will not operate properly. An example fault is shown in *Figure 3-3b*. In this example, the open is in the wire from the output of gate 2 to input B of gate 3; therefore, gate 2 has no control over gate 3. That is, the circuit output is a function of only X and Y and will be 1 only when X and Y both are 1. The circuit output again is totally independent of the signals on W and Z.

Measurements must be made to isolate a fault in a logic circuit because an open in a logic circuit can give the same type of circuit indications, in many cases, as a short.

At this point, it becomes obvious that the short in *Figure 3-2b* and the open in *Figure 3-3b* result in the same overall system behavior. The only way to determine whether the fault is an open or short is to make voltage measurements on the portion of the circuit involving gate 2. If a voltmeter is placed on the output of gate 2 in *Figure 3-3b*, the voltmeter will indicate a 1 when both W and Z are 1 which indicates that gate 2 is functioning properly. However, in *Figure 3-2*, the output of gate 2 would be stuck-at-0 regardless of the signals on W and Z. This would lead one to the conclusion for *Figure 3-3b* that there is an open between the output of gate 2 and input B of gate 3 or that gate 3 is defective. The open would be isolated if the resistance of the path between the output of gate 2 and input B of gate 3 were measured with an ohmmeter. Instead of indicating the normal 0 ohms for a wire, the ohmmeter would indicate a very high resistance or infinity, which would indicate a break in the electrical connection between the two points.

The cases of *Figures 3-2* and *3-3* indicate that merely reasoning through the operation of a circuit is not enough to isolate the fault. Knowing that the circuit is responding properly to the signals X and Y and not to signals W and Z isolates the problem to a smaller area of the circuit, but it is not possible without measurements to determine if gate 2 is bad, gate 3 is partly bad, there is a short in the path, or there is an open in the path. Thus, reasoning through the operation of the system indicates the portion of a circuit where measurements should be made to finally isolate the fault to a particular component or wire.

IMPROPER VOLTAGE LEVELS

In between the conditions of a short circuit and an open circuit is a condition where the signal at a given point is not stuck at either 0 or 1, but has a voltage level that is too low to reliably indicate a 1, yet too high to reliably indicate a 0. Of course, a system with this fault won't operate properly, but what's worse, it won't operate the same way all the time. In order to understand how an improper voltage level occurs requires a closer examination of how transistors work in digital circuits.

Transistor Inverter Circuit

A very simple transistor circuit with no faults present is shown in *Figure 3-4a*. This circuit will be used to illustrate the operation of the basic

Figure 3-4.
Faults in Transistor
Circuits

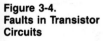

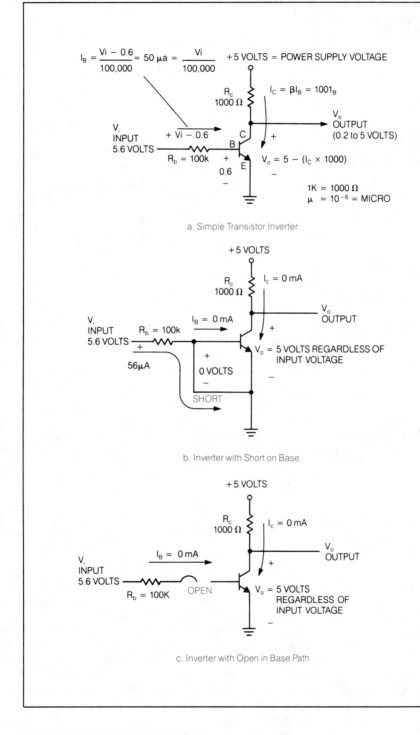

a. Simple Transistor Inverter

b. Inverter with Short on Base

c. Inverter with Open in Base Path

**Figure 3-4.
Faults in Transistor
Circuits (cont.)**

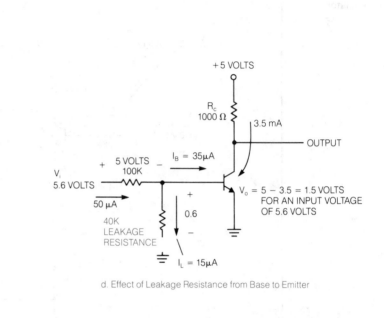

d. Effect of Leakage Resistance from Base to Emitter

Switching circuits operate
at one of two logic levels.
A simple inverter is an
example.

transistor digital circuit. The chief feature of transistor operation is that it
provides considerable current gain. If a signal is applied to the input such that
a base current is produced, the collector current will be 50 or more times as
large as the base current. The output voltage is determined by multiplying the
collector current (in amperes) by the collector resistor value (in ohms) and
subtracting the resulting voltage from the power supply voltage.

Normal Operation

In the example of *Figure 3-4a*, a base current of 50 microamperes
(0.000050 ampere) is produced by the logic 1 applied to the circuit input
terminal. The current gain is assumed to be 100 so this causes a 5 mA collector
current which in turn causes a 5 volt drop across the 1,000 ohm collector
resistor. When this 5 volts is subtracted from the 5 volts of the power supply,
the output voltage is 0 volts which is in the logic 0 range. Thus, the transistor
circuit acts as an inverter because a 0 is output when a 1 is input.

On the other hand, when a logic 0 (0 volt signal) is applied to the
input, the base current is zero; therefore, the collector current is zero. This
causes a 0 volt drop across the 1,000 ohm collector resistor so the output
voltage is $5 - 0 = 5$ volts which is within the voltage range for a logic 1. Again,
the transistor acts as an inverter so that a logic 0 input produces a logic 1
output. More complicated circuits can be reasoned through in much the same
way to determine the effect of a 0 or 1 input level on the output voltage and
logic level.

The on voltage between base and emitter is about 0.6V to 0.7V and about 0.2V to 0.4V between collector and emitter for a saturated silicon transistor.

There is one other aspect of transistor operation that has not been mentioned to this point: When current flows into the base of the transistor, the internal voltage drop between the base and emitter terminals is between 0.6 and 0.7 volt if the transistor is made from silicon. Thus, the input voltage must be greater than this voltage to cause base current to flow.

Similarly, when collector current is flowing, the internal voltage drop between the collector terminal and the emitter terminal prevents a true 0 volt output because the voltage never gets lower than around 0.1 to 0.2 volt for a silicon transistor. Thus, when a logic 1 is applied to the input of the circuit of *Figure 3-4a*, 0 volt output is not possible. The output voltage saturates at about 0.2 volt so slightly less than 5 mA flows through the collector resistor. However, the range of output voltage for a logic 0 (for the TTL family) is from 0.0 to 0.4 volt; therefore, a logic 0 is still output and the transistor is said to be in its saturated state. When the input voltage is not greater than the transistor's base-to-emitter voltage drop, base current does not flow. Therefore, collector current does not flow, a logic 1 is output, and the transistor is said to be in its off state or high-resistance (millions of ohms) state.

Effect of a Short

A short across the base emitter of a transistor inverter causes collector current to be zero, places the transistor in its off-state and outputs a logic 1.

Now, with the transistor circuit's normal operation in mind, we can determine the effect of shorts or opens on the output of a transistor circuit. *Figure 3-4b* shows a circuit with the base shorted to the emitter. In this case, all input current flows through the short circuit and no current flows through the base of the transistor. Thus, the collector current is zero and the transistor is in its off state. Thus, the output voltage is high and the output is stuck at a logic 1 whether the input is a logic 0 or 1.

Effect of an Open

A similar situation occurs if there is an open in the base circuit.

Another situation which could cause the transistor to output a 1 regardless of its input signal is shown in *Figure 3-4c*. In this case, there is an open in the base circuit so that no matter what input voltage is applied, no base current can flow, thus no collector current can flow. Again, the output is stuck-at-1.

Effect of Leakage Resistance

Another type of circuit failure is shown in *Figure 3-4d*. In this case there is an unwanted and unexpected leakage resistance path from the base to the ground. Application of a logic 0 to the input still will turn off the transistor with the resulting logic 1 level output. However, when a logic 1 is applied, not all of the input current will go into the base of the transistor because some current will go through the leakage resistance. In the example of *Figure 3-4d*, the 0.6 volt base-emitter voltage drop causes 15 microamperes to flow through the 40,000 ohm leakage resistance. Since the input voltage in this case is 5.6 volts and 0.6 volt is dropped from base to ground, 5.0 volts must be

Unwanted leakage current
can cause unusual effects.

dropped across the 100K ohm resistor. Since I = V/R, I = 5/100,000 which is 50 microamps. Subtracting the 15 microamps of leakage current from the total input current of 50 microamps leaves only 35 microamps to flow into the transistor base. This means that the collector current will be reduced to 3.5 mA so that the output voltage is 5 minus 3.5 or 1.5 volts. The 1.5 volts is neither a logic 0 or a logic 1 level so that the following transistor (not shown) may be turned on or it may be turned off depending on the particular characteristics of the transistor. Thus, its output may be a logic 0 or it may be a logic 1. Furthermore, the output may be different from time to time depending upon temperature and supply voltage.

For example, if a normal inverter circuit like the one shown in *Figure 3-4a* is coupled to the output of the circuit of *Figure 3-4d*, only 1.5-0.6 volts or 0.9 volts would be dropped across the 100K ohm resistor. Thus, the base current would be 9.0 microamperes. This would cause an output voltage of 4.1 volts, which is in the range for a logic 1. Thus, the circuit of *Figure 3-4a* would respond to a 1.5 volt input as if it were a logic 0 input. However, another inverter of slightly different design might respond to the 1.5 volt input as if it were a logic 1 input. In either case, the improper voltage level can be found by working backward through the circuit and measuring the output voltage of each transistor in the path to determine where the improper level first occurs.

Component Failure

All of the conditions of *Figure 3-4b*, *3-4c*, and *3-4d* could be a fault external to or internal to the transistor. If internal, it would be classified as a component failure. If the transistor is a discrete component, then the transistor could be replaced. If the transistor is in an integrated circuit, the entire circuit must be replaced. All the troubleshooter can do is determine through measurements and analysis that a given component is faulty and replace that component. Whether the fault is in the component or in the wiring usually can be resolved by a process of elimination through the course of measuring the component in place or by measuring the component out of the system with a suitable test instrument.

OTHER TRANSISTOR TYPES

Before leaving the topic of faults in transistor circuits and their effects on circuit output voltage levels, it should be mentioned that the bipolar NPN transistor shown in *Figure 3-4* is only one of the types of transistors found in digital circuits. Other types are the bipolar PNP transistor, P-channel FET and N-channel FET. (The letters P and N refer to the type of material in the transistor. The letters FET are an abbreviation for Field Effect Transistor.) The basic circuits and operational features of these devices are shown in *Figures 3-5* and *3-6*.

Figure 3-5.
PNP Transistor Inverter

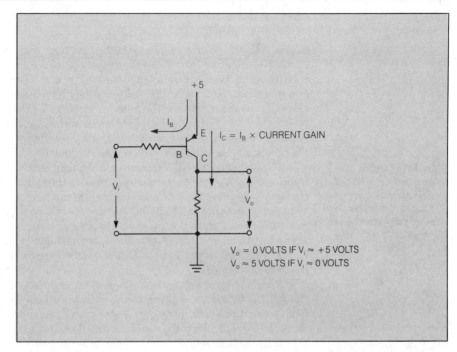

$I_C = I_B \times$ CURRENT GAIN

$V_o = 0$ VOLTS IF $V_i \approx +5$ VOLTS
$V_o \approx 5$ VOLTS IF $V_i \approx 0$ VOLTS

Figure 3-6.
FET Operation

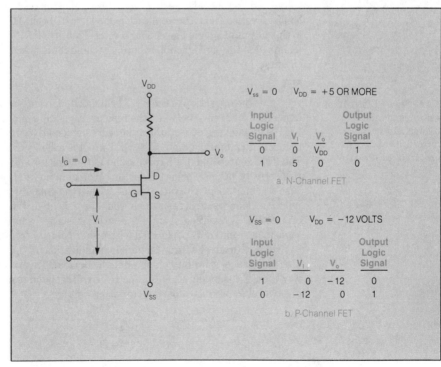

$V_{SS} = 0$ $V_{DD} = +5$ OR MORE

Input Logic Signal	V_i	V_o	Output Logic Signal
0	0	V_{DD}	1
1	5	0	0

a. N-Channel FET

$V_{SS} = 0$ $V_{DD} = -12$ VOLTS

Input Logic Signal	V_i	V_o	Output Logic Signal
1	0	-12	0
0	-12	0	1

b. P-Channel FET

PNP

The PNP bipolar transistor, shown in schematic form in *Figure 3-5*, has operational features similar to those of the NPN transistor in *Figure 3-4a*. Comparison of these two figures shows that the main difference is in the polarity of the voltages connected to the emitter and collector and the current flow directions. Notice that the emitter of the PNP is connected to the positive side of the power supply and the collector is connected through a collector resistor to ground which is the negative side of the power supply. The base circuit is connected to the input voltage, and the output voltage is taken from the collector of the transistor with respect to ground.

Just as in the NPN transistor, if the base terminal of the PNP transistor is connected to the same potential as the emitter terminal, base current cannot flow, thus, no collector current can flow. As a result, the voltage at the output will be 0 volts because there is no voltage drop across the collector resistor, thus, the top end of the resistor is at the same voltage level as the bottom end; that is, 0 volts. Therefore, an input voltage of 5 volts (a logic 1) will result in an output voltage of 0 volts (a logic 0) and logic inversion has been performed.

If the input voltage is at a logic 0, say at 0 volts, current will flow through the forward biased emitter-base diode through the base resistor to the 0 volt connection at the input. A collector current equal to this base current times the current gain of the transistor will flow. If the transistor is saturated so that the emitter-to-collector voltage is a few tenths of a volt, the output voltage will be the voltage drop across the collector resistor which will be almost 5 volts. Thus, the application of a logic 0 (0 volts) to the input will result in the output of a logic 1 level near 5 volts. Faults in PNP circuits would be found using the same troubleshooting techniques as discussed for the NPN circuits.

FET

The operation of the FET is illustrated in *Figure 3-6*. The most important difference between the bipolar transistors and the FET is that the FET is voltage sensitive rather than current sensitive. Its input current is zero regardless of input voltage. (The FET input is called a gate rather than a base. The FET source and drain correspond to the emitter and collector, respectively, of the bipolar transistor.) If an ohmmeter is connected across the base and emitter of a bipolar transistor with the polarity to forward bias the junction, a low value of resistance would be indicated. If the polarity of the connections is reversed, a higher value of resistance would be indicated. If this same measurement is performed with either polarity from the gate of an FET to either its drain or source terminal, an indication on the ohmmeter of very high resistance or infinity ohms would be normal. This is true because of the way the FET is made. Even so, the FET will respond to an input voltage of a given level to produce a particular output voltage.

Operation of a PNP transistor is similar to that of an NPN transistor except that voltage polarities are reversed and current flows are opposite to what they were in an NPN.

A FET (Field-Effect Transistor), is controlled by voltage rather than current. Its circuits have a very high resistance.

N-Channel FET

N-Channel FETs have a positive voltage applied to the drain and zero or positive voltage applied to the gate, when operating as an inverter.

In the N-channel device, the V_{DD} is a positive voltage and V_{SS} is 0 volts or ground. Application of a voltage at the same level as the $\overline{V}_{SS}$ voltage to the gate would provide no gate-to-source voltage; therefore, drain current would not flow and the output voltage would be at the V_{DD} level because no voltage drop occurs across the resistor. In this case, a 0 volts (logic 0 level) input would produce a positive V_{DD} voltage output (logic 1 level) and logic inversion is accomplished. Similarly, if a voltage near V_{DD} (logic 1) is applied to the gate, enough gate-to-source voltage occurs to cause maximum drain current flow which reduces the output voltage to near the V_{SS} level or 0 volts. Thus, a logic 1 input results in a logic 0 output. These inputs versus outputs are shown in *Figure 3-6*.

P-Channel FET

P-Channel FETs have a negative voltage applied to the drain and zero or negative voltage applied to the gate when operating as an inverter.

The P-channel FET works with voltage polarity opposite to that of the N-channel FET; thus, it requires a V_{SS} voltage that is positive with respect to the V_{DD} voltage. For example, if V_{SS} is 0 volts then V_{DD} must be some negative voltage supply. If the input voltage is at the V_{SS} level of 0 volts, there is no gate-to-source voltage so no drain current flows and the output voltage is at the V_{DD} level. If the more positive voltage (0 volts in this case) is taken as the logic 1 level, and the more negative voltage (the V_{DD} level in this case) is taken as the logic 0 level, it can be seen that a logic 1 input will produce a logic 0 output. Similarly, if V_i is at the V_{DD} level (a negative voltage) there is significant gate-to-source voltage of the proper polarity to produce maximum drain current flow so that the output voltage is near the V_{SS} level of 0 volts. Thus, a logic 0 (-12 volts in this case) input will produce a logic 1 output (0 volts).

Notice that all previous examples have used this same convention where logic 1 is the more positive voltage and logic 0 is the more negative voltage. This is referred to as "positive" logic. What is different about this circuit is that ground or 0 volts is logic 1 rather than a positive ($+$) voltage, and a negative ($-$) voltage is logic 0 rather than ground or 0 volts. In other words, the logic is the same, but the different ground reference point causes different voltages to produce that logic.

If a circuit consists of two or more of the transistor types shown in *Figure 3-4, 3-5,* and *3-6*, interface circuits may be required between them to adjust the logic 0 and logic 1 voltage levels that occur in the different transistor inverters. Such an interface circuit definitely would be required to interface a circuit of the NPN transistor of *Figure 3-4* to the P-channel FET circuit of *Figure 3-6*.

Using a FET Transistor as a Resistor

The inverters discussed in *Figures 3-4, 3-5,* and *3-6* use a resistor from the collector or drain of the transistor to the dc supply voltage (V_{cc} or

In MOS Integrated circuit design, an MOS field-effect transistor is used for high resistance because it is less costly to make in IC form.

V_{dd}). In integrated circuits, it is often expensive to make a large value resistor because of the amount of space the resistor takes up on the silicon chip surface. It is much more economical to make transistors on the silicon. Fortunately, a transistor can act like a resistor under certain operating conditions.

The relationship between I_d and V_{ds} for a MOSFET transistor is shown in *Figure 3-7a* for the case in which the gate terminal is connected to the drain terminal. This causes the V_{gs} voltage to be relatively large so the transistor is on and conducting current. Also shown in *Figure 3-7a* is the linear plot of the current versus voltage for a resistor. By comparing the curves, it can be seen that for small values of V_{DS}, the FET acts like a resistor. Even for large values of V_{DS}, the FET is still behaving like a resistor, but the resistance is varying with applied voltage. Thus, the FET resistance is non-linear, but it would work just as well as the linear resistor for the applications considered in the circuits of *Figure 3-6*. In *Figure 3-7b*, the linear resistor is shown replaced by the physically smaller (with regard to silicon area), but equivalent value resistance FET. This is the standard design used in MOS integrated circuits. The operation of the circuit is the same as for the MOS transistor circuits shown in *Figure 3-6*.

Figure 3-7.
Using MOSFET as a Resistor

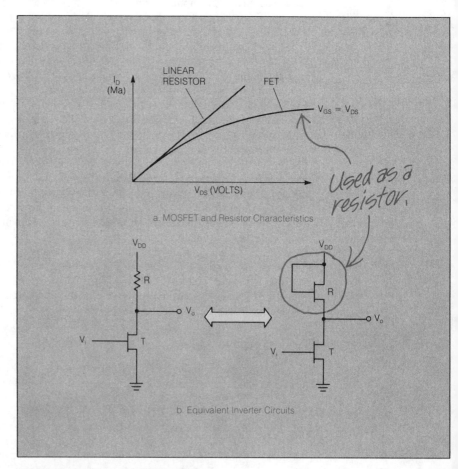

a. MOSFET and Resistor Characteristics

b. Equivalent Inverter Circuits

Faults in circuits using the P-channel FET or the N-channel FET would be found using troubleshooting methods as discussed for the NPN bipolar transistor of *Figure 3-4* except that gate current would not be measured. The test instruments used for troubleshooting transistor circuits — the voltmeter, ammeter, ohmmeter and a device known as a logic probe — will be considered in more detail in the next section.

MEASUREMENT TECHNIQUES

The test instruments considered in this chapter provide information about voltage, current, or resistance levels in a circuit. They indicate the level of the measured quantity by a movement of a needle across a calibrated meter scale (analog meter), or by a digital display of the actual numerical value (digital meter), or by turning on or off a light-emitting device (logic probe). All are useful in determining the location and nature of faults in a digital system.

Multimeters

A general purpose test instrument that is capable of measuring voltage, current, and resistance is called a multimeter. It can be either an analog type as shown in *Figure 3-8a* or a digital type as shown in *Figure 3-8b*. The analog type is generally less expensive than the digital type, though the analog type is not as convenient to use and often is not as accurate as the digital type.

Function and Range Selection

Multimeters measure voltage, current and resistance and can display readings in analog or digital form. Scales and ranges can be changed easily with selector switches.

Both have control switches to select the function (voltage, current or resistance) and the range or scale. Thus, if DC voltages with values expected to be under 10 volts are to be measured, the switches would be set to select the DC voltage function and a range of 0 to 10 volts. For an analog meter, the scale on the meter face that corresponds to the range selected is read at the position of the pointer. For a digital meter, a number between 0.000 and 9.999 would be displayed to directly indicate the actual value of the voltage measured. That's one of the conveniences of the digital meter. Another is "autoranging" where the meter itself selects the best range for the input voltage. Thus, the digital meter does all the work — the operator simply connects the input.

Polarity

Make sure that the polarities of the measuring probes of any meter used for testing are correctly matched to the polarities of the points being tested in the circuit.

Both meters have jacks on the meter case into which the measuring probes can be plugged. The jacks are marked + and − and/or of a red (for +) and black (for −) color. For voltage and current measurements, the red probe is connected to the more positive point in the circuit and the black probe is connected to the more negative point in the circuit. Except for *Figure 3-6* for the P-channel circuit, the example circuits that have been shown have the more negative point as ground, but in many circuits, as is true for the P-channel circuit, the more positive point is ground.

Figure 3-8.
Multimeters
(Courtesy of Simpson Electric Company, Elgin, Illinois)

a. Analog Meter

b. Digital Meter

CAUTION: Always turn off the circuit power before measuring resistance.

For resistance measurements, the two probes are placed across the circuit whose resistance is to be measured and a voltage from the meter is applied to the circuit. For resistors, the polarity (+ or −) of this voltage doesn't matter, but for transistors and diodes it does. In some meters, the red lead is positive as you would expect; but in other meters, the black lead is positive.

Input Resistance

When any measurement is being made with any instrument, the instrument selected should be designed so that connection of the instrument will not affect the operation of the circuit being measured. For dc measurements, the input dc resistance is the meter parameter that is most likely to affect circuit operation. *Figure 3-9* illustrates the effect of meter input resistance on the circuit operation and the measured voltage values. *Figure 3-9a* shows a voltmeter that has a relatively high input resistance of 1 megohm so that it will draw very little current from the circuit being measured. (Some meters have more than 10 megohms input resistance.)

How much the meter affects the circuit and the voltage measurement is determined by the ratio of the meter resistance to the circuit resistance that the meter is connected across. The combination of these two resistances in parallel determines the equivalent resistance of the circuit when the meter is connected. The formula for computing the equivalent resistance of two resistances in parallel is shown in *Figure 3-9b*. The equivalent resistance (R_{eq}) of two resistors (R_1 and R_2) in parallel is computed by dividing the product of the two resistors by the sum of the two resistors. In the circuit of *Figure 3-9a*, the 10K ohm circuit resistor (R_2) in parallel with the 1 megohm meter resistance results in an equivalent resistance of 9,901 ohms. Therefore, the voltage across R_2 is indicated to be about 2.49 volts instead of the actual value of 2.50 volts when the meter is not connected. Thus, the act of measuring the voltage has changed the voltage by about 0.01 volt, but this is less than 0.5% error in the measurement which is acceptable for most troubleshooting.

If a voltmeter with only a 10,000 ohm internal resistance is used in the measurement, as shown in *Figure 3-9c*, the equivalent resistance of the two 10,000 ohm resistances in parallel is 5,000 ohms. Now the voltage indicated by the meter is 1.67 volts, which is a major error of over 30%. Besides the measurement error, the operation of a circuit could be changed to the point that it may appear to be malfunctioning when it is not.

This condition is referred to as "test instrument loading the circuit" and must be avoided during troubleshooting. In general, to avoid "loading down" the circuit and changing circuit voltages, the input resistance or impedance of the test instrument should be at least 100 times the resistance across which it is placed. This is true of all measurement equipment, including the simple logic probes that will be considered in the next section.

When taking circuit measurements, make sure that test instrument circuit loading does not occur, it can adversely affect circuit operation.

**Figure 3-9.
Effect of Meter Input
Resistance on Measured
Voltages**

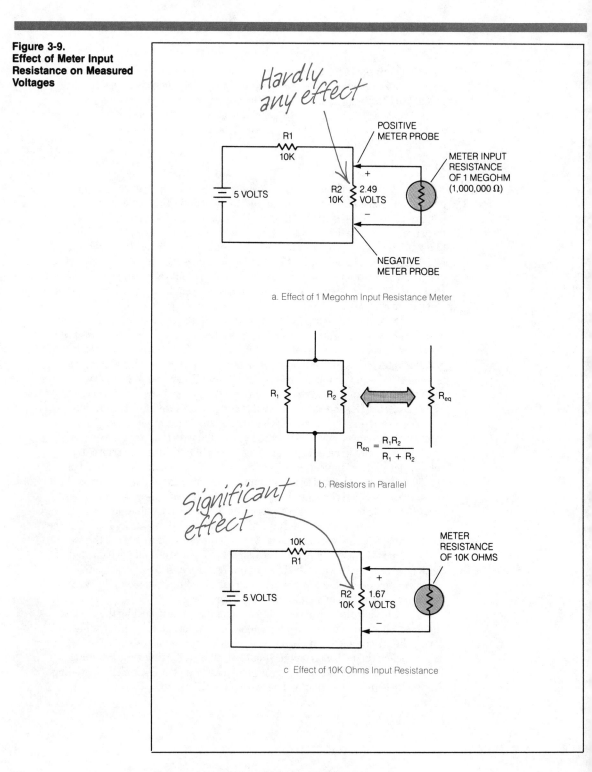

a. Effect of 1 Megohm Input Resistance Meter

$$R_{eq} = \frac{R_1 R_2}{R_1 + R_2}$$

b. Resistors in Parallel

c. Effect of 10K Ohms Input Resistance

Logic Probe

The logic probe is a type of voltmeter that provides information about the logic level of a particular signal line. If the level is a 1, the light turns on; if it is a 0, the light is off.

A logic probe is a form of a voltmeter. There are several forms of logic probes and there are some related devices such as logic pulsers that are available to aid in circuit evaluation. Some of these devices are shown in *Figure 3-10*. A logic probe will provide the troubleshooter with information about the signals on one line. A logic clip will provide the troubleshooter with information about the signals on sixteen lines. When a signal is at a logic 1, the light on a logic probe will turn on. When the signal is at a logic 0, the light will be off. Thus, the troubleshooter has a positive indication of the status of a signal path.

Logic Clip

Effectively, a logic clip with 16 contacts is 16 logic probes in one package. It allows connection to all pins of a 16 pin IC package at one time.

A second type of logic probe is shown in *Figure 3-10*. It sometimes is called a logic clip because it is a clip-on probe with 16 contacts that connect to the 16 pins of an integrated circuit. There are sixteen small lights, one for each pin, so that the signals on all 16 pins can be monitored at the same time. Such a probe is generally level sensitive as opposed to being able to detect momentary 1 levels that occur in fast digital pulses. By connecting such a clip to a circuit and providing known input conditions, the entire operation of the circuit can be observed quite readily by the light pattern.

Figure 3-10.
Logic Pulser and
Logic Clip
(Courtesy of
Hewlett Packard Co.)

Logic Pulser

A logic pulser is used to inject signal pulses into a circuit for tracing.

A device that can be used in conjunction with the logic probe or the logic clip is the logic pulser shown in *Figure 3-10*. The logic pulser produces pulses which are inserted or injected into the circuit at the point of contact. Generally, the troubleshooter has control over when and how often pulses are injected by a push-button switch. Usually, one pulse is generated each time the button is depressed and released. By successively depressing and releasing the button, a pulse train of relatively low frequency can be injected into the circuit On some pulsers, a pulse train is produced simply by holding the button in the depressed position.

By using the pulser in conjunction with the logic probe or logic clip, the passage of the pulses generated by the pulser through the circuit is indicated by flashing lights on the logic probe or logic clip. Such a combination test would allow the troubleshooter to trace the pulses along any path of a circuit to determine which paths are working properly and which are not.

TROUBLESHOOTING METHODS

The procedure for determining the location of a fault in a system involves reasoning through the operation of a system to isolate first the general functional unit that is operating improperly. This reasoning process may be aided by evidence collected from a series of well-planned measurements. Once the fault is isolated to a given functional unit, the fault can be pinpointed by following the same reasoning process and plan of detailed measurements within the functional unit. In all such measurement plans and system analysis, the troubleshooter must think of the system as a number of series paths of signal flow, all of which must be operating properly for the system to operate properly.

Functional Analysis

A thorough understanding of how a system works when operating properly is a very valuable tool when observing the operation of a system that has a fault.

An example of the functional flow that exists in every system is indicated for the general case in *Figure 3-11a*. Each system must have an input function, a processing function, and an output function. If any one of these functions fail, the system will not operate properly. The observed operation of the system can provide a great deal of information about which input function or processing function or output function is causing the problem.

A more specific example of the functional nature of an electronic system, a color television receiver, is shown in *Figure 3-11b*. The system described is not a digital system, but the techniques involved in troubleshooting are the same in analog and digital systems. Sometimes troubles may be caused by a fault in a not-so-obvious function; however, in the following discussion, only the more obvious are considered.

**Figure 3-11.
System Functional
Relationships**

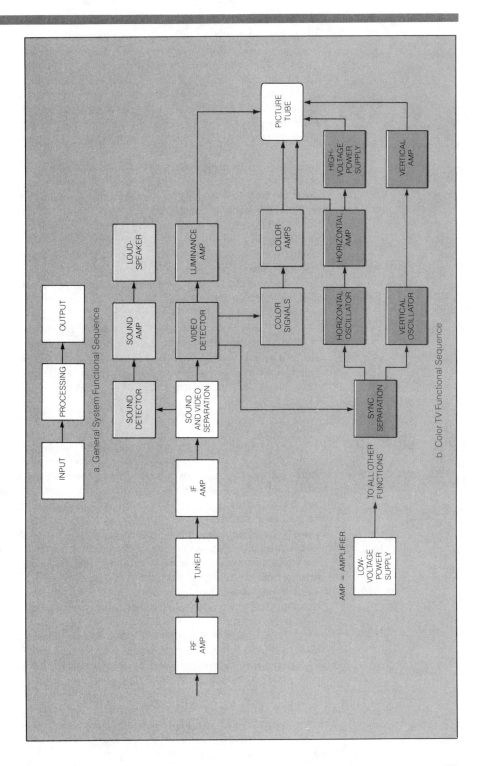

a. General System Functional Sequence

b. Color TV Functional Sequence

AMP = AMPLIFIER

Functional Operation of a TV

A functional TV receiver
is used as an example.

The input circuits or functions consist of amplification and tuning. The RF amplifier boosts the weak antenna signal to a level that can be operated on by the tuner section to select one television channel from all the channels available. This function is followed by specially tuned amplifiers called IF amplifiers which reject unwanted signals and boost the signal strength of the desired signal.

The next function is that of separating the sound signal and video signal. From this point in the system, the sound path is independent of the other functions. The sound signal proceeds to a sound detector which recovers the audio frequency signals from its carrier. The audio is amplified to the level required to drive the loudspeaker.

The video detector recovers the video signal from its carrier. The picture signals are separated into the luminance signal (which determines the black and white portions of a picture) and the burst and chroma signals (the color information signals). The chroma or color determining signals are processed and amplified to produce the color control signals which are sent along with the luminance signal to the electron guns of the picture tube to reproduce the original picture in color.

The synchronization signal is sent to control the horizontal and vertical oscillators. These circuits generate the waveforms that cause the electron beams generated by the electron guns in the picture tube to be deflected across and down the screen to produce an entire rectangular picture. These signals are shaped and amplified and sent to the deflection coils of the picture tube.

Troubleshooting a TV

When a fault occurs, by
reasoning through the
subsystem functions and
the symptoms caused by
the fault, the probable
faulty subsystem should
become evident. More
detailed troubleshooting
techniques are required to
pinpoint the exact cause of
the problem.

Even with this brief description, it is possible to analyze the symptoms of almost any fault and develop a list of most likely locations of the fault within the system. For example, if the observed failure is that there is no sound (not even noise) or picture and the screen is black, the troubleshooter is faced with the unlikely possibility that two or more independent circuit paths have failed at the same time, or that all circuits in the system have lost their power. The latter case is much more likely and the low-voltage power supply would be examined first. If the set is not producing sound, but is providing a good color picture, the fault must lie somewhere between the sound separation function and the loudspeaker. It is not possible to further localize the problem without making some system measurements or performing some other troubleshooting procedure such as part replacement or component measurement.

If the sound is present and a black-and-white (no color) picture is present, the fault likely would be in the sections handling the color signals such as the chroma bandpass or the burst oscillator sections. Again, more information would be required to determine the exact cause of the problem. If there is neither program sound nor picture, but the screen is uniformly illuminated with a white background and noise is heard from the speaker, there is system power and the fault must lie in functions that are common to both sound and picture; those from the antenna (assuming a signal is present from the antenna) to the sound and video detectors. As a final example, assume that program sound is heard and the picture has color, but the picture is rolling vertically. The main functional elements that involve picture vertical and horizontal placement are the sync separator and vertical and horizontal oscillators and amplifiers. There are other, more remote possible causes, but the troubleshooter probably would begin making measurements on the vertical oscillator and amplifier circuits to locate the fault.

Regardless of the system being examined, this reasoning process from input functions through processing functions to output functions must be made to get an idea of which function is faulty. Once the problem function has been determined, it is then possible to use various troubleshooting techniques and make some measurements that will lead to the actual fault. Two of the most powerful troubleshooting strategies are visual inspection and component substitution.

Visual Inspection

Often the exact fault in a subsystem can be determined simply by visually inspecting the subsystem.

Once a system problem has been related to a functional element or portion of the system through analysis and measurement procedures, it is possible that the fault may be detected visually; that is, simply by looking at the wiring and components in the circuit. For instance, in the color television example, if the low-voltage power supply is considered at fault because the screen is black and there is no sound, and if vacuum tubes are used, looking at the tubes to see if the filaments are glowing red will indicate if the problem lies in the tube filament supply or if it lies elsewhere. Similarly, if the color television fault lies in the color producing circuitry (burst or chroma circuits), that region of the printed circuit board or chassis wiring should be examined for loose wires, sockets, shorted wires, and so on.

Intermittent

If faults are intermittent, moving components or wiring slightly may help to detect the problem.

In one such case (no color), the author visually examined the area involving these circuits and found no obvious problem. By physically moving wires, tubes, sockets and other components with a wood dowel, it was found that the color would come in when one of the coils in the section was moved. This coil's electrical connections had deteriorated with age and was providing an intermittent (off and on) open connection in that portion of the circuit. By soldering the coil connections, the problem was solved and color was restored without ever making a voltage measurement or checking any of the components in the system.

Other examples of the types of problems that can be found by visual inspection of the suspected portion of a system are shown in *Figure 3-12*. In the situations shown in this figure, either a short or an open is suspected through analysis of the system operation or has been confirmed through voltage and resistance measurements. The problem is to physically locate the short or open visually if possible.

Short

The short, shown in schematic form in *Figure 3-1c*, is shown pictorially in *Figure 3-12a*. By looking at the printed circuit pattern and the components, it is possible to detect the presence of a small piece of conductive material, possibly a solder drop or a small piece of wire, bridging the printed circuit metallization. In this example, the effect of the conductive particle is to short out the resistor R1 in *Figures 3-12a* and *3-1c*. By removing the particle

**Figure 3-12.
Visual and Electrical
Detection of Physical
Faults**

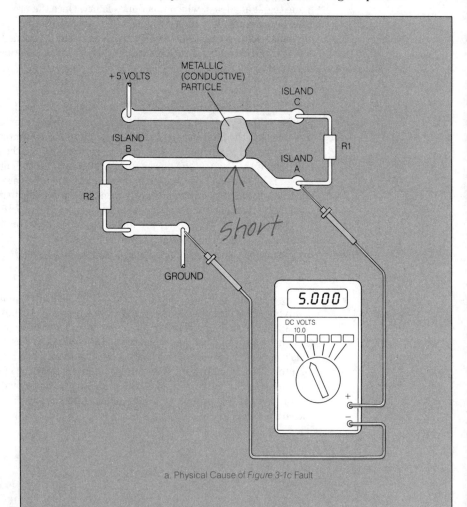

a. Physical Cause of *Figure 3-1c* Fault

with the probe of a multimeter or other pointed metal object such as a screwdriver, the short can be removed and the circuit repaired. (Do not lose the particle by "flicking" it; it may cause another short where it lands.)

Loose conductive particles that have fallen onto a printed circuit can short out wiring and cause malfunctions.

The circuit should be checked with a voltmeter or ohmmeter before and after the particle is removed to confirm that the particle was causing the problem. It is not always possible to determine if a particle is conductive by looking at it, but even if the particle is obviously metallic and conductive, it still may not be possible to determine visually if it is making electrical contact to both runs of the printed circuit board conductors. However, if 5 volts is measured at both islands A and C as illustrated in *Figure 3-12a*, the particle is causing the short. After the particle is removed, the removal of the short can be verified by measuring 2.5 volts at island A with respect to ground. This last measurement also helps confirm that R2 was not damaged by excessive current due to the short across R1.

**Figure 3-12.
Visual and Electrical
Detection of Physical
Faults (cont.)**

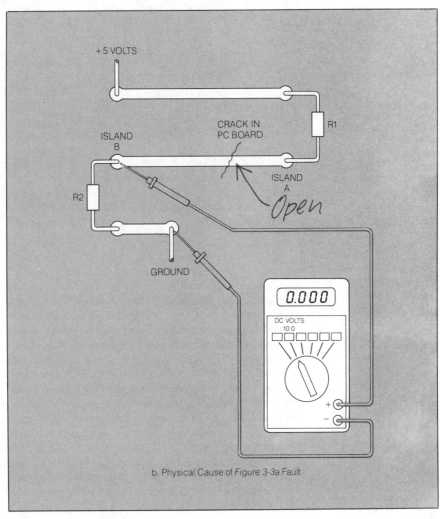

b. Physical Cause of *Figure 3-3a* Fault

**Figure 3-12.
Visual and Electrical
Detection of Physical
Faults (cont.)**

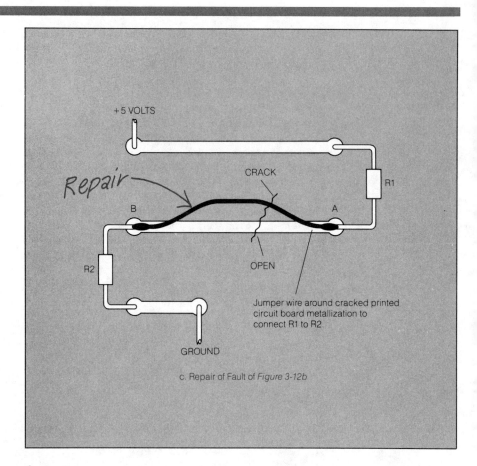

c. Repair of Fault of *Figure 3-12b*

Open

A crack in a PCB's printed
conductor is one type of
open that usually can be
visually detected. Mea-
surements before and
after repair assure the
crack is the problem and it
is repaired.

In the example of *Figure 3-12b*, an open has occurred that is
represented in circuit form in *Figure 3-3a*. The open is a crack in the printed
circuit board that runs through the printed conductor that connects R1 to R2.
Such cracks may be difficult to see because a hair-line crack can break the
circuit. If the presence of the open has not already been confirmed by voltage
or resistance measurement, the measurement should be made at this time.
Measure the resistance by placing the probes of an ohmmeter on the two
circular solder islands A and B with the system power off, or measure the
voltage by placing a voltmeter from island B to ground as shown in *Figure
3-12b* with the system power applied. If the voltage reads 0 volts at island B
and 5 volts at island A, there is an open circuit between these two points and
the troubleshooter can proceed with the repair of the circuit. The reason the
measurement is necessary is that the crack may not have cut open the metal
layer and may not actually be the cause of the circuit problem. Once it has been
confirmed that the crack has caused an open circuit, the circuit can be repaired
by soldering a wire from island A to island B as shown in *Figure 3-12c*. It would
be wise to determine what caused the crack to prevent future problems.
Perhaps a fastener came loose and allowed the board to bend.

As an actual case history of the situation depicted in *Figure 3-12b*, the author once was faced with the repair of a color television set that had neither picture (black screen) nor sound. It was a tube set and a visual inspection indicated that all tubes were glowing properly. The symptoms (no sound and black screen) pointed to the low-voltage power supply. A visual examination of that circuit detected a crack that looked much like the one shown in *Figure 3-12b* in the printed circuit coming directly out of the output connection to the power supply. A voltmeter measurement indicated that the power supply was producing 300 volts on one side of the crack, but the voltage was 0 volts on the other side. The set power was turned off and a jumper wire was soldered over the cracked area. Presto, the set was restored to normal operating condition.

Of course, simple shorts and opens are not the only types of failures that can occur, but when they do, a combination of visual examination and electrical measurements can pinpoint the fault. When an open or short or leakage current path occurs inside one of the components of the system, many of the same reasoning and measurement techniques that are used in finding shorts and opens in the system wiring can be used to find the defective component. Sometimes defective components, or at least the circuit at fault, can be located by the physical appearance of the component; for example, burned resistors.

Component Failures

Circuit faults consist not only of opens, shorts and leakage currents, but also of component failures.

If a component has an internal short or open or if it does not have the proper output voltage level, one must determine whether the fault is in the component or in some portion of the circuit external to the component. Several techniques for checking component operation will be considered in this section.

Out-of-Circuit Test

One technique for checking a component requires removal of the component from the system and testing it with a suitable test instrument.

CAUTION: Turn off system power before removing a part and do not turn on power while the part is removed unless you are sure the system will not be damaged. If power is on, turn it off before installing a part.

If a component is removable, an important troubleshooting technique is to remove the suspected component from the circuit and test it externally. A variation of this technique is to replace the suspected component with a known good one, and observe system performance.

For example, when dealing with a color television that has vacuum tubes, and no obvious short or open circuit problems have been detected by measurement and visual examination, then the tubes of the suspected circuits would be removed and checked with a tube tester, or known good tubes would be substituted temporarily. The same procedure could be used with transistors and integrated circuits if the appropriate test equipment is available. If a component tests bad or marginal, replace the component. If, after replacement, the system still fails to operate properly, the new component should be tested out of the circuit. If it is now bad, then something else in the system circuitry is bad and is causing the replaced component to fail. The most likely causes of such a problem are a short on the output of the component, or the supply voltage or input voltages being too high for the component. In either case, the other fault must be detected and repaired first. However, most of the time, replacement of only one faulty component will repair the system.

Removal and external testing of a device is practical only if the device or component is plugged into a socket that is connected to the printed circuit board metallization. If the component is directly soldered to the printed circuit connections, removal of a component is very tedious and may damage the component or the printed circuit board if the removal is not made very carefully.

In such cases, the component should be removed only if it is known to have failed; therefore, the component testing must be done while the component is still in the system. Even if the component is in a socket and can be removed easily, it may be possible to isolate the failure of the system to that component by testing the system with the component in place. The techniques involved in testing components still connected to the system involve voltage measurements with and without all of the pins of the component connected to the system. An alternative procedure, called signal tracing, involves using logic pulses and logic clips or probes in combination to trace the flow of signals through various paths in the system to determine which paths and which circuits are faulty. Both methods will be discussed in the following sections.

In-Circuit Test

When it is impractical to remove a component from a circuit, faults may be isolated by selected voltage, current, or resistance measurements or by signal tracing.

In order to examine the general concepts of testing components, and specifically testing components in place in the system, the situations of *Figures 3-2b* and *3-3b* will be considered again. In *Figure 3-2b* where the short is somewhere in the path from gate 2 to gate 3, it is a relatively simple matter to determine that a short is present; however, determining where the short actually is located is somewhat more difficult. If each gate is in a separate socket, each could be removed one at a time and each time check for the short with a voltmeter. For example, if the short exists in the circuit with both gate 2 and gate 3 in the circuit, but the short is not present when gate 2 is removed from the circuit, one can assume that gate 2 has failed with a stuck-at-0 condition. If the short still exists when gate 2 is removed, then the short must be along the interconnecting wire or in the B input of gate 3. The latter case can be checked by removal of gate 3 (with or without gate 2 back in the circuit). If removal of gate 3 removes the short on the line, then the B input of gate 3 is shorted to ground and gate 3 must be replaced. If removal of both gates do not remove the shorted condition, the wire is somehow shorted to ground and the short must be removed as necessary.

The open circuit condition of *Figure 3-3b* could be pinpointed with a similar sequence though the wire conditions can be readily checked by making a resistance measurement from the output terminal of gate 2 to the B input terminal of gate 3. If the resistance is 0 ohms, the wire is not open and the fault must be in one of the gates.

If the gates of *Figures 3-2b* and *3-3b* are not in separate packages, but are all in one integrated circuit, it is not recommended to remove the entire IC. In that case, only the output lead of gate 2 could be disconnected and, for *Figure 3-2b*, the shorted condition checked. (How to identify the various leads will be discussed shortly.) If the short is not removed by this action, the B input lead of gate 3 could be disconnected. If either gate is found faulty, then the entire component would be removed and replaced.

In some cases it may be necessary to remove an IC's individual pin connections, or a discrete component in order to isolate the circuit fault.

The disconnection of a single lead of a component from a circuit is illustrated in *Figure 3-13a* for an IC in a socket on the system board and in *Figure 3-13b* for an IC soldered to a system circuit board. The case of *Figure 3-13a* is the easiest because all that is required is to remove the IC from the socket, bend the output lead slightly outward, and then replace the component in the socket with all pins of the circuit entering the socket except for the bent lead. Now gate 2 can be checked for an output short by measuring the voltage on the dangling lead. This voltage should not be stuck at ground if the gate is operating properly. With two logic 1 inputs on gate 2, it should have a logic 1 output in accordance with the AND gate truth table. If the device output lead appears shorted to ground regardless of input conditions, then gate 2 is faulty. If gate 2 is operating properly, open the input B pin on gate 3 and check the operation of gate 3 with this input lead. If gate 3 operates properly, check the resistance of the wire to ground. The resistance of the wire to ground should be very high or infinity with both the output lead of gate 2 and the B input lead of gate 3 disconnected from the circuit. Although this has served to illustrate the method of isolating one pin at a time, the simplest way to find this particular short is to remove the IC and check for the short between the appropriate socket pins and ground. If neither shows a short, the IC must be replaced because both gates are in the same IC.

The pin isolation technique is more useful when the device is soldered into the circuit board as shown in *Figure 3-13b*. The measurements are done the same as with the socket example of *Figure 3-13a*, but it is more difficult to disconnect the pin from the board. Generally this is accomplished by carefully holding the IC lead with needle nose pliers while heat is applied to melt the solder at the solder island. When the solder melts, the lead is pulled gently upward and clear of the connection. If the measurements show that the component is good, the process is reversed by heating the island until solder again melts and gently pushing the lead back into the hole in the island. Some new solder should be added to complete the connection.

In the process of removing the lead, it is also possible (and makes the job easier) to remove the solder from the hole as it melts with a device called a solder sucker. The simplest one is similar to an ear syringe, but has a heat resistant tip. With the solder removed, a slight lifting of the lead should disconnect the lead from the board. The reconnection is a simple matter of pushing the lead back in the hole, reheating the island and lead, and applying new solder.

Of course, such soldering and resoldering is tedious, slow work and may damage good components if extreme care is not taken. This method should be used only as a last effort to determine the system problem. A more desirable and less destructive approach is to trace signals through circuit paths using logic pulsers and probes. This technique is known as signal tracing.

Great care must be taken in removing a component's individual pin connections to prevent damage to the component or circuit.

**Figure 3-13.
Pin Isolation Techniques**

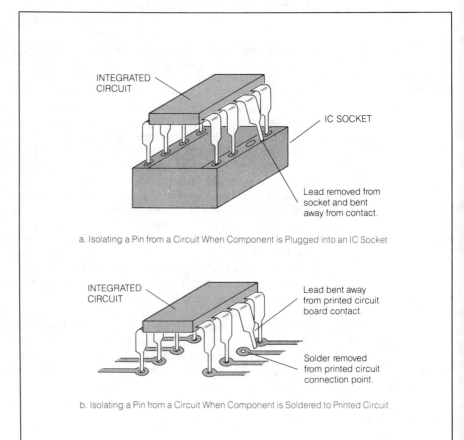

INTEGRATED
CIRCUIT

IC SOCKET

Lead removed from
socket and bent
away from contact.

a. Isolating a Pin from a Circuit When Component is Plugged into an IC Socket

INTEGRATED
CIRCUIT

Lead bent away
from printed circuit
board contact.

Solder removed
from printed circuit
connection point.

b. Isolating a Pin from a Circuit When Component is Soldered to Printed Circuit

Signal Tracing

Signal tracing is a fault detection technique where a known signal is injected into a system at a particular point and the resultant system performance observed for malfunctions.

The technique of signal tracing, which has been used extensively in radio and television repair work, also is useful for the detection of faults in digital systems. Instead of simply using a voltmeter or a logic probe to indicate the voltage or logic level of a point in an operating system, the signal tracing method uses the injection of a known signal at one point in the system and then uses the measurement instruments to determine how that signal passes through the system.

The technique can be illustrated by again using the basic circuit of *Figure 3-2a*. The circuit is redrawn in an equivalent all NAND gate form in *Figure 3-14a*. Any logic that consists of a group of input AND gates feeding a group of output OR gates can be converted to all NAND gate form by simply leaving the interconnections as they are and directly replacing all gates (AND and OR) with NAND gates.

It is possible to buy four two-input NAND gates in a single IC package. The type of diagram shown in *Figure 3-14b*, which shows how these four gates are connected to the external pins of one particular type, is available from manufacturer's data. *Figure 3-14b* also shows how the external pins can be connected to provide the logic circuit of *Figure 3-14a*. Notice that these pin numbers are identified on the logic diagram of *Figure 3-14a*. On an actual printed circuit board, the connecting conductors between pins 6 and 9 and between pins 3 and 10 probably would run underneath the IC.

Signal Tracing Using Logic Probe

The logic probe and logic pulser can be used for signal tracing. The probe can be used as a signal detector and the pulser as a signal source.

The procedure for signal tracing this circuit can be illustrated using the diagrams of *Figure 3-15*. The pulser is connected to one of the inputs of gate 1 and the probe is connected to the circuit output. During this test, the non-pulsed input of gate 1 must be connected to a logic 1 to allow the test pulses at the other input to pass through the gate. If the non-pulsed input is tied to a logic 0, the pulse train cannot get through the NAND gate even though the circuit is operating properly. In this example, in order for the pulses applied to the input of gate 1 to reach the probe at the output of gate 3, both inputs of gate 2 are connected to a logic 0.

The circuit is similar to that of *Figure 3-2b*, but with the line between gate 2 and 3 shorted to +5 volts. By generating a sequence of pulses on input line X and with the logic probe connected to the circuit output (pin 8), the presence of the pulse train is indicated by a blinking light on the logic probe. Thus, the path from the X input to the output is working properly. Similarly, by placing the pulser on line Y, connecting line X to a logic 1 and repeating the test, the path from Y to the output is verified. This verifies the operation of gate 1 and one input of gate 3.

**Figure 3-14.
All NAND Gate Logic
Circuit**

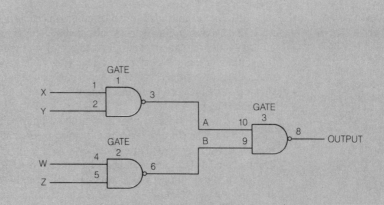

a. All NAND Gate Equivalent of Circuit in *Figure 3-2*

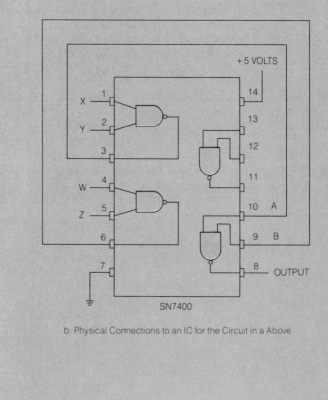

b. Physical Connections to an IC for the Circuit in a Above

**Figure 3-15.
Signal Tracing to Isolate
Faults**

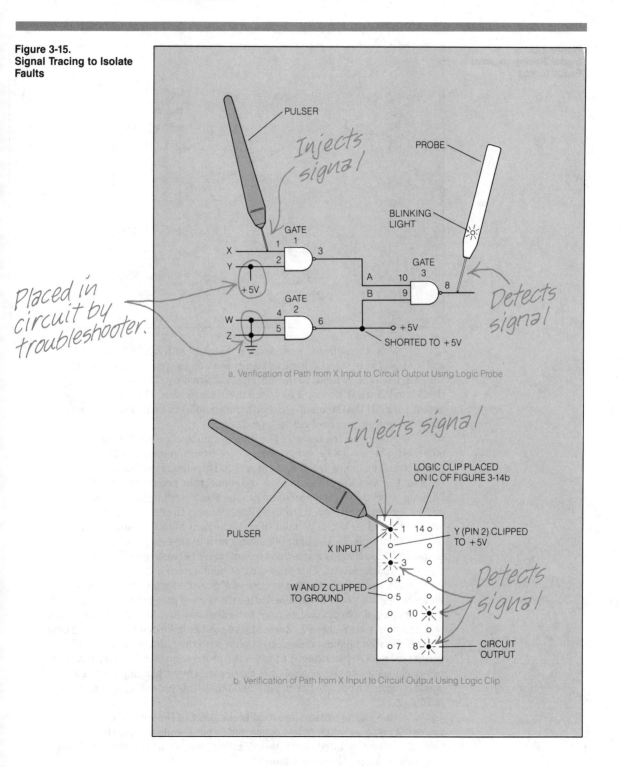

a. Verification of Path from X Input to Circuit Output Using Logic Probe

b. Verification of Path from X Input to Circuit Output Using Logic Clip

Figure 3-15.
Signal Tracing to Isolate
Faults (cont.)

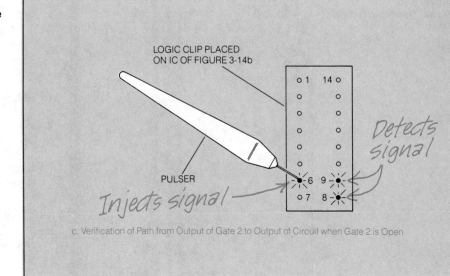

LOGIC CLIP PLACED
ON IC OF FIGURE 3-14b

Detects signal

PULSER

Injects signal

c. Verification of Path from Output of Gate 2 to Output of Circuit when Gate 2 is Open

Now, the pulser is moved to the W input (with Z at +5 volts and X and Y at 0). There is no blinking or steady light on the probe, indicating that the path from the W input to the output is not working. The pulser is moved to the Z input (with W now at +5V) with the same results. Thus, there is a fault in that path. (If the circuit of *3-3b* (with the open) were being analyzed in this way, the same sequence of events would occur.)

Now move the probe to the B input (pin 9) of gate 3. Still no light is observed. There must be a short somewhere from and including the output of gate 2 to and including the B input of gate 3. Disconnect pin 9 to isolate it from the line. Connect the pulser to pin 9 and connect the probe to pin 8. The blinking indication on the probe verifies the short is not in gate 3. Now disconnect pin 6 to isolate it from the line. Connect the probe to pin 6 and connect the pulser to the W input (pin 4). The light blinks. Connect the pulser to the Z input (pin 5). The light blinks and verifies that gate 2 is working properly. Thus, there is a short on the conductor between pins 6 and 9. Find the short and remove it. This procedure is summarized in *Table 3-1*.

If, instead of a short, the open of *Figure 3-3b* were the problem, different results would be obtained after the tests of gate 1 through gate 3 path were completed. No pins would need to be disconnected. When gate 2 is tested with the pulser on W, then Z, it would test good as indicated by a blinking light at pin 6. Next, a blinking indication at pin 8 with the pulser at pin 9 would verify that gate 3 is working. But when the probe was moved to pin 9 with the pulser connected to either pin 4 or 5, there would be no blinking light. This would indicate an open between pin 6 and pin 9. This procedure is summarized in *Table 3-2*.

One way to isolate the actual break point (if the conductor is accessible) is to leave the pulser connected to pin 4 while moving the probe along the wire or printed circuit metallization from pin 6 toward pin 9. When the blinking stops, the open is found.

Signal tracing results should be analyzed carefully. Circuit opens give different results than circuit shorts.

Table 3-1.
Signal Tracing the Circuit in Figure 3-14a with Short to +5 Volts from Conductor Between Pin 6 and Pin 9

Connect Pulser to IC Pin	Connect Probe to IC Pin	Probe Indication	Conclusion
1	8	Blinks	
2	8	Blinks	Gate 1 OK
4	8	Off	
5	8	Off	
9	8	Off	
Isolated 9	8	Blinks	Gate 3 OK
4	Isolated 6	Blinks	
5	Isolated 6	Blinks	Gate 2 OK External Short to +5V

Table 3-2.
Signal Tracing the Circuit in Figure 3-14a with Open in Conductor Between Pin 6 and Pin 9

Connect Pulser to IC Pin	Connect Probe to IC Pin	Probe Indication	Conclusion
1	8	Blinks	
2	8	Blinks	Gate 1 OK
4	8	Off	
5	8	Off	
4	6	Blinks	
5	6	Blinks	Gate 2 OK
9	8	Blinks	Gate 3 OK
4	9	Off	
5	9	Off	External Open Between Pins 6 and 9

Signal Tracing Using Logic Clip

Using a logic clip rather than a logic probe speeds signal tracing in ICs tremendously because voltage levels on all pins of the IC are indicated at the same time.

The use of the logic clip and pulser can speed up the analysis. In *Figure 3-15*, the presence of the clip is illustrated by circles that represent the light emitting devices for each pin of the IC. Filled in circles with rays indicate the light is on. For this example, let's assume that the output of gate 2 is open inside the IC. Connect the pulser to the X input as shown in *Figure 3-15b*, and blinking lights appear on the logic clip at pins 1, 3, 8 and 10 as indicated to verify that the circuit path from X to the output is good. Now connect the pulser to the W input and blinking lights appear at pins 2, 3, 8 and 10 to verify that the circuit path from Y to the output is good.

UNDERSTANDING DIGITAL TROUBLESHOOTING

Move the pulser to the W input and the only blinkling light is at pin 4. Move the pulser to the Z input and the only blinking light is at pin 5. Move the pulser to pin 6 and blinking lights appear at pins 6, 8, and 9 as indicated in *Figure 3-15c*. This verifies the path from pin 6 to the circuit output; therefore, gate 2 must be defective.

The best way to accomplish the repair is to replace the IC. If the circuit were in a development breadboard where actual wires are used for connections, the faulty gate could be disconnected from the circuit and the unused fourth gate in the IC wired in its place.

The advantage of the signal tracing method is that it is fast and simple and allows the operation of each portion of a suspected circuit to be evaluated without removing the circuit or any of its components. Signal tracing along with voltage and resistance measurements will allow the troubleshooter to detect and correct a great majority of the simple and common faults that occur in digital (and other) electronic systems.

WHAT HAVE WE LEARNED?

1. The common faults that occur in any digital system are short circuits, open circuits, and voltage level problems.
2. These faults can be readily detected by making appropriate voltage and resistance measurements throughout the suspected portions of the system.
3. These measurements can be made with either an analog meter, a digital meter, or a logic probe.
4. The troubleshooter must observe how the system is operating and use his/her knowledge of the system's functions to determine which is the most likely function to cause the observed problem.
5. Once the problem is localized to a given functional portion of the system, the techniques of visual examination, voltage and probe measurements, and signal tracing can be used along with external component testing or component replacement to locate and correct the fault.

Quiz for Chapter 3

1. In the circuit of *Figure 3-1a*, if the value of R2 is increased to 9,000 ohms, what would be the voltage across R2?
a. 0
b. 0.5
c. 4.5
d. 5.0

2. In the circuit of *Figure 3-1b*, if R2 develops an internal open circuit (no current can flow through R2), what will be the circuit current in mA (power supply current)?
a. 0
b. 2.5
c. 5.0

3. If the fault described in problem 2 occurs in the circuit of *Figure 3-1c*, what will be the power supply current in mA?
a. 0
b. 2.5
c. 5.0

4. In the circuit of *Figure 3-2a*, if a short develops from the output of gate 1 to the power supply voltage of 5 volts, what will the output of the circuit depend upon?
a. The X input
b. The Y input
c. The W and Z inputs
d. None of the above

5. In the circuit of *Figure 3-2a*, if a short occurs from a power supply line to the output of gate 2, what will be the output logic level?
a. 0
b. 1
c. 0 or 1 depending on the values of X and Y

6. In the circuit of *Figure 3-3a*, if the open circuit occurs internally in R2 instead of in the wire, what will be the power supply current in mA?
a. 0
b. 2.5
c. 5.0

7. For the same conditions of problem 6, what will be the voltage across R2?
a. 0
b. 2.5
c. 5.0

8. In *Figure 3-4a*, the output voltage is approximated as 0 volts based on the base current being 50 microamperes. If the 0.6 volt base-emitter voltage drop is considered, what would be the value of the collector current in mA for an input voltage of 5 volts?
a. 3.0
b. 4.0
c. 4.4
d. 4.7

9. For the same conditions of problem 8, what would be the output voltage?
a. 2.0
b. 1.0
c. 0.8
d. 0.6
e. 0.2

10. In the circuit of *Figure 3-4d*, what would be the collector current in mA if the 40K ohm resistor is increased to 100K ohms, assuming the input voltage is 5.6 volts?
a. 3.0
b. 4.0
c. 4.4
d. 4.7

11. What would be the output voltage in the circuit of *Figure 3-4d* if an input voltage of 5 volts were applied?
a. 2.1
b. 2.7
c. 1.6
d. 0.8

12. In the circuit of *Figure 3-4d*, if the value of R_c is decreased to 500 ohms, what will be the output voltage?
a. 0
b. 1.5
c. 3.25
d. 4.0

13. If a 50K ohm resistor is connected in parallel with a 25K ohm resistor, what is the equivalent resistance of the parallel combination?
   a. 25K
   b. 20K
   c. 16.67K
   d. 16K

14. In the circuit of *Figure 3-6a*, if the meter has an input resistance of 100K ohms, what will be the voltage measured across R2?
   a. 1.78
   b. 2.38
   c. 2.43
   d. 2.50

15. In a signal tracing exercise, a logic probe is placed on the output of gate 3 in *Figure 3-2a*. When a pulser is applied to each of the inputs of gate 3, a blinking indication is present on the probe. If the pulser is moved to the output of gate 1, the blinking does not occur. What is the fault in the circuit?
   a. There is a short from gate 1 to the +5 supply voltage.
   b. There is a short in the wire connecting gate 2 to gate 3.
   c. There is an open in the wire connecting gate 1 to gate 3.
   d. There is an open in the wire connecting gate 2 to gate 3.

16. In the circuit of *Figure 3-2a*, if applying a pulser to each of the W, Y and Z inputs results in a blinking probe connected to the output of gate 3, but applying it to X does not cause blinking, what is the fault in the circuit?
   a. Gate 1 is defective.
   b. The input line from X to gate 1 is open.
   c. Gate 3 is defective.
   d. a or b above.

17. In the circuit of *Figure 3-2a*, if applying a pulser to any input X, Y, W or Z will cause a blinking probe at either input to gate 3, what is the problem?
   a. Gate 1 is defective.
   b. Gate 2 is defective.
   c. The two inputs of gate 3 are shorted together.

18. If in a color television receiver, there is sound but no picture, but the screen is illuminated, what is the most likely functional element that has failed?
   a. RF amplifier
   b. Tuner
   c. Video detector
   d. Color circuits
   e. Deflection amplifiers

19. In the circuit of *Figure 3-1a*, 0 volts is measured across R2 and the resistance measured from the left side of R1 to ground with the power supply disconnected is 2,000 ohms. What is the problem with the circuit?
   a. Short across R2
   b. Open in R2
   c. Short across R1
   d. Defective power supply

20. In the circuit of *Figure 3-1a*, if 0 volts is measured across R2, what are the possible faults?
   a. An open circuit
   b. A shorted R2
   c. A defective power supply
   d. A short across the power supply
   e. All of the above
   f. a and b above

Combinational Logic Problems

ABOUT THIS CHAPTER

Chapter 3 introduced the electrical causes of most faults that are found in electrical and electronic systems along with the measurement techniques that can be used to detect the location of such faults. Some of the faults that occur in combinational logic circuits also were introduced. This chapter continues the examination of such faults and gives some methods that can be used to repair combinational logic systems. The emphasis will be to understand the component and system operation because this knowledge is necessary to find a fault.

FAULTS IN SSI DIGITAL CIRCUITS

Simple gate combinations are used in even the most complex systems to control subsystem operation and input/output functions.

The basic gates used in modern digital systems are fabricated in small-scale integration (SSI) circuits which have less than 100 gates per chip. The operating characteristics and logic symbols for the AND, OR, NOT, NAND, and NOR gates have been covered in previous chapters. If the reader is not sure how these gates work, go back and review the material because this knowledge is basic and necessary to further understanding.

Typical systems consist of a group of input NAND gates connected to a group of output NAND gates or a similar structure consisting of all NOR gates. Even relatively complex systems such as computers still use some of these gates to control the operation and input/output functions of system components. In these cases, the combinational logic may consist of a single NAND gate with an associated medium- or large-scale integration component. (A medium-scale integration (MSI) component has over 100 gates per chip and a large-scale integration (LSI) component has over 1,000 gates per chip.) A simple example of such a situation is illustrated in *Figure 4-1*, which is the circuit of an 8-switch keyboard. The circuit consists of eight resistors, one 8-input NAND gate, eight momentary-contact pushbutton switches and one octal three-state buffer.

**Figure 4-1.
Combinational Logic
Using Simple Gates**

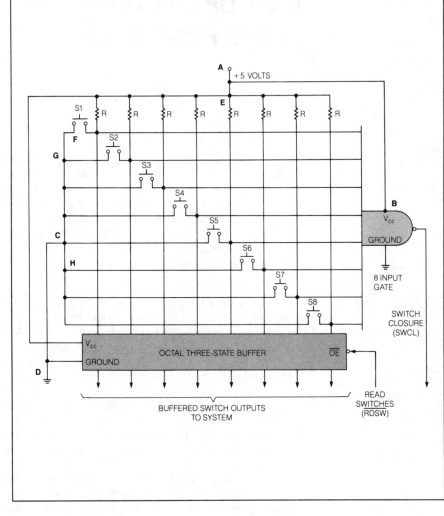

Three-State Buffer Operation

Three-state buffers, controlled by a common enable signal, are used to transfer bits in parallel onto a common bus in microcomputers and other digital systems.

In order to understand the operation of the circuit of *Figure 4-1*, let's review the basic operation of the three-state buffer. (Recall its operation was described in Chapter 2.) The logic diagram for the octal three-state buffer, shown in *Figure 4-2a*, consists of eight (octal means eight) single-bit three-state buffer symbols with the $\overline{OE}$ (Output Enable Not) lines connected together in parallel. The input logic 0 and 1 level signals will appear on the output lines only when the control signal $\overline{OE}$ is at its active level, which is the low or 0 level. Remember that this is indicated by the circle on the buffer control inputs and the bar over the signal name. Thus, only when the $\overline{OE}$ control line is brought to a logic 0 level will the output lines receive the input voltage levels. On the other hand, when the $\overline{OE}$ line is at a logic 1, the output lines are electrically disconnected from the input lines and essentially appear

**Figure 4-2.
Operation of Octal
Three-State Buffer**

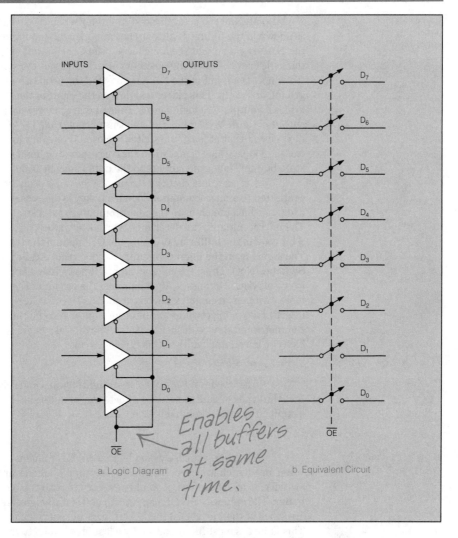

a. Logic Diagram   b. Equivalent Circuit

Enables all buffers at same time.

as open circuits. Thus, the buffers can be thought of as electrical switches whose closure is controlled by the signal $\overline{OE}$ as illustrated in *Figure 4-2b*. The three-state buffer is used commonly in microcomputers to control various circuit connections to a common bus.

Circuit Operation

Now that the basic operation of the three-state buffer is understood, the operation of the circuit of *Figure 4-1* can be analyzed to provide the background necessary to reason through the faults that can occur in such a circuit. In the circuit of *Figure 4-1*, there are 8 momentary-contact, push-button switches. One terminal of each switch is connected to electrical ground (0 volts). The other terminal is connected to a resistor, one of the inputs of the NAND gate, and to one of the inputs of the octal three-state buffer. Since the other end of the resistor is connected to +5 volts, a logic 1 is applied to the

Using a combination of a NAND gate and an octal three-state buffer, inputs from an 8-key keyboard are interfaced to a microcomputer.

NAND gate and the octal three-state buffer when the switch contacts are open as shown in the figure. If all switches are open, all inputs to the buffer and to the NAND gate are at the logic 1 level, thus, the output of the NAND gate is at the logic 0 level. When the pushbutton is depressed, the switch contacts close to connect the input of the NAND gate and the octal three-state buffer to ground or 0 volts. This places a logic 0 on the input to the NAND gate which forces its output to a logic 1 level. Thus, if one or more switches are closed, the output of the NAND gate is a 1 and this output, called SWCL, indicates to the next circuit that at least one switch is closed. For every line that has a switch closed, a logic 0 also is placed on the corresponding input of the octal three-state buffer. Thus, some inputs to the buffer may be 0 and some may be 1.

Let's assume that the circuit of *Figure 4-1* is an 8-switch keyboard connected to a microcomputer. When any key is depressed, SWCL changes to a logic 1 which indicates to the microcomputer that a key has been depressed. The microcomputer can determine which key was depressed by reading the 8-bit code in the buffer by bringing the $\overline{OE}$ input of the three-state buffer low. The signal from the microcomputer that does this is called $\overline{RDSW}$ (for Read Switches Not). Thus, the microcomputer knows that a key is depressed for every bit that is at logic 0. By expanding the circuit of *Figure 4-1* to include more switches, a complex keyboard such as a typewriter-style keyboard can be interfaced to a microcomputer or other digital system. Since a keyboard is a common input device in such systems, the digital system troubleshooter is likely to encounter faults in this type of circuit.

Troubleshooting

The circuit of *Figure 4-1* is straightforward and relatively simple so that the types of faults and their effects can be determined fairly easily. Let's examine the most likely faults.

SWCL Stuck at Zero

If in the example keyboard, the control signal SWCL remains stuck at 0, the points to check are failure of the +5 volts supply, a possible NAND gate failure, or the failure of a line common to all eight switches.

The simplest case would be that SWCL remains stuck at a logic 0 when any switch is closed. The microcomputer would never be informed of a switch closure, therefore, it would never try to read the binary code from the buffer. The only way SWCL can remain at 0 is if all eight NAND gate inputs are stuck at the 1 level or if the NAND gate output itself is stuck at the 0 level. This failure is most likely caused by a loss of +5 volts to the NAND gate, a fault in the NAND gate, or in some line that is common to all eight switches.

Check for the presence of +5 volts at point B (the V_{cc} input to the NAND gate). If not present, check at point A. If +5 volts is present at point A but not at point B, then probe along the connecting wire between the two points to find the open circuit.

The logic probe and pulser are used to determine if the NAND gate is at fault or if the problem is in the switch matrix.

If +5 volts is present at point B, the NAND gate can be checked in the circuit by using a logic probe and pulser to determine if SWCL can be brought high when any input is brought low. Thus, placing a pulser on any input line and placing the probe on the SWCL line should cause a blinking probe light if the gate is working properly. If it is not, the gate should be replaced. If the gate seems to be responding properly to all input lines, then the fault lies in some other part of the circuit.

If pulsing the NAND gate shows it to be in good operating condition, the switch connection matrix must be checked. The only part of the switch circuit that is common to all switches is the wire from point C to point D that connects the switches to ground. If this common connection is open, none of the switches can deliver a logic 0 to the NAND gate inputs. Checking this path with an ohmmeter should locate the open which is most likely to occur at the connections at point C or D, but could occur anywhere along the path. Of course, the circuit could be repaired by installing a jumper wire around the open.

SWCL Stuck at One

Another failure symptom is when SWCL is stuck at 1. In this case, the microcomputer would be continually reading the buffer only to find that no switches are closed, or that one switch is always closed, or that all switches seem to be closed.

When the control signal is stuck at 1, one of three possible situations is indicated by the buffer to have occurred: one switch closed, all switches stuck closed, or no switches closed.

The first case to consider is that SWCL is 1 even when all switches are in the open position. The most likely problem is a faulty NAND gate or an open in the NAND gate ground connection. Either of these problems would prevent the NAND gate from generating a logic 0 even when all gate inputs are at their 1 level.

For the case where it appears that one switch is closed at all times, there may be an open circuit from a switch terminal to point E. This includes the resistor which is a likely cause of the problem. Another cause of the problem may be a short to ground on the path that connects that switch to the NAND gate or on the path that connects the switch to the buffer. This short could be in the switch, in the input circuitry of the NAND gate, in the input circuitry of the buffer, or in the wiring. Component isolation and testing, as described in Chapter 3, would determine the location of the short to ground. Still another case to be considered when SWCL is stuck at 1 is when it appears that all switches are permanently closed (all buffer outputs at 0). The probable cause of this is an open circuit between the power supply connection point A and the common resistor connection point E with the path A to B intact. A short on the path A to B is ruled out because SWCL could not be a 1 if the +5 volt line is shorted.

Improper Operation of Only One Switch

One final fault in the circuit of *Figure 4-1* will be considered. Suppose that the circuit responds normally to all switch closures but S1. This problem is localized by the symptom. Either the switch is faulty and cannot make contact, or there is an open in the path from the switch (point F) to the ground connection (point G), or there is an open between the switch and the NAND gate input, or that particular input to the NAND gate is faulty. Resistance measurements and logic probe checks should isolate the problem. If the switch is faulty, it should be replaced. However, in an emergency, if the contacts can be reached, buffing the contact points with sandpaper or an abrasive cloth may restore the switch to an operating condition.

There are other faults that can occur in the circuit of *Figure 4-1* that have not been discussed. For example, the buffer may not respond to the signal $\overline{\text{RDSW}}$ or may not reliably pass one of the inputs to the output. However, these and other faults in this circuit can be isolated using similar reasoning and procedures as given in the examples. These examples have illustrated that even in a simple gate combinational circuit, there can be many causes of circuit failure. However, by examining the operation of the circuit rationally, the fault usually can be isolated by using simple test equipment and procedures. This same approach also will work in the more complex medium-scale integration (MSI) circuits and large-scale integration (LSI) circuits considered in the remainder of this chapter.

While even simple gate combinational circuits can have several failure sources, analyzing circuit operation and using simple test equipment and procedures will isolate the fault.

FAULTS IN MSI DIGITAL CIRCUITS

MSI circuits include such devices as decoders, multiplexers, counters, shift registers, and encoders. These devices are used with simple gates to perform relatively complicated digital functions with only one or two integrated circuits. The result is a subsystem with fewer interconnections and a lower chance of failure. And when failure does occur, the fault is relatively easy to isolate since it must be in one of the few circuits or in the small amount of wiring that is used to interconnect the circuits. In this section, the operation and faults of some of the more common MSI components will be considered.

MSI circuits have fewer interconnections and a lower failure rate. The result is a subsystem in which faults are relatively easy to isolate.

Analog Multiplexer Circuit

The most commonly used MSI circuit is the decoder. An application using the simplest digital logic decoder with discrete MOSFET transistors to perform the function of an analog signal multiplexer is shown in *Figure 4-3*. The digital control signals, the lines A_8 through A_{15}, the signal $\overline{\text{IOW}}$, and the signal $\text{IO}/\overline{\text{M}}$, would come from a microcomputer or other digital control system.

Figure 4-3.
8-to-1 Analog Signal
Multiplexer

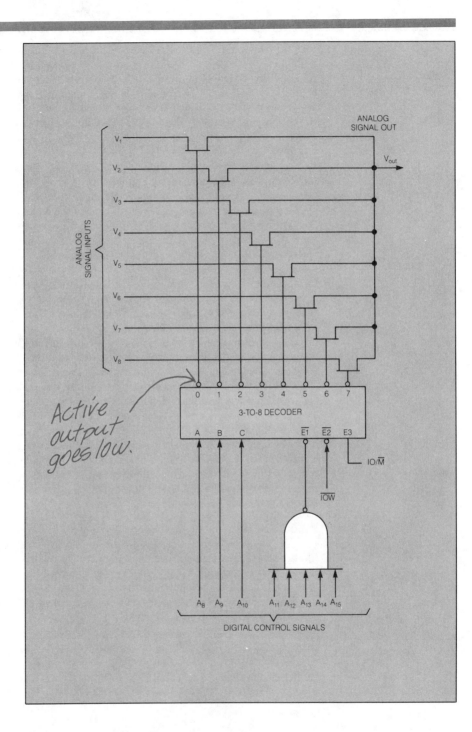

The decoder is the most common MSI circuit and is designed so that only one of its output signals can be low at any one time.

The signals that control the operation of the circuit have fairly common names if they are generated by a microprocessor. The lines A_8 through A_{15} are called address lines because they select or address a given decoder output line. The signals $\overline{IOW}$ and $IO/\overline{M}$ are timing and control signals that determine when the analog multiplexer is enabled or activated. The $\overline{IOW}$ (Input Output Write Not) signal goes low when the processor wants to send information to or activate a selected I/O device. The $IO/\overline{M}$ signal is used by the processor to indicate whether the Input-Output subsystem or Memory subsystem is to be turned on. If the signal is at 0, the memory subsystem is turned on; if at 1, the input-output subsystem is turned on.

Inputs A, B, and C of the decoder are known as the decoder select lines so the signals on lines A_8, A_9 and A_{10} select the output of the decoder. The lines A_{11} through A_{15} are connected to a NAND gate whose output will be at a logic 0 level only if all five of these signal lines are at the logic 1 level. The output of the NAND gate as well as the control signals $\overline{IOW}$ and $IO/\overline{M}$ are connected to the enable inputs $\overline{E1}$, $\overline{E2}$, and E3. The eight active low outputs of the decoder are labeled 0 through 7. These outputs are connected to the gates of the eight MOSFET transistors to control whether they are in their conducting or non-conducting state. (The control input to a FET is called a gate rather than a base.)

When a logic 0 level is applied to the gate of one of these transistors, the transistor acts as a very low value resistor so that the analog input voltage is connected to the output line V_{out}. On the other hand, when a logic 1 level is applied to the gate of one of these transistors, the transistor acts like an electrical open circuit and the input analog signal does not appear on the output line V_{out}. The purpose of the decoder is to control which transistor is in its low resistance state and thereby control which analog signal appears at V_{out}. The decoder is designed so that only one of its output signals can be at the logic 0 level at any time. Thus, the circuit of *Figure 4-3* acts as a digitally controlled switching network for the eight input analog signals. That is, the circuit multiplexes the analog signals onto the V_{out} line under the control of the digital signals into the decoder.

Decoder Operation

The decoder function of *Figure 4-3* is relatively straightforward. First, all three enable lines must be in their true or active state in order for one of the outputs 0 through 7 to go to a logic 0 level. Thus, if a logic 0 is not applied to both $\overline{E1}$ and $\overline{E2}$ at the same time that a logic 1 level is applied to E3, none of the decoder outputs will go to a logic 0 level, regardless of the logic levels applied to the select inputs A, B, and C.

In the decoder, all three enable lines must be in their active state before an output line will go to a logic 0 level. Which output line goes to a logic 0 level is determined by the binary code sent over lines A, B, and C.

If all enable inputs are in their true or active levels, then the binary code on lines A, B, and C determine which output line goes to a logic 0 level. If A, B, and C are all at the logic 0 level, the output 0 (the decimal equivalent of the binary number 000) will go to a 0 level, turning on the top transistor in *Figure 4-3* which allows the voltage V_1 to appear at V_{out}. Similarly, if the A, B, C lines are all at logic 1, output 7 (7 is the decimal equivalent of the binary code 111) will go to a logic 0 level. This would cause the bottom transistor to go into its low resistance state and the voltage V_8 would be connected to the V_{out} line. Thus, this circuit allows a digital controller to electrically gate any desired one of the input analog signals onto the output line.

An application of this circuit would be in a system that automatically collects data from up to eight different inputs. The eight analog voltage inputs are selected one at a time by the decoder under control of the digital control system. In such a system, the analog voltage V_{out} would be applied to an A/D converter to obtain a digital signal for processing by a digital system.

Troubleshooting

Even though MSI ICs like the decoder fail ocassionally, the most likely failure is in a connection to the decoder. Therefore, carefully checking the surrounding circuits and their connections is the first step when a fault occurs.

There are only a few different types of failures that can occur in the circuit of *Figure 4-3*; most of them deal with connection problems though component failures also have to be considered. For example, if, when a logic 1 is applied to each of the lines A_{11} through A_{15} and to E3, and a logic 0 is applied to E2, a low output should appear on the output line corresponding to the 3-bit select code on A_8, A_9, and A_{10}. By stepping through the eight possible 3-bit select codes, the complete operation of the decoder can be verified. Further, by placing one of the enable lines to its inactive level, all decoder outputs should go the logic 1 level. If the decoder outputs do not have the correct levels, the failure must be in the decoder itself or its input connections, or the input NAND gate itself or its input connections. These failures can be isolated using methods previously described, then the faulty component can be replaced or the wiring problem corrected.

If the decoder is operating properly in response to the input control signals and there is no V_{out} for any 3-bit select code (assuming V_1 through V_8 are present), there would have to be an open circuit between the common transistor connection point and the V_{out} terminal. If only one voltage input is not present at V_{out} when the 3-bit select code for that input is used, but each of the other input voltages is present at V_{out} when each is selected, the failure is due to: (1.) a faulty transistor, or (2.) an open wire between the transistor and the input voltage, or (3.) an open wire between the transistor and the V_{out} connection, or (4.) an open wire between the gate of the transistor and the decoder output. By observing the type of failure, the fault can be localized to a small portion of the circuit and diagnostic tests performed only on that portion.

Digital Multiplexer Circuit

Depending on the logic level of the control signal, a multiplexer switches the 8-bit binary signals from either an 8-bit register or an 8-bit counter to the output lines.

Another common configuration of MSI digital circuits is the digital multiplexer shown in *Figure 4-4*. The purpose of this multiplexer is to act as a digital switch to connect either the 8 binary signals from the 8-bit register or the 8 binary signals from the 8-bit counter to the output lines A_0 through A_7. Which set of 8 signals appears on the output lines depends on the state of the control signal REF. If REF is at the logic 0 level, the register outputs are sent to the output lines. If REF is at the logic 1 level, the counter outputs are delivered to lines A_0 through A_7.

This figure introduces two MSI circuit types that haven't been discussed: the octal two-to-one multiplexer and the 8-bit counter. The multiplexer is a combinational circuit and the counter is a sequential circuit.

As the name implies, the function of the counter is to count. It counts the number of pulses that appear on the line INC. Remember that a pulse is a digital signal that changes (makes a transition) from one logic level to another at one time and makes the reverse transition a short time later. Generally, a counter changes its count on one of the transistions. In the circuit of *Figure 4-4*, the count increases each time the signal INC makes a low-to-high level transition. The maximum count is 2^8 or 256 since it has an 8-bit output code. Thus, the counter can count from a state containing 8 zeros to a state containing 8 ones for a total of 256 different binary codes. The counter is said to be modulo 256 since on every 256th pulse the counter resets to all zeros and starts counting up again.

**Figure 4-4.
Digital Multiplexing
Circuit Example**

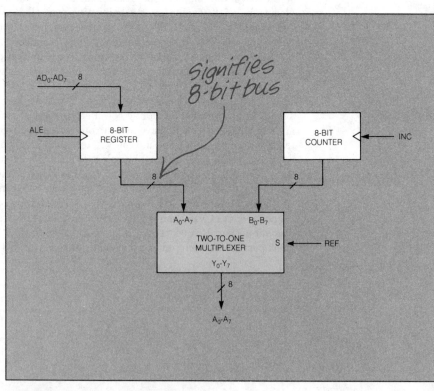

The 8-bit register in *Figure 4-4* is a synchronously latched register. The signals on lines AD_0 through AD_7 are stored in the register when the control signal ALE makes a low-to-high level transition. The stored values then appear on the output of the register and are applied to the multiplexer.

Troubleshooting

Two types of common failures that occur in a multiplexer are: none of the outputs change regardless of the state of the control signal, or one output does not change even if the corresponding inputs are at different logic levels.

Several failure observations could be made in a circuit of the type shown in *Figure 4-4*. One is that none of the outputs A_0-A_7 change regardless of the state of REF. This would imply a fault in the multiplexer or an open or short in the REF line. Similarly, if the outputs of the 8-bit register never change, either the register is faulty or there is an open or short in the ALE line. The same conditions apply to the counter and its INC control line.

If the counter code increases by 1 for each low-to-high transition on the INC line and this code is measured on the B_0 through B_7 inputs, the counter and its connection wires are operating properly. Similarly, if the register outputs change to be the same values as the inputs on lines AD_0 through AD_7 when a low-to-high transition occurs on the ALE line, and these same values are measured both on the A_0-A_7 inputs of the multiplexer, the register and its wiring are operating properly. Under these conditions, the fault causing no change on output lines A_0-A_7 would have to be due to a faulty multiplexer or opens in the multiplexer wiring or connections.

Another failure mode is that one multiplexer output does not change even though the corresponding inputs to the multiplexer are at different logic levels. For example, if the register is outputting 8 zeros and the counter is outputting 8 ones, the multiplexer outputs should change from all 0's to all 1's as REF is changed from a logic 0 to a logic 1 level. If, under such a test condition, all multiplexer outputs except Y_1 change from a 0 to a 1, the cause could be one of the following: (1.) a flaw in the multiplexer in its input circuit for B_1, or (2.) a flaw in the Y_1 output circuit, or (3.) a short on the Y_1 output wire or (4.) an open on the B_1 input wire. Once the multiplexer is found to be operating properly with a separate component test fixture or by using signal tracing techniques, the failure analysis can be limited to the connections and wiring on the B_1 and Y_1 leads. By knowing that the fault is limited to a small area of the entire circuit, the troubleshooter can reduce testing time considerably over what would be required if every wire and component had to be examined in detail. Of course, this is true in all troubleshooting.

FAULTS IN LSI DIGITAL CIRCUITS (READ-ONLY-MEMORIES)

The most complicated combinational circuit types are the Read-Only Memory (ROM) and Programmable Logic Array (PLA). Both types of circuits have thousands of transistors within a single integrated circuit package; thus, they are known as large scale integration (LSI) circuits. Both provide storage of information through the wiring pattern that exists between the gate elements within the device.

ROMs are complex combinational circuits used to store function curves, code conversion tables, or other tables of constants used in a specified system. Typical ROMs output an 8-bit code (a byte) when addressed with the appropriate code.

The simple example of a read-only memory, shown in *Figure 4-5*, has only four storage locations (four input NAND gates labeled G1-G4) and four bits per location (four output NAND gates labeled G5-G8). The interconnection between the outputs of G1-G4 and the inputs of G5-G8 determine what binary pattern is stored in each memory location. Gates G1-G4 provide an m-to-2^m line decoder. In the example of *Figure 4-5*, m is 2, so G1-G4 comprise a 2-to-4 decoder. Only two address lines, A_0 and A_1, are needed to address the four locations. When both of these lines are at the 0 level, only G1 has ones on both its input leads so only G1 will output a logic 0 signal level. This logic 0 will cause a 1 output on the NAND gates to which it is connected, which in this case, are G7 and G8. Thus, the 4-bit output code is 0011 in response to an address code of 00. Similarly, when the address code is 01 (0 on A_1 and 1 on A_0), only G2 has ones on both its inputs and only that gate will output a 0 level. This 0 level output will cause G5 and G6 to have 1 outputs. Thus, an output code of 1100 will be generated whenever an address code of 01 is applied to the inputs of the ROM. The reader can verify that an address code of 11 will cause an output code of 0110 and an address code of 10 will produce an output code of 1101. Since the output code generation with respect to address code is fixed at the time of manufacture, the storage pattern cannot be changed; that is, the memory cannot be written into. This is why it is called a read-only memory.

The simple example in *Figure 4-5* with only 16 bits is only for explanation. Normally, a ROM provides thousands of 8-bit locations. An example of a small 256-byte ROM that might be available as a high-speed memory device is shown in *Figure 4-6a*. For microcomputers, a byte normally consists of eight bits, thus, this device provides 256 locations with 8 bits of storage per location. Since $256 = 2^8$, 8 address line inputs are required so that an external digital system such as a microprocessor can select any one of the 256 locations for output. To eliminate line clutter in the drawing, only one input is shown to each output NAND gate, but interconnection dots indicate which gate has a 1 output for each active (0) row line. The codes stored in the memory as shown are given with respect to address inputs on A_0-A_8 in *Figure 4-6b*.

Application of such ROMs is to store function curves or code conversion tables or other tables of constants used in a particular system. Generally, if the ROM is to be used in microcomputer systems, an octal three-state output buffer is connected between the output NAND gates and the integrated circuit pins as shown. The buffer is enabled by a control signal indicated as a $\overline{CS}$ (Chip Select Not) in the figure.

Figure 4-5.
Simple 4-Location ROM
with 4 Bits per Location

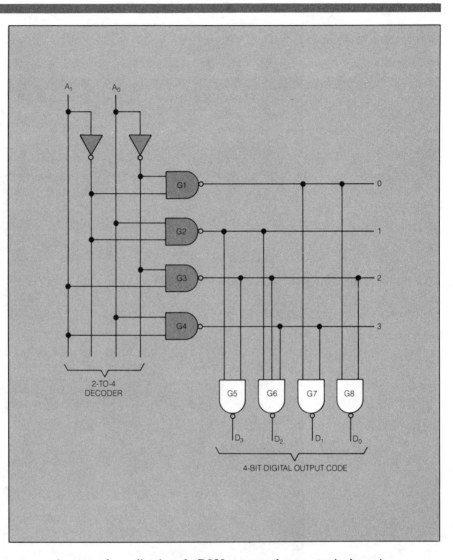

Sound can be generated
by storing the sound en-
velope in a digital code in
ROM and addressing the
ROM location in the cor-
rect sequence and at the
correct rate.

An example application of a ROM as a sound generator is shown in
Figure 4-7. The address is provided by an 8-bit counter whose count is
increased by 1 on each low-to-high transition on the INC line. Thus, if the INC
signal makes a low-to-high transition once every millisecond, the count value
would increase by one every millisecond which provides 1,000 increments per
second. This 8-bit code is sent to the address lines A_0-A_7 of the ROM causing
the ROM to deliver the stored code that corresponds to each address. Thus,
the output code on D_0-D_7 changes every millisecond. The digital-to-analog
(D/A) converter converts the 8-bit code from the ROM to one of 256 different
analog voltage levels. (Recall that the D/A converter was discussed in Chapter
1.) This analog signal is amplified by an audio amplifier and applied to a
loudspeaker.

**Figure 4-6.
256-Byte ROM Structure**

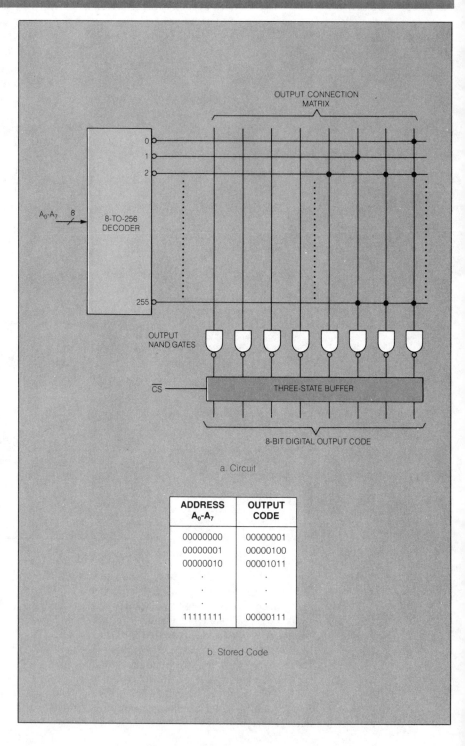

a. Circuit

ADDRESS A_0-A_7	OUTPUT CODE
00000000	00000001
00000001	00000100
00000010	00001011
.	.
.	.
.	.
11111111	00000111

b. Stored Code

By storing in the ROM the envelope of the sound to be generated and by pulsing the counter at an appropriate rate, the desired sound can be generated at the speaker. Since the counter will continually cycle through the codes 0000 0000 through 1111 1111, the same sound will be repeated over and over again. If a sine function is coded into the ROM (recall the sine wave from Chapter 1), an almost pure tone would be produced. By providing the speech pattern for a letter or word and using the proper rate (rather than a constant rate) on the INC signal, the circuit could produce synthesized human speech. This latter application, however, would require a larger capacity ROM than the one shown in *Figure 4-7*.

Figure 4-7.
Simple ROM Application
in a Sound Generator

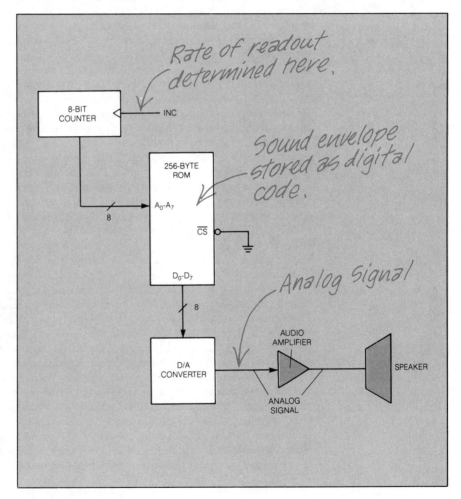

Troubleshooting

The circuit of *Figure 4-7* could fail in any of several ways. Failure would be observed as the wrong sound, weak sound, or no sound coming out of the speaker. Since this is a combination analog and digital system (a hybrid system), both analog and digital troubleshooting methods must be used.

A hybrid system, like the sound generator example, requires both analog and digital troubleshooting methods to find faults. First signal tracing through the analog circuitry is used to check the analog circuits. If O.K., the counter and ROM are tested for proper operation.

One approach would be to begin with a signal tracing procedure to test the analog portion of the circuitry. This could be done by isolating the output pin of the D/A converter and injecting a sinusoidal waveform of 1,000 hertz (or any other convenient audio frequency) through a suitable amplifier to the speaker. An appropriate clear tone should be heard if the speaker and its connecting wires are not faulty. If the speaker is alright, the audio signal should be injected into the input of the audio amplifier. Again, if a clear tone is heard, the amplifier is operating properly. If the speaker or audio amplifier or their interconnection wiring is found to be defective through the signal tracing procedure, the fault can be corrected or the faulty component replaced. If the analog portion is alright, then digital measurements must be made.

The simplest component in the digital portion to check is the counter. By pulsing the INC line with a logic pulser, the voltage levels on the outputs of the counter should change in an orderly manner. A logic probe on the line A_0 should blink at half the frequency of the INC line. The A_1 line would indicate a frequency one half that observed on the A_0 line and so on through the A_7 line. By using a logic clip and a pulser on the INC line, the bits that represent the counter output should count from 0000 0000 to 1111 1111 in increments of 1. If the light pattern on a logic clip is steady when INC is pulsed, either the INC line is open or shorted to ground, or the counter circuit is faulty. If the counter seems to be operating alright except one output line is always in the low or high state, either the counter circuit is faulty or there is an open or short in that output line. Once the counter and its associated wiring have been verified to be operating properly, the operation of the ROM can be considered.

One simple approach, if the storage pattern of the ROM is known, is to apply the pulser to the INC line and attach a logic clip on the ROM circuit. The inputs to the ROM should show the counter binary pattern changing at a rate equal to the INC pulse rate. The lights on the output lines D_0 through D_7 should change in a pattern that is representative of the binary coded function table stored in the ROM. For example, if a triangular or sine wave is stored in the ROM, the output should be a repeating binary pattern that starts at or near all zeros, gradually builds up to all ones, and decreases gradually to near all zeros again. If all the outputs are stuck at 1 or 0 even when the codes on lines A_0 through A_7 are continually changing, the most likely faults include problems in the $\overline{CS}$, ground, or V_{cc} (power supply) connections. A faulty ROM also could cause such an indication. Checks for opens and shorts in the wiring can be made by normal continuity or voltage measurement techniques. If the wiring is alright, the ROM would need to be checked in a microcomputer or by using a test circuit that will permit comparison of the ROM output pattern with the known coding pattern of the ROM.

It is very tedious to check each ROM location by hand. A simpler method uses a microcomputer to address each location of ROM and compare the output to a known code.

One technique for verifying the ROM encoding and operation is to check each location in the ROM with a special purpose test circuit. With such a circuit, the exact 0 and 1 pattern stored in each location can be verified by making pin-by-pin voltage measurements or by using a logic clip, but this is a tedious procedure. A more convenient procedure is to use a microcomputer system to exercise the ROM by reading each storage location bit-by-bit and comparing the code with the known code supposed to be in the ROM. This method is especially useful for a ROM that has thousands of storage locations.

If all but one of the outputs of the ROM seem to be working properly, the possible faults are a wiring problem in that lead or a faulty ROM output circuit on that line.

If the ROM and counter combination are working properly to produce the correct sequence of codes on lines D_0 through D_7 at the rate determined by INC, the only remaining possibility is a faulty D/A converter or its associated wiring.

The D/A converter converts the 8-bit input code to a corresponding analog level output. If the wiring into and out of the D/A converter can be verified as working properly, the fault would probably be in the D/A converter or its power supply or ground connections.

The D/A converter is tested by introducing digital codes from the system and measuring the output with a voltmeter.

One simple way to test the D/A converter is to use the circuit of *Figure 4-7* to produce digital codes into the D/A converter while measuring the resulting output with a voltmeter. However, to observe any changes in the voltage with a voltmeter requires that the INC pulse rate (frequency of low-to-high transition occurrences) be reduced to a slow rate. For example, an INC pulse from 2 to 10 pulses per second would cause the D/A input and output to change at a rate slow enough to be observed with a voltmeter.

By monitoring the input digital code with a logic clip and the analog output voltage with a voltmeter, it would be possible to verify the operation of the converter. For example, when all clip lights are off (all zeros input), the voltmeter indication should be at its lowest. When the most significant inputs (bits A_7 and A_6) are at the 1 level, the voltmeter indication should be high. The voltmeter indication should vary between these low and high levels as the binary code increases from 0000 0000 to 1111 1111 as indicated by the changing light patterns on the logic clip. If the voltage stays in the high range, then one of the digital input lines between the ROM and converter for the most significant bit inputs (A_7 and A_6) must be stuck at the 1 level, or the converter itself is faulty. If the voltage stays in the low range, these same input lines must be stuck at 0, or the converter itself is faulty. In either case, replacing the converter or correcting the wiring faults should repair the system.

AN MSI ENCODER CIRCUIT EXAMPLE

The encoder's function is basically opposite to that of the decoder's. It converts a single line input into an output 3-bit code unique to the input line.

One MSI circuit that has not been discussed is the encoder. To introduce this device and look at one more example of troubleshooting in an MSI system, the example of *Figure 4-8* will be considered. This circuit most likely would be found in a microcomputer system. The encoder basically performs the operation that is opposite to that performed by a decoder. Recall that a decoder converts an m bit code to a one-of-2^m line action. The 3-to-8 decoder again is used in the example of *Figure 4-8*. In this example, one of the decoder output lines, $\overline{G}_0$ through $\overline{G}_7$, goes to a logic 0 level when selected by the 3-bit code on input lines A, B, and C and when the enable input $\overline{E}$ also has a logic 0 on it.

The encoder generates a m-bit binary code that corresponds to the input line that has a logic 0 on it. The specific encoder used in *Figure 4-8* is a priority encoder that determines which of two or more inputs having a logic 0 level at the same time will produce an output. It must output a 3-bit code that corresponds to only one of these lines. The priority scheme is built in and cannot be changed. In an application, the way that the external circuits are connected to the encoder will determine which of the external circuits receive the higher priority. In the example of *Figure 4-8*, the inputs are numbered from lowest priority (input 0) to highest priority (input 7). Thus, if there is a logic 0 simultaneously on both lines 0 and 5, the 3-bit code output by the encoder would be the 3-bit code that corresponds to an active line 5.

**Figure 4-8.
Encoder-Decoder
Application Example**

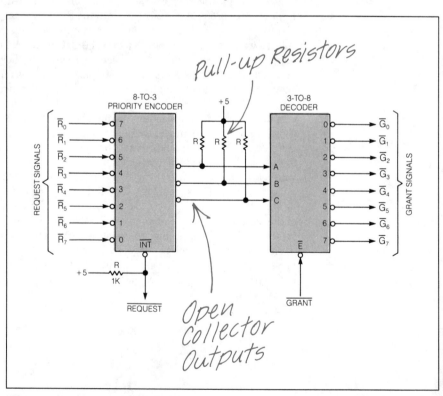

These outputs are different in a way we haven't discussed. They have what is called an open collector transistor output which requires that a resistor be connected from each output to the 5 volt power supply. Most digital devices such as the decoder provide this resistor internally, thus, the decoder outputs don't require these external resistors.

The encoder outputs are inverted and this is indicated by the small circles on each output. Thus, if input 7 has a logic 0 on it, the internal 3-bit code that corresponds to the decimal number 7 is 111. However, the inversion or complement of 111 is 000; therefore, the bit pattern 000 is sent to the three output lines. Thus, when line $\overline{R}_0$ (input 7) has a logic 0 applied, the output of the encoder will be 000 and the $\overline{INT}$ output will be a logic 0. This is true regardless of the binary signals applied to the other inputs since the $\overline{R}_0$ line has the highest priority. The inputs and outputs are summarized in *Table 4-1*.

**Table 4-1.
Encoder Inputs and
Outputs**

Request Signal Active	Corresponding Encoder Input Active	Output Code to Decoder A B C Inputs		
$\overline{R}_0$	7	0	0	0
$\overline{R}_1$	6	0	0	1
$\overline{R}_2$	5	0	1	0
$\overline{R}_3$	4	0	1	1
$\overline{R}_4$	3	1	0	0
$\overline{R}_5$	2	1	0	1
$\overline{R}_6$	1	1	1	0
$\overline{R}_7$	0	1	1	1

When any input line receives a logic 0, the $\overline{INT}$ output goes to a logic 0. Only if all input lines are at logic 1 will the INT output be at logic 1.

Now that the operation of each separate component in the circuit of *Figure 4-8* is understood, the overall operation of the circuit can be determined. The simplest case is when only one of the request signals is active; that is, at a logic 0. Assume, for example, that only request signal $\overline{R}_3$ is a logic 0 and all other request signals are logic 1. The priority encoder will produce outputs of 0 on INT and 011 on the 3-bit code output lines (refer to *Table 4-1*).

The system of which this circuit is a part monitors the $\overline{\text{INT}}$ output by means of the $\overline{\text{REQUEST}}$ line. When it detects the logic 0 level, it knows that a request input is active. At the proper time, it responds by placing a low on the $\overline{\text{GRANT}}$ line to enable the decoder. At that time, the decoder output line $\overline{G}_3$ will go to logic 0. This 0 is used by the system to activate the subsystem that pulled request line $\overline{R}_3$ low to request service. However, if another subsystem had requested service at the same time so that two request lines were active low at the same time, the priority encoder would output a low on $\overline{\text{INT}}$ and would output only the 3-bit code that corresponds to the higher priority request of the two.

Troubleshooting

Once the overall operation of the circuit of *Figure 4-8* is understood, it is possible to consider some failure symptoms and determine their probable cause. Here's the first problem to be considered: During operation of the system, the grant lines $\overline{G}_2$, $\overline{G}_3$, $\overline{G}_6$, and $\overline{G}_7$ never go to logic 0 even when request lines $\overline{R}_2$, $\overline{R}_3$, $\overline{R}_6$, or $\overline{R}_7$ are the highest priority line receiving a logic 0. The other grant lines work normally in response to logic 0's on their appropriate request lines. Where in the overall circuit is the fault most likely to be?

It is not likely that the decoder or the encoder has failed in this particular manner (but the possibility does exist). Also, it is not reasonable to think that the wires connecting the faulty R inputs or the faulty G outputs have simultaneously failed in a combination to yield the observed circuit behavior. Thus, the most likely area of the failure is in an input or output circuit or an interconnection wire that is in some way common to the observed circuit operation. If one examines the 3-bit codes that correspond to the failed output conditions and the codes of the working outputs as shown in *Table 4-2*, a common feature is observed.

The bit that separates all the working codes from the non-working codes is the middle bit on line B. Only outputs that have a 0 on line B work properly. Apparently it is not possible to drive line B to a 1 to generate the outputs that are failing. Thus, line B must be stuck at 0. One way to confirm this to request $\overline{R}_2$. If line B is stuck at 0, the $\overline{G}_0$ output should go low because the encoder output would be 000 (refer to *Table 4-1*). Similarly, requesting $\overline{R}_3$ would result in a $\overline{G}_1$ output.

Table 4-2.
Three-Bit Code Outputs

Working Outputs	Failed Outputs
0 0 0	0 1 0
0 0 1	0 1 1
1 0 0	1 1 0
1 0 1	1 1 1

If a check for shorts or opens by making voltage measurements on the IC pins does not reveal the problem, pin isolation, logic probing and signal tracing would have to be used to determine if the IC has a fault.

The most likely cause of line B to be stuck at 0 would be an open from the power supply lead to the decoder B input or encoder output. This includes the resistor, wiring and connection points. A short to ground along line B between the encoder and decoder is another likely cause. Measuring the resistor and making continuity checks from the power supply terminal to line B should determine the location of an open to the power supply. Probing for continuity along the wire from encoder to decoder should locate an open in that connection. Applying power to the circuit and measuring the voltage on line B with a logic 0 applied to input $\overline{R}_0$ should determine the presence of a short to ground on the B wire. If the wiring and resistor are alright, then the decoder input B or the encoder output B must be internally faulty. Pin isolation and logic probing techniques should reveal which of these needs to be replaced.

As in all circuits, there are many possible points of failure and only one has been considered in this example. The procedure for fault isolation and correction remains the same. By understanding the basic operation on the circuit and observing the symptoms of the failure, reasoning through the operation should narrow the location of the fault to a small portion of the circuit to reduce the testing requirements to reasonable proportions. If the troubleshooter had to make all possible measurements on even a simple circuit of the types discussed in this chapter, the amount of work and the amount of data to be interpreted would be overwhelming.

WHAT HAVE WE LEARNED?

1. The basic combinational components, which include three-state buffers, decoders, encoders, and read-only memories, can be combined with each other and with simple gates to perform useful functions.
2. We learned how some of these circuits work and that most of the common faults that occur in them can be found by reasoning and with simple tests.
3. The binary counter is a sequential circuit. These circuits are harder to troubleshoot because their operation depends on a sequence of often rapidly changing signals and the time relationships between such signals.

Quiz for Chapter 4

1. A three-state buffer is a device that:
  a. has three different output lines.
  b. has three different logic levels.
  c. has a high impedance state in addition to normal 0 and 1 levels.
  d. is a special type of storage register.

2. To cause a three-state buffer to output 0 or 1 levels, the following must be true:
  a. the information must have been stored within the buffer.
  b. the output enable must be true.
  c. the output enable must be false.
  d. the signal $\overline{OE}$ must be at a logic 1.

3. A decoder is an MSI circuit whose output lines are controlled by:
  a. a binary input select code.
  b. a similar set of input lines.
  c. an output enable.
  d. a clock input.

4. If the decoder shown in *Figure 4-3* is enabled with a 3-bit input code of 010, the following output would result:
  a. only line 5 would be at a logic 0.
  b. only line 5 would be at a logic 1.
  c. only line 2 would be at a logic 0.
  d. only line 2 would be at a logic 1.

5. If a multiplexer circuit has four input lines and a single output line, how many bits of line select code are required?
  a. 0
  b. 1
  c. 2
  d. 4

6. An encoder is an MSI circuit that:
  a. provides for delivering one of two or more inputs to an output.
  b. selects a given output line based on an binary input code.
  c. provides an output code that corresponds to which of a set of input lines is true.
  d. provides a storage of a certain number of binary bits.

7. A ROM containing 512 bytes of storage will have how many output gates?
  a. None
  b. 4
  c. 8
  d. 16
  e. 512

8. In the example of *Figure 4-8*, if only $\overline{R}_0$ through $\overline{R}_3$ inputs can produce correct outputs, what is the most likely circuit fault?
  a. A line stuck at 0
  b. A line stuck at 1
  c. B line stuck at 0
  d. C line stuck at 0
  e. C line stuck at 1

9. If in *Figure 4-1* the circuit fails to respond to closing of any of the switches S6, S7, and S8, what is the most likely fault?
  a. The line from C to the switches is shorted to ground.
  b. The line from point C to point H is open.
  c. All three switches are faulty.
  d. The NAND gate is faulty.

10. If in *Figure 4-7* the outputs of the ROM are all independent of the ROM inputs and do not produce a logic 1 or logic 0 voltage, what is the most likely fault?
  a. The counter is faulty.
  b. The D/A converter is faulty.
  c. There is an open in the $\overline{CS}$ connection.
  d. The ROM input circuitry is faulty.

Sequential Logic Problems

ABOUT THIS CHAPTER

The examples of the previous chapters have been limited to faults and their effects in combinational circuits. These circuits have the feature that their output is directly related to the combination of input signals that is present at any given time. The type of logic that will be considered throughout this chapter and the remainder of the book is sequential logic. Most digital systems of any complexity, including microcomputer systems, use sequential logic.

Recall that sequential logic systems have their output state determined both by what happened in the past and by the current input. Memory-type components, such as flip-flops and registers, make up sequential systems.

Sequential logic systems have the characteristic that the outputs and the sequence of operations of the system are dependent on both the present system inputs and inputs that were present in the immediate past. Stated another way, what happens at the output of the system and the next step to be taken in the system operation is determined by what is present at the input at the moment and by what was present at the input at the last step. Sequential logic systems have memory devices such as flip-flops, registers, or semiconductor memory circuits to keep track of what has happened in the past. Even though sequential logic systems often are more complicated in their design and operation than combinational logic systems, the basic procedures used in troubleshooting combinational logic systems apply equally well to troubleshooting sequential logic systems. Recall that reasoning through the circuit functions to isolate a fault to a small area is one of the troubleshooting techniques. Since the basic circuit operation must be understood in order to reason through the problem, the operation of some typical circuits will be discussed.

GENERAL SEQUENTIAL LOGIC ANALYSIS

The basic structure of a sequential logic system is shown in *Figure 5-1*. The functions shown in *Figure 5-1* are split into two types of combinational logic blocks (the output logic block and the memory control logic block) and a memory block. The purpose of the output logic block is to develop the system output signals from the system input signals and the signals present on the outputs of the memory elements.

The output signals from the memory are considered as a binary number that represents the state of the system. The state number is the decimal equivalent of the binary number. For example, if the memory consists of three flip-flops whose outputs are 0, 1, and 0 respectively, the system is said to be in state S010 or state 2 (since 2 is the decimal equivalent of the binary number 010).

Figure 5-1.
Classical Sequential
System Structure

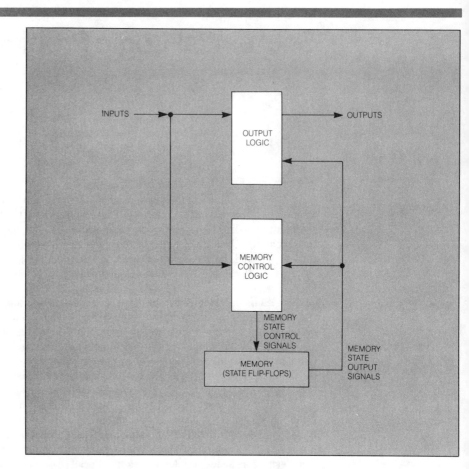

Sequential logic systems are synchronous when they are synchronized by a master clock.

The memory control logic block is used to generate the memory output signals that represent the next state from the present state and the input signals. For example, if the machine is in state 2 and is supposed to go to state 3 under the input conditions that are present, then the memory control logic block will generate signals into the state flip-flop inputs that will cause their outputs to become 0, 1, and 1. Generally, the state flip-flops are clocked D-type or J/K flip-flops; therefore, the flip-flop outputs (the state) change on either the leading edge or trailing edge of the system clock. This type of system is called a synchronous sequential system because the state changes are in step (synchronized) with the system clock. All of the examples considered in this book and most non-military systems are synchronous digital systems.

In an actual system, the combinational portion usually consists of various logic gates, decoders, multiplexers, encoders, and so forth; however, read-only memories and their variations may be used for portions of the combinational logic functions. (A special type of ROM called a programmable logic array (PLA) also may be used to perform combinational logic operations.) The system memory usually is in the form of flip-flops and registers, though random access memories may be used in complex systems.

In all such systems, the troubleshooter must determine how and under what circumstances the outputs are generated, and what sequence of operations the machine will go through as the inputs change. Generally this requires tracing the logic that generates the system outputs and the next state inputs. As information is gathered, it should be summarized in a listing, flowchart, or other form that can be analyzed.

VENDING MACHINE BLOCK DIAGRAM

One example of a relatively simple sequential logic system is shown in block diagram form in *Figure 5-2*. The machine is a simple coin vending machine which is sequential by its very nature. As the coins are entered by the customer one after another, their values are added together and the total value stored. Then the customer selects the item to be purchased. If the total of the coins entered is greater than or equal to the value of the selected item, the item will be delivered to the customer. If not, the item will not be vended and the coins will be returned to the customer. If the value of the coins is greater than the value of the item, change will be returned to the customer. Once the coins have been returned or the item and any change have been delivered to the customer, the machine must return to its "wait-for-coin-input" condition.

The controller makes sure the operational sequence described above is followed. This controller monitors the coin entered signal, the item selection signal, and the signals from the comparator to determine what action must be taken next by the machine. The action may be to return all the coins that were entered, or to deliver the selected item only, or to deliver the selected item and return change in the form of nickels or dimes.

The coin detector determines which coin denomination is entered (nickel, dime, or quarter) and generates a pulse on the appropriate signal line (N, D, or Q) to the adder. It also delivers a pulse C when any coin is entered. The coin value adder adds the value of the entered coins and holds the total. The item selection logic determines the value of the item selected. The electromechanical mechanisms return all coins if the DUMP signal is received or deliver the selected item to the customer if the VEND signal is received. The change control mechanism releases a dime, nickel or combinations of these to return the correct change. The general operation or purpose of each of the blocks and the overall vending machine must be understood before the detailed circuits that make up each block can be analyzed. Once that is done, it is a straightforward matter to determine the likely location of a fault in the system.

The major events in a simple coin vending machine example are: coin identification and computation after a coin is inserted, the decision to return the coins or vend the merchandise, and the amount of change to be returned.

Item Selection Logic

The simplest block in *Figure 5-2* is the item selection logic. The basic features of this logic are shown in circuit form in *Figures 5-3* and *5-4*. The logic in *Figure 5-3* has two functions: One is to store the item selection input from the closed contacts of one of the switches S1 through S30; the other function is to determine the item value and pass the proper item value signal to the next circuit. The logic is arranged so that if a customer depresses more than one item selection button, the most expensive item is selected.

**Figure 5-2.
Vending Machine Block
Diagram**

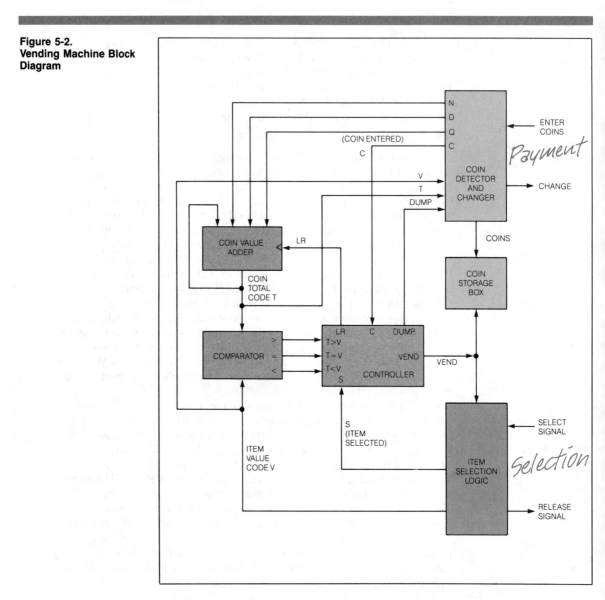

Logic circuitry to identify
the item selected includes
these functions: Store item
selection, determine item
value, pass on the data.

In *Figure 5-3*, depressing a single item selection switch, S1, causes
the logic 1 level on the D input of FF1 to appear on the Q_1 output and a 0 to
appear on the $\overline{Q}_1$ output. This low on $\overline{Q}_1$ will cause the $\overline{V50}$ output of the AND
gate G1 to go low indicating that a 50 cent item has been selected. The Q_1 high
enables the output AND gate G31 so that when a VEND pulse occurs high, the
R1 output of AND gate G31 will go high to release the selected item. Notice
that once $\overline{Q}_1$ goes low, it inhibits gates G2 through G36 so no other switch signal
can get through to any of the other flip-flops, thus only item 1 can indicate a
selection. In general, an output of a 0 on any flip-flop's $\overline{Q}$ terminal will inhibit
the switch signal from all flip-flops to the right of the selected flip-flop.

Figure 5-3.
Item Selection Logic

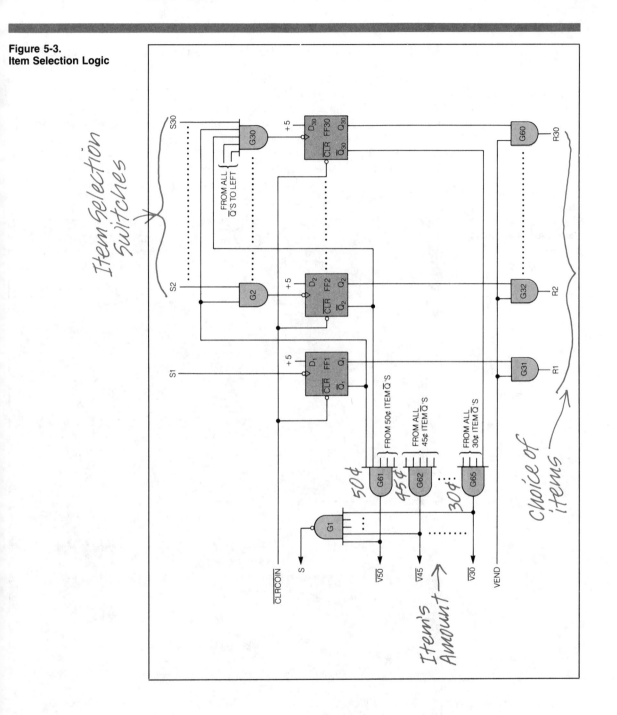

Assuming the items are arranged so that the most expensive are at the left and the least expensive are at the right, this logic selects the most expensive item if more than one button has been depressed.

An encoder generates an 8-bit BCD code representing the coin value, and sends this data to the controller.

Once a flip-flop has been set in *Figure 5-3*, the signals $\overline{V50}$ through $\overline{V30}$ are sent to the item value code logic shown in *Figure 5-4*. The logic in *Figure 5-4* generates an 8-bit code to indicate the value of the item selected to the controller in binary-coded decimal (BCD) code. The BCD code represents each decimal digit as a 4-bit binary code. Thus, if the item value is 35 cents (a low occurs on $\overline{V35}$), the code on lines V_7 through V_0 will be <u>0011</u> <u>0101</u> which are the 4-bit codes for 3 and 5. The reader can verify the other code on lines V_7 through V_0 for other values.

Figure 5-4.
Item Value Code Logic

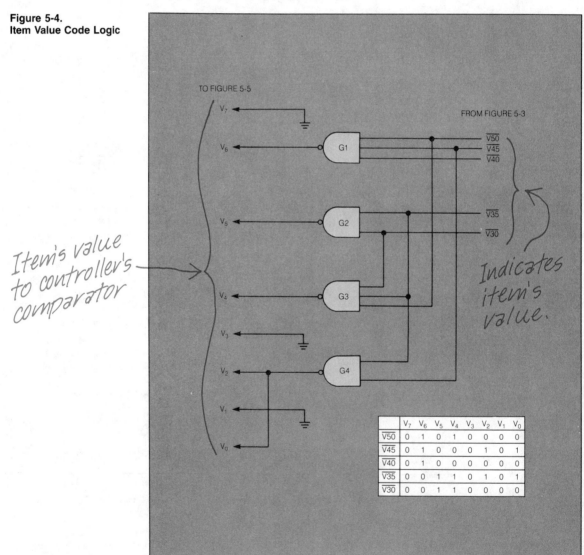

	V_7	V_6	V_5	V_4	V_3	V_2	V_1	V_0
$\overline{V50}$	0	1	0	1	0	0	0	0
$\overline{V45}$	0	1	0	0	0	1	0	1
$\overline{V40}$	0	1	0	0	0	0	0	0
$\overline{V35}$	0	0	1	1	0	1	0	1
$\overline{V30}$	0	0	1	1	0	0	0	0

Item's value to controller's comparator →

Indicates item's value.

Any low on the $\overline{V50}$ through $\overline{V30}$ lines will cause the outputs of the respective NAND gates G1-G4 to go high. Notice that outputs V_1, V_3, and V_7 are connected directly to ground. Their value is always 0 because a 1 will never be required in these positions for the numbers used. The binary values on V_0, V_2, V_4, V_5 and V_6 are generated by the NAND gates G1-G4 shown in *Figure 5-4*. The binary values for these outputs are shown in the chart. The outputs of V_0 through V_7 are sent to the comparator to compare with the amount of money entered.

Coin Value Adder and Comparator

The next part of *Figure 5-2* to be considered is the coin value adder and the comparator. This circuit is shown in *Figure 5-5*. Actually, the adder and the comparator, shown in block diagram form, would consist of several integrated circuits.

The circuits to generate the coin value and to generate the signal C from the signals N, D, and Q generated by the coin detector mechanism are shown in more detail. A pulse on the N, D, or Q line generated by the coin detector mechanism will in turn cause a 1 to occur on the Q output of the corresponding flip-flop. The $\overline{Q}$ output goes low which causes the C output of G2 to go to a 1 level. The $\overline{Q}$ signals of FF1 and FF3 are applied to G1 whose output along with the Q output of FF2 generate the BCD code as shown in the chart that corresponds to the input coin value in much the same way the item value code was generated in the circuit of *Figure 5-4*. The BCD code is applied to the A_7 through A_0 inputs of the adder.

The other set of inputs, B_7 through B_0, receive the value of the total from the 8-bit total register. The sum outputs of the BCD adder (S_7 through S_0) are always the sum of the current total and the new coin value. Thus, if the current total represents 15 cents (S_7-S_0 = 0001 0101) and a quarter is entered (A_7-A_0 = 0010 0101), the new sum outputs will represent 40 cents (S_7-S_0 = 0100 0000). This value also is applied to the D_7-D_0 inputs of the total register. When the LR pulse generated by the controller of *Figure 5-2* is delivered to the total register, the value on D_7-D_0 is stored in the total register and appears on Q_7-Q_0. It also is applied to T_7-T_0, one set of inputs to the comparator. The other set of comparator inputs receive the BCD code for the item value as determined in the circuits of *Figures 5-3* and 5-4.

The purpose of the comparator is to indicate the relation between the amount of money entered and the value of the selected item. It indicates this by making one of its outputs a logic 1. The possible outputs are T>V (coin total greater than item value), T = V (coin total equal to item value), or T<V (coin total less than item value). Of course, these outputs are meaningful only after the last coin has been entered and the item has been selected, therefore, the controller ignores these signals until the S (item selected signal in *Figure 5-2*) is received.

Logic and adder circuits determine the value of the coins deposited, which is sent to the comparator. The comparator, determines the relationship between the coin value entered and the merchandise value.

Figure 5-5.
Coin Value Adder and
Comparator

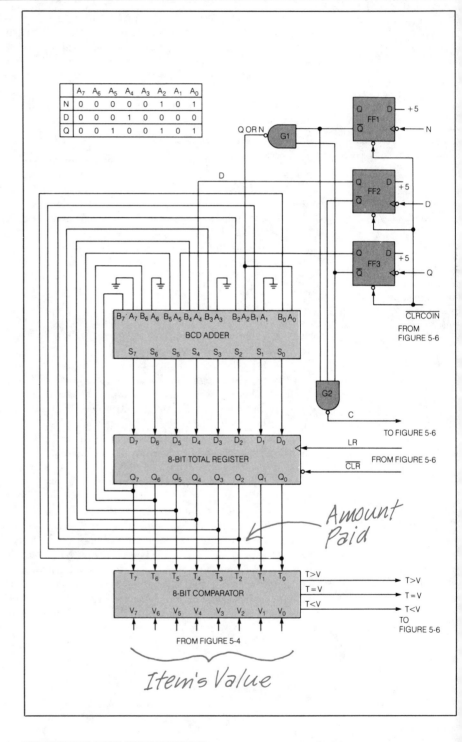

Controller

Based upon input signals from the comparator, item selection logic, and the coin detector, the controller outputs signals to either vend the item purchased and give change, if necessary, or else to return the money deposited.

So far the basic input and output circuits have been examined. These operate under the direction of the system controller which implements a certain sequence of events depending on events that have already occurred and the value of the present input signals. Thus, the system of *Figure 5-2* is a sequential logic system.

The controller circuit is shown in *Figure 5-6* and is somewhat more complicated to analyze than the circuits in *Figures 5-3* through *5-5*. *The key to understanding the controller portion of a sequential system is to determine the sequence of states and the outputs generated in each state.* Recall that the *current state* is the binary code at the output of the state flip-flops at a particular moment of time. The *next state* will be the binary code presently at the input to the state flip-flops.

The particular controller design shown in *Figure 5-6* is a state decoder. The 3-bit state code at the output of the state flip-flops is sent to the 3-to-8 decoder. Then the decoder output which is at 0 indicates which state the controller is in. Thus, if the outputs of the flip-flops are 000, the decoder output 0 will be low and the controller is said to be in state 0 or S000. By looking at the controller outputs generated by the decoder output and the inputs generated at the D terminals of the state flip-flops, it is possible to determine what activities are performed in the present state and what state will be next. *These two facts completely define what a state does and what happens next.* Once this information is known for all states, the total behavior of the machine can be understood and summarized.

The simplest approach to sequential machine analysis is to start with the first state code and see what the outputs and next state are. This process is repeated for all state codes until the analysis is complete.

State 0

Because the circuit is sequential, each state depends on the input signals present and the state the system is in when the input arrives. State 0 is the initial state which sends the controller to State 1.

State 0 is entered when power is first applied because the three state flip-flops FF1, FF2 and FF3 are cleared by the action of the RC network connected to the power supply and to the state flip-flops. This circuit is in the lower right corner of *Figure 5-6*. When power is turned on, the voltage at the junction of the capacitor and resistor is zero for a short time, therefore, a logic 0 is applied to the $\overline{CLR}$ inputs of the state flip-flops. This sets Q_0, Q_1 and Q_2 at 000 and establishes state 0 through the decoder. After a short time, the capacitor charges to the $+5V$ level (logic 1) so the clear is removed and the flip-flops are free to respond to their D inputs. Reset to state 0 can be caused at any time by pushing the reset button which discharges the capacitor to zero volts to clear all three flip-flops. After the switch is opened, the capacitor again recharges to the logic 1 level.

Figure 5-6.
Controller Logic

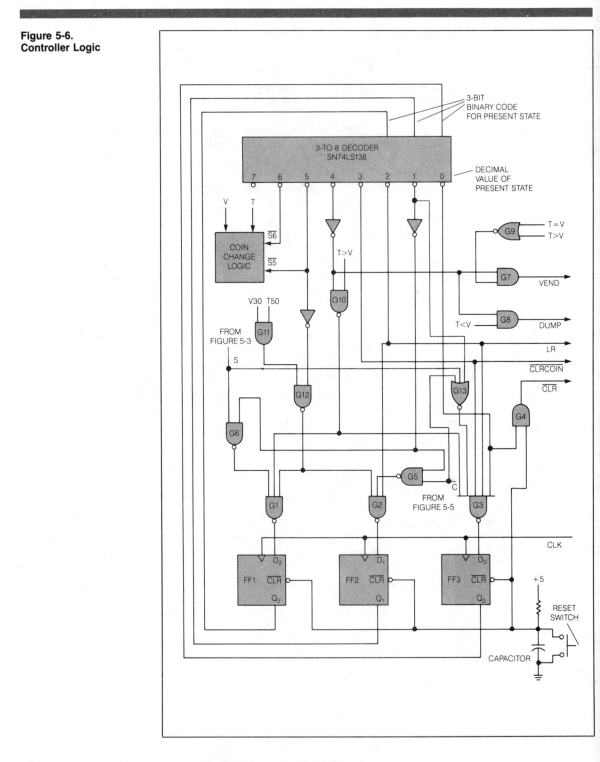

To determine what outputs are generated in a state, follow the decoder output line for that state to all destinations. For state 0, the decoder output goes to gates G3 and G4. Gate G4 produces the $\overline{CLR}$ signal that clears all selection and coin flip-flops and the total register to all zeros. Thus, state 0 is a state that resets the machine to its starting conditions. The state 0 input to gate G3 produces a 1 at D_0. This causes the next state (which occurs on the leading edge of the CLK (clock signal) to be 001 or state 1.

State 1

The controller waits in State 1 until a coin is received to generate a C signal or a S is received for an item selection.

When the controller is in state S001 (state 1), no output is generated, but a 1 is applied to one input of G5 and G6 to enable them. Until a C or S signal is input, the controller is held in state 1 by the decoder output through G13. If C occurs, the 0 output of G5 is applied to G2 which applies a 1 to D_1. Thus, the flip-flop outputs go to 010 or state 2. If S occurs, the outputs go to 100 or state 4. Thus, while in state 1, the next state will be state 1 (no S or C inputs), state 2 (C input), or state 4 (S input).

States 2 and 3

When a coin is received the controller goes to State 2, then 3 and returns to State 1 to wait for the next coin.

When any coin is entered, C is generated so the controller goes to state 2 and the LR signal is generated to latch the new coin total into the total register. The decoder output 2 also is sent to G2 and G3 so that the next state code is 011. The D-type flip-flops receive the code 011 which advances the decoder to state 3 on the next CLK low-to-high transition. In state 3, the $\overline{CRLCOIN}$ signal is generated to clear the coin flip-flops to get ready for a new coin. Decoder output 3 also goes to G3 to force a 1 on FF3 so the next state is state 1. Again the controller waits for another coin input or an item selection.

State 4

When a selection is made, the controller goes to State 4 to determine if the item should be vended because enough money was paid or if the coins should be returned.

When all coins have been entered and a selection is made, the S signal causes the controller to move from state 1 to state 4. This is the point where the logic must determine if enough money has been entered for the selected item. From the state 4 decoder output, an enable 1 is applied to G7 and G8. If enough money has been entered as indicated by either T = V or T>V, G7 will produce the VEND output to release the selected item. However, if T<V, then G8 will produce the DUMP output to release the coins entered. The next state also is determined by the comparison of V and T. If T<V or T = V, the next state is 0. If T>V, the next state is 5 because a 1 is forced on FF1 and FF3 by the output of G10.

States 5 and 6

The controller enters State 5 and 6 if change is to be made. After change is made it goes to State 0.

The controller reaches state 5 when T>V; that is, too much money was entered for the selected item and change must be returned to the customer. The state 5 decoder output enables the circuit that generates the change control signals to deliver a nickel or a dime or both in change. The controller then goes to state 0 to prepare for the next selection unless the item value is 30 cents ($\overline{\text{V30}}$ is low) and the coin total is 50 cents (T50 is high). In this case, the output of G11 goes high which, along with the state 5 signal, causes a low to be delivered from G12 to the inputs of G1 and G2. This produces the code of 110 to send the controller to state 6 which tells the coin change logic to dispense another dime in change. Then the controller goes to state 0.

Change Control Circuit

The circuit that generates the signals NC (nickel change) and DC (dime change) to drive the coin change mechanism is shown in *Figure 5-7*. The DC signal is generated when state 6 is active ($\overline{\text{S6}}$) or because of the occurrence of one of 6 different combinations of item value versus coin total when in state 5 ($\overline{\text{S5}}$). For example, if the item value is 30 cents and the total is 40 cents (V30 AND T40), a dime would be returned. Similarly, NC is generated when any of six item value and total combinations occur. For example, if the item value is either 5 cents or 15 cents less than the coin total, NC must be generated to return a nickel. The reader should verify each of the combinations shown.

The change control circuit drives the nickel and dime change mechanism when state 6 is active. The change returned is based upon the data inputted during state 5.

Figure 5-7.
Change Control Circuit

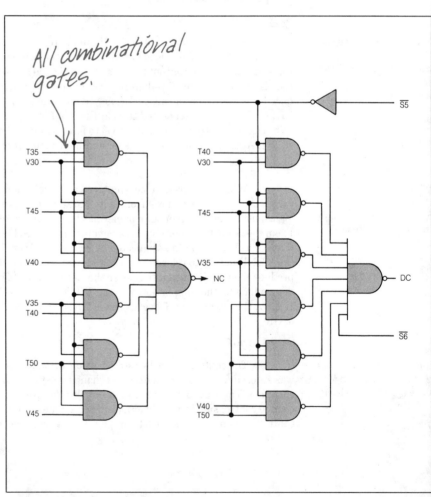

Controller Sequence Description

Once the individual combinational input and output circuits and the controller sequencing are understood, they can be summarized in a form for easy reference. This can be done with a step-by-step list of operations or a flow chart. This is done for the vending machine example in *Figure 5-8* as a control sequence program.

With the machine behavior described in this form, its overall behavior can be easily understood and referenced. Further, it is easy to see the effect of a given fault on the sequence of operations. It is also possible to determine the effect of a fault on the combinational circuit behavior using the same techniques described in the last two chapters. Some typical faults and their effect on the vending machine operation will be considered next.

FAULTS IN SEQUENTIAL SYSTEMS

Sequential systems exhibit the same types of failures as combinational systems. Reasoning through system functions to localize faults and then pinpointing them with the aid of test instruments is the best troubleshooting technique.

The same shorts, opens and component failures that are found in combinational systems also occur in sequential systems. Many of the same procedures used to isolate faults in combinational logic systems also apply to sequential systems. Certainly the reasoning process used to localize the fault to a certain functional unit in the system is a procedure that is used in all troubleshooting efforts. Then, measurements with test instruments help locate the problem that is causing the system failure.

**Figure 5-8.
Summarizing the
Vending Machine
Operation**

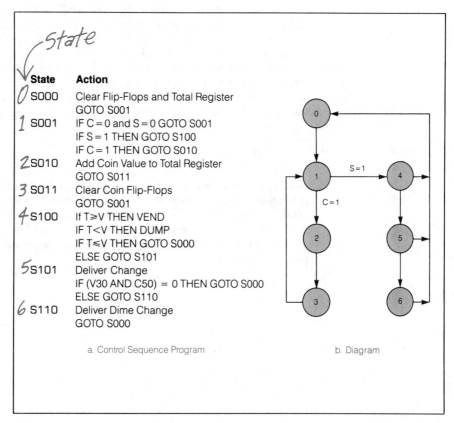

State	Action
S000	Clear Flip-Flops and Total Register GOTO S001
S001	IF C = 0 and S = 0 GOTO S001 IF S = 1 THEN GOTO S100 IF C = 1 THEN GOTO S010
S010	Add Coin Value to Total Register GOTO S011
S011	Clear Coin Flip-Flops GOTO S001
S100	If T≥V THEN VEND IF T<V THEN DUMP IF T≤V THEN GOTO S000 ELSE GOTO S101
S101	Deliver Change IF (V30 AND C50) = 0 THEN GOTO S000 ELSE GOTO S110
S110	Deliver Dime Change GOTO S000

a. Control Sequence Program   b. Diagram

Faults in Storage Devices

Storage devices are common only to sequential systems and consist of flip-flops and registers; both function in the same manner. The most common D-type flip-flop fault is an output not responding to the input.

The only types of elements that occur in the example used in this chapter that were not used in the combinational logic systems are the storage devices. These include the flip-flops and the coin total storage register. These are basically the same types of components since the register is simply a collection of eight flip-flops which share the same clock line. Thus, the only new type of component that must be considered from a component failure viewpoint is the D-type flip-flop. This flip-flop has a D input, outputs of Q and $\overline{Q}$ (complements of each other), a clock input, and a clear input. There may be other control inputs as well, but for the example considered in this chapter, it will be sufficient to consider only these basic inputs and outputs.

The basic fault that would be observed in a D-type flip-flop is that its output does not respond to the inputs. In other words, the output Q is stuck at either a 0 or a 1 level. The other output $\overline{Q}$ would be stuck at the opposite level unless there is a fault in the output circuitry of the device. Either the stuck-at-0 or stuck-at-1 faults in a flip-flop can have disastrous effects on the operation of a sequential system, particularly if the faulty flip-flop is one of the state flip-flops.

Stuck-at-0

One output fault case is the stuck-at-0 condition in which Q remains at 0 and $\overline{Q}$ remains at 1 regardless of the input conditions. If a 1 is applied to the D input and a clock pulse is applied to the clock or latch input and Q still remains at 0, then either the $\overline{CLR}$ input is shorted to ground in a permanent clear condition or there is an open in the clock or D input lines. These faults could be internal to the flip-flop or in the external wiring. Component testing with isolated leads or replacement with a known good component would rule out the internal fault possibility. Wiring faults can be determined with the same signal tracing or voltmeter measurement techniques discussed in previous chapters.

Stuck-at-1

If the flip-flop will not clear when a low is applied to the $\overline{CLR}$ terminal, then there is a fault internally in the clear circuit or externally in the clear wiring (probably an open circuit). If the flip-flop is stuck at a 1 level (Q is permanently 1 and $\overline{Q}$ is permanently 0) regardless of the 0 applied to the D input and the application of a suitable clock pulse, again there must be an internal fault or a fault (probably an open) in the D or clock lines. Such problems can be detected and corrected using the same procedures for the stuck-at-0 condition.

Sequential System Fault Analysis

In a faulty sequential system, the troubleshooter will observe some system behavior that is not normal, and by reasoning, must determine the most likely cause of the behavior. Then he/she must use test instruments to find the exact cause. This will be the approach considered in this section. Of course, not all problems that might occur in a given sequential system can be examined in the limited space available here, but representative problems can be covered. The vending machine system covered by *Figures 5-2* through *5-8* will serve as the example system since its operation has already been analyzed in detail.

Symptom 1

One machine malfunction that is slightly annoying to the customer is the case in which the machine accepts the coins and does not vend the selected item, but does return the coins to the customer. Refer to *Figure 5-8* and examine the actions. Since the coins are returned, the machine apparently gets to state 4 to generate the DUMP signal, but never generates the VEND signal. This behavior could occur only if the machine always determines that the coin total is less than the item value when it reaches state 4. At this point, it returns the coins and goes back to state 0 and then to state 1.

Notice in *Figure 5-8* that state 4 can be reached directly from state 1 without ever entering states 2 and 3 where the coin values are added. If this happens, then T will always be 0 and the observed fault will be present. Therefore, a good point to begin troubleshooting is to check that the state flip-flops go to state 2 and 3 as each coin is entered. If they don't, then check that the C signal (*Figures 5-5* and *5-6*) is generated for each coin entry. If not, then isolate the problem to G2, FF1, FF2, or FF3 in *Figure 5-5*. If C is generated, then isolate the problem to G5, G2, FF2, or the decoder in *Figure 5-6*. *Figure 5-9* summarizes this and the following troubleshooting sequence.

If the controller is cycling from state 1 to 2 to 3 to 1 properly, then the problem may be the coin detection and adding circuit, the item value circuit, or the comparator. Whether the observed problem occurs regardless of coin combination entered or of item selection, or if the problem occurs for only certain coin and item combinations, helps determine the next troubleshooting steps. Let's assume the problem occurs regardless of combinations.

Since the comparator lies at the center of the suspected area, it would be a good point to begin troubleshooting. Monitor the binary code at the T_7-T_0 inputs while entering two or three coins. If the code changes correctly to show the accumulated total, then the coin detection and adding circuits are working.

If the machine returns coins entered but does not vend, a check to see that the flip-flops go to states 2 and 3 as the coins are entered is the best starting point.

**Figure 5-9.
Troubleshooting
Flowchart**

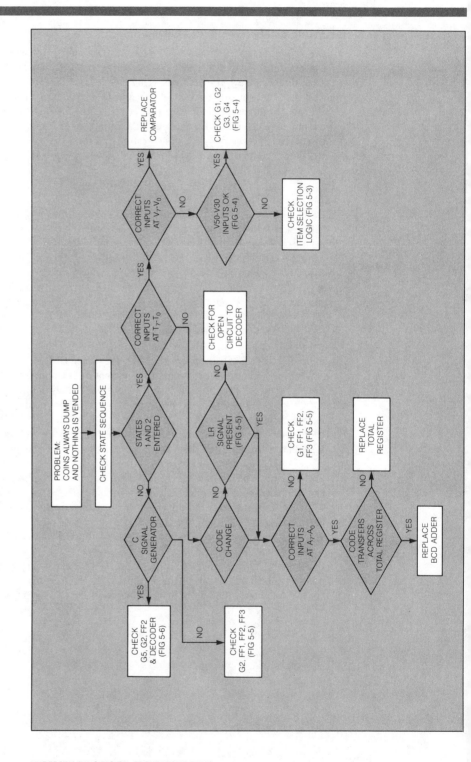

If the code doesn't change at all, the LR signal generated by the decoder state 2 output may not be reaching the total register or the LR input itself may be defective. If the code changes, but incorrectly, monitor the A_7-A_0 inputs while entering coins. If these codes are correct for each coin as shown in the chart, then probably the BCD adder is defective, but the total register is also suspect. If the code at the input to the total register is transferred to the output when LR occurs, then the problem is in the BCD adder. If the A_7-A_0 inputs are not correct, isolate to G1, FF1, FF2, or FF3 (*Figure 5-5*).

If the T_7-T_0 inputs to the comparator were correct, then monitor the V_7-V_0 inputs to the comparator while entering coins and selecting an item. If the BCD code is correct for each item selected (see chart in *Figure 5-4*), then the comparator must be defective. If the BCD code is not correct, then the item value or item select logic (*Figures 5-3* and *5-4*) is defective. Work backwards to the V30 through V50 signals and item select gates to isolate the problem.

Symptom 2

When the machine alternates between state 4 (VEND generation) and state 5 (change delivery) the machine will "Jackpot" until empty; an open between the G12 to G2 line is the likely fault.

One machine behavior problem that is a delight to the customer is "hitting the jackpot" where the machine continues to deliver the selected item and change until it is empty. Refer to *Figure 5-8* again. This could occur only if the machine alternates between state 4 where VEND is generated and state 5 where change is delivered. The action described could occur if the machine considered the next state of 5 to be 4 rather than 0 or 6 as is correct. This could occur if the circuit that generates the 1 on state flip-flop FF2 (*Figure 5-6*) when in state 5 is faulty. The only fault that could cause this problem is an open in the line from G12 to G2 (*Figure 5-6*). This fault would cause the next state for state 5 to be state 4 and the machine would oscillate between states 4 and 5.

Symptom 3

A fault in Gates G7 or G9 or in the common vending solenoid power line will cause the machine to take money but not return change or vend the selected item.

The most maddening machine problem from the customer's viewpoint is the case in which the machine takes the money, but does not vend the selected item and does not return the coins entered. It may or may not deliver change on the basis of the coins entered and the value of the item selected. If the machine delivers change, it is reaching state 5 of *Figure 5-8*. Either VEND is not generated because of a fault in G7 or G9 (*Figure 5-6*) or there is an open between the controller VEND line and the gates G31-G60 (*Figure 5-3*) that deliver the release signal to the release solenoids in the vending mechanism. Of course, another possible cause not in the logic is the common power line to the vending solenoids.

If change is not returned, the machine may not be able to reach state 4 because the S signal is not generated properly (*Figure 5-3*) because G1 is faulty. If the problem occurs only for certain items, but not all, then one of the NAND gates or flip-flops in the item select logic may be faulty. If S is being generated, then G6, G1 or FF1 (*Figure 5-6*) may be faulty.

When a fault occurs that prevents the system from reaching State 4, no coins are returned and no items are delivered.

The machine could be stuck in state 0 because of several reasons. FF3 (*Figure 5-6*) could be stuck at 0 because FF3 is faulty or because a $\overline{CLR}$ is always present. A constant $\overline{CLR}$ could be caused by a short to ground on the line, in G4, in the capacitor, or in the reset switch. The decoder may be defective or the line from the decoder output 0 to G3 may be open, or G3 may be defective. Any of these faults would cause the machine to stay in state 0.

The machine could get stuck in the state 1, 2, 3 sequence if the C signal remains at a 1 due to the coin detection flip-flops FF1, FF2 and FF3 in *Figure 5-5* not being cleared by the $\overline{CLRCOIN}$ produced by state 3 in *Figure 5-6*. This could happen if there were an open in the $\overline{CLRCOIN}$ line. Actually, if both C and S are present because of this condition, the machine would go to state 7 which is a no operation and the next state is state 0. Thus, the net effect of C being stuck-at-1 is that state 4 is never reached and no coins are returned and no item is delivered.

Coins could be entered until the coin box filled up with no response from the machine. Notice that the logic is biased to protect the vendor rather than the customer. Only one unlikely fault can cause a "jackpot" situation, but any of several faults will allow the machine to keep the customer's money without vending.

Symptom 4

Faulty gates in the change control circuit, a comparator fault, or a decoder fault can cause the machine to fail to return change. The system never gets to State 5, or the machine might be out of change.

As a last example of problems that can occur in the vending machine, suppose the machine accepts the coins and vends the selected item, but does not return change. Of course, this could be a simple problem like the coin changer is out of coins. However, it could be due to the machine never getting to state 5 or the change gates (*Figure 5-7*) never receiving the enable $\overline{S5}$ from state 5. One or more of the gates in the change control circuit may be faulty; however, this probably would not always withhold change under all conditions. The machine might always go from state 4 to state 0 if the output of G10 (*Figure 5-6*) is stuck at 1 because of a fault in G10, a fault in the T > V line, a fault in the line from the decoder output 4 to G10, or a fault in the decoder itself. Any of these faults would prevent change from being delivered.

There are many other fault conditions that could occur in the vending machine. The reader may want to propose some component or wiring faults and try to determine how the machine would behave under such a condition.

Faults in MSI Sequential Devices

The counter is related to the register and flip-flop and is used for timer and clock circuits in sequential systems design. Faults in timing circuits can confuse the operation of a sequential system. Some of these faults will be considered in this section by using the clock generation circuit for the vending machine as an example.

Oscillator Clock

A possible clock generation circuit is shown in *Figure 5-10*. It is designed to produce a frequency of 100 hertz which has a period of 10 milliseconds. The basic operation of the device of *Figure 5-10a* is fairly straightforward as connected. The value of the capacitor sets the frequency of the internally generated square wave in accordance with the approximate relationship:

$$F_o = 500/C$$

where the frequency F_o is in megahertz (millions of hertz) and C is in picofarads (one millionth of a microfarad). (This particular device can produce an output frequency up to a maximum of 40 MHz.) Thus, with a capacitor value of 5 microfarads (5 million picofarads) as shown, the frequency is set to 500/5,000,000 or 100 hertz.

The terminal $\overline{EN}$ enables the output square wave when $\overline{EN}$ receives a low. In this application, it is enabled all the time by connecting it to ground. The terminals RNG and FREQCONT allow an external voltage to control the frequency of the output around a value as fixed by the capacitor. However, in this application, these are fixed at +5 volts and have no further control on the frequency of the output.

The most obvious problems that could occur with this circuit are no output or incorrect frequency. No output would probably be caused by a defective IC or an open in the connections to V_{cc}, GND, or $\overline{EN}$. An open in the connections to terminals RNG and FREQCONT might cause the frequency to be other than the desired value, but the circuit would still produce a square wave of approximately the correct frequency. If the FREQCONT terminal connection were shorted to ground, a very low frequency would result. An open in the connections to the capacitor or the capacitor itself would cause the frequency to increase to near the maximum of around 40 megahertz. If no fault is found in the wiring, the circuit must be assumed bad and replaced.

Faults in timing and clock circuits can produce confusing sequential system operation. The most obvious problems are faulty clock generators and counter circuits.

Counter Clock

The circuit shown in *Figure 5-10b* is a simple 4-bit binary counter connected to divide by 16. The device shown has two clock inputs (A and B), four flip-flop outputs of Q_A (least significant bit), Q_B, Q_C, and Q_D (most significant bit), and two reset control lines R_{o1} and R_{o2}. Both R_{o1} and R_{o2} must be high to clear the counter to all zeros. Since R_{o2} is wired high, R_{o1} controls the clear function. If R_{o1} is low, the count will be increased by one each time the system clock A signal undergoes a high-to-low transition. For this device, the maximum clock frequency typically is 42 MHz. The B clock input is connected to the Q_A output to provide the divide-by-16 function. The counter output that is of interest is Q_D which is called output Y.

Figure 5-10.
Oscillators and Counters

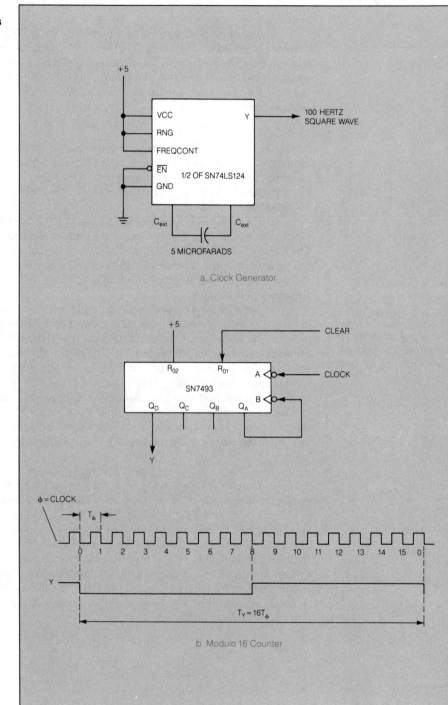

a. Clock Generator

b. Modulo 16 Counter

The output Y is shown in relation to the input clock A in the waveform. When eight trailing edges have occurred in the A signal, the Y signal will complement (change from a 0 to a 1 or vice versa). Thus, output Y is a square wave that has a period of 16 times the period of the input clock. Since frequency is the reciprocal of the period, the frequency of the Y square wave is 1/16 that of the input clock frequency. This is why the counter is described as divide-by-16 or modulo 16.

If the counter of *Figure 5-10b* fails to count, either the R_{01} line is stuck at the 1 level (possibly an open in the wiring), or there is an open in the A input lead, or the A input signal is stuck at a 0 or a 1 level (no transitions from level to level), or the power supply and/or ground leads are open. If only the Q_A line changes and the other outputs are stuck at a 0 or a 1, then there is probably an open in the line from Q_A to B or a short to ground in this line. Otherwise, the IC probably is defective.

Thus, we see that, like combinational components, the proper operation of the sequential components; the timer, counter, and square wave generator (oscillator), depends primarily on a working component and good connections to the component terminals. Thus, such components in themselves are not much different from a combinational device from a troubleshooting viewpoint. The troubleshooter must determine if the component is good and if it is, then the wiring fault must be determined. Alternatively, if the component is soldered into the circuit, the wiring may be determined to be alright using signal tracing and lead isolation techniques before the effort is made to remove and replace the component. What is different about sequential MSI and LSI circuits is their basic behavior and analysis of their circuit operation as has been seen from the vending machine example. The differences are more significant in the LSI and VLSI (very large scale integration) devices used in microcomputers. Much of the rest of the book will be concerned with this very important class of system and the supporting equipment, beginning with an overview of their operation in the next section.

> Even though LSI and VSLI basic behavior is different, sequential troubleshooting involves the same techniques used in combinational troubleshooting.

INTRODUCTION TO MICROCOMPUTERS

While the components of a microcomputer may be very complex circuits internally, their functional behavior is quite straightforward, which greatly simplifies system design. However, since such devices operate primarily on parallel digital data codes (many signals appear on a set of wires at one time), the task of the troubleshooter is complicated by having to know the state of many signals at once. The fault analysis and detection task is also complicated by the fact that the sequence of operations the machine must perform is not wired into gate and decoder connections, but is stored in the system memory as a series of coded instructions. With such a system, the troubleshooter not only has to verify hardware component and wiring operation, but also must understand the operation of the computer program as well. In many cases, these tasks may require the use of special test equipment.

> Fault analysis and detection in microcomputers requires the troubleshooter to know component interconnections, work with many simultaneous signals changing states, and understand how the software runs the system.

Before the subject of faults in microcomputers can be tackled, the basic operation and structure of a microcomputer must be understood. This will be the object of the remainder of this chapter.

Microcomputer Components and Operation

The basic subsystems of the microcomputer are the microprocessor, the memory, and the I/O sections.

A block diagram of the three basic subsystems of a microcomputer is shown in *Figure 5-11*. The central control element is the microprocessor. It determines the operation of all other components in the system as well as being responsible for providing the sequence of machine behavior dictated by the microcomputer program stored in the system memory. The system memory stores the binary codes which represent the computer program, system data, and system constants and messages. The input and output subsystem (usually referred to as I/O) provides the communications and control signals to and from the external environment.

A typical controller microcomputer consists of a microprocessor IC, one or two memory ICs, and one or more input/output controller circuits along with appropriate interface circuits to connect external equipment and signals to the microcomputer input and output circuits. Alternatively, the memory, basic I/O, and microprocessor can be purchased as a single integrated circuit called a microcomputer. The system then would consist of this microcomputer IC and additional interface circuits that might be needed to connect the microcomputer circuit to external equipment and devices. A larger microcomputer system such as a personal computer would consist of one or more microprocessors, many memory circuits, many input and output circuits and associated interface circuits, a keyboard and CRT terminal, disk drive units, and a printer. However, all of these types of microcomputers would still use the same basic structure shown in *Figure 5-11* with the same types of components used in all such systems.

Memory Operation

Memory is organized into 8 or 16-bit words (bytes).

The memory is organized as a large number of 8-bit storage locations with each 8-bit group called a byte. These bytes are transferred one at a time (or two at a time depending on the processor type) to and from the processor under processor control. Processors that perform work on 16-bit data and instruction codes internally are called 16-bit processors. They can transfer either one or two bytes at a time, with the two byte codes called a word. Processors that perform operations on 8-bit codes internally are called 8-bit processors. They can transfer data and instruction codes only one byte at a time.

Figure 5-11.
Microcomputer Structure

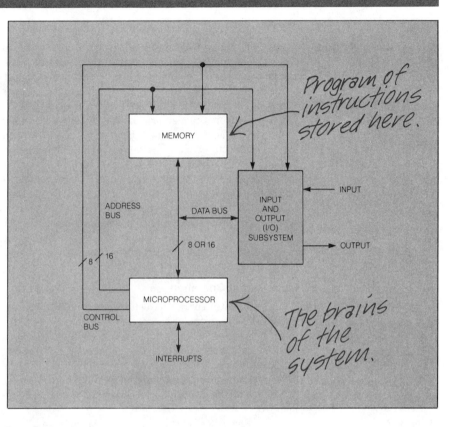

Data Bus

Data is transferred
bidirectionally between
subsystems along a paral-
lel conductive path, called
a bus.

The information is transferred between memory and the processor
and between input and output devices and the processor along 8 or 16 wires
(depending on the processor) in parallel fashion. These 8 or 16 wires are called
the data bus. They are shown in *Figure 5-11* as a single line with arrows on both
ends of the line to indicate that the codes can go in either direction along the
wires. The number next to the slash mark indicates how many wires are
represented by the single line.

Memory Write

Data is transferred into
the memory from the pro-
cessor through a sequence
called a write operation.

In order to transfer information from the processor to the memory,
the processor must perform a memory write operation in which the data is
placed on the data bus by the processor and appropriate address and control
signals are sent to the memory from the processor. (This procedure is called
"accessing the memory.") Typically, the processor will generate an address
code of 16 or more bits (depending on the processor) to indicate which memory
storage location is to receive the data. Then, with the data on the data bus, the
processor will bring a memory enable line to its active state to turn on the
memory and bring a write enable line to its active state to cause the memory to
perform the write operation; that is, store the information.

Memory Read

Data is transferred out of the memory into the processor through a sequence called a read operation.

The opposite transfer from the memory to the processor is handled similarly. In this case, the operation is called a memory read and the processor will be receiving either the code for the next instruction of the microcomputer program that is to be executed or it will be receiving some data code from the memory. The processor will place its data lines into the input mode so it can receive data from the memory and it will place the address code for the location to be read on the address lines. Then it will bring the memory enable signal into its active state and bring the read enable signal into its active state. The memory circuit will place the requested binary code onto the data lines and the processor will store this code into one of its internal registers. If the code represents the next instruction to be executed by the processor, the code will be stored in the internal instruction register of the processor and the entire memory read operation will be known as an instruction fetch or instruction read. If the code is a data code, the data will be latched into one of the data registers in the processor for further operation and manipulation depending on the instruction being executed.

Input/Output Operation

Data transfers between the input/output devices and the processor are done in a way similar to memory transfers. In fact, in many designs, the input and output locations are simply considered to be just another memory location and there is no difference between an input or output transfer and a memory transfer. This is called memory-mapped I/O. Other designs use a different address and enable signal for input and output devices. Such processors are said to support a separate I/O space and they are said to be I/O mapped.

When performing an I/O operation, the processor addresses control gates in the I/O sections just as if they were memory, enables the unit, and sends a control signal to input or output data on the data bus.

Regardless of the type of I/O transfer used, the process of sending data from the processor to the output device is considered an I/O write and is very similar to the memory write. The processor would output the data on the data bus, the address or location code for the desired output device on the address bus, and would then enable the output write conditions. Similarly, a read of an input device would consist of the processor placing its data bus circuits in their input mode, placing the address for the desired input device on the address bus, and providing an input read enable signal. The data would be placed on the data bus by the input device in response to these signals and the processor would then latch the data into one of its internal data registers to complete the input transfer operation or instruction.

Processor Operation

The processor completely controls all read and write operations by specifying which location is to be accessed by the code it places on the address lines and by enabling appropriate control lines. Thus, if there are 16 address lines, a code of 16 zeros would access location 0 (the very first location) in either memory or the I/O space. If a code of all 1's were placed on the 16 address lines, the 65,535th memory location would be accessed. Thus, a 16-bit address code (usually just called "address") can locate one of 65,536 different locations or bytes in memory for accessing by the processor.

The processor must generate the address for the location of either the next instruction or the data it needs to execute the instruction presently in its instruction register. Next, the processor enables (turns on) its input register for a read operation or enables its output register for a write operation. Then the processor enables the memory or the I/O subsystem to perform a read or write operation as required.

The main functions of the processor are to access the memory at any location, control all read and write operations, and perform the operations to support these functions in the correct sequence.

This process is performed over and over again by the processor as it works its way through the microcomputer program, one instruction after another, and as it accesses the data needed to execute each instruction. In fact, the main function of the microprocessor is to fetch and execute program instructions in the proper order to cause the machine it is controlling to behave in the desired manner.

A MICROCOMPUTER VERSION OF THE VENDING MACHINE CONTROLLER

As an example of the design of a microcomputer and its application to a physical control problem, we will consider a microcomputer version of the vending machine circuitry discussed earlier in the chapter. This example will help clarify some of the concepts introduced in this section.

A single microcomputer containing memory, processor and I/O circuits replaces all of the previous circuitry used for the vending machine. It must have interface circuits to couple inputs and outputs and a program to run it.

The approach used is to implement all components of the block diagram of *Figure 5-11* with a single integrated circuit microcomputer known as the TMS9940. This microcomputer contains memory for data and program as well as for the processor and I/O circuits. The processor is of the 16-bit type in that it processes internal instruction codes and data codes 16 bits at a time. Since the memory and basic input and output circuits are all internal to the device, there is no need for an external address bus or data bus.

To use the microcomputer as the vending machine controller, only the vending machine external inputs must be connected to the TMS9940. Then a program to generate the vending machine control signals to cause the sequence of behavior shown in *Figure 5-8* can be written and stored in the memory.

Hardware Connections

The basic hardware connections are shown in *Figure 5-12*. The coin detector outputs of N, D, Q, and the resulting signal $\overline{C}$ are input to the microcomputer. Each of the 30 item selection switches are connected to the 32-to-5 line priority encoder circuit. This circuit generates a 5-bit binary code for the highest priority switch closed. These 5 bits are inputted to the microcomputer and also are sent to a 5-to-32 line decoder. The decoder output, when enabled by the $\overline{VEND}$ signal, causes the release of the selected item. The $\overline{S}$ signal is generated when any one of the selection switches is closed. The power-on and push-button reset circuit is the same as in the earlier version.

The microcomputer generates the outputs DUMP to dump the coins if the coin total is less than the item value, $\overline{VEND}$ to deliver the selected item, and NC and DC to return change. The microcomputer also generates outputs to clear the coin and selection event flip-flops. These flip-flops generate signals called interrupts. The $\overline{INT1}$ signal will interrupt the microcomputer to notify it that a coin has been entered. Similarly, the $\overline{INT2}$ signal will interrupt the microcomputer to notify it that an item switch has been pushed. The interrupt will cause the computer program to respond to the $\overline{C}$ or $\overline{S}$ event as indicated by the sequence in *Figure 5-8*.

Program

The program stored in the memory of the microcomputer directs the microcomputer to monitor inputs, execute instructions on the basis of inputs received, and generate output signals to perform the action required.

While the diagram of *Figure 5-12* shows signal inputs and outputs, it does not indicate how the microcomputer responds to any of the input signals or under what conditions it generates any of the output signals. This information is contained in the computer program which is stored in the memory inside the microcomputer. Only by examining the program and relating it to machine operation can it be verified that the design of *Figure 5-12* will behave the same as the design of *Figures 5-3* through *5-8*. All that can be determined from the hardware design of *Figure 5-12* is that the design is a very simple one and that the expected signals are monitored and generated.

If the program contained in the microcomputer memory were examined, it would be seen to consist of many bytes of instruction codes in binary ones and zeros, called machine code. These codes would have to be converted to a form called assembly language that could be easily understood by a person familiar with the instruction set for this microcomputer. Conversion of a program from machine code to assembly language is called disassembly. An assembly language program is written as a sequence of assembly language statements consisting of instruction abbreviations called mnemonics and data location indicators called operands. An example assembly language program that might be used for the vending machine example is shown in *Figure 5-13* along with explanatory comments. The reader should examine this program in detail to understand that it implements the behavior of the original design described in *Figure 5-8*.

**Figure 5-12.
Microcomputer Vending
Machine Logic**

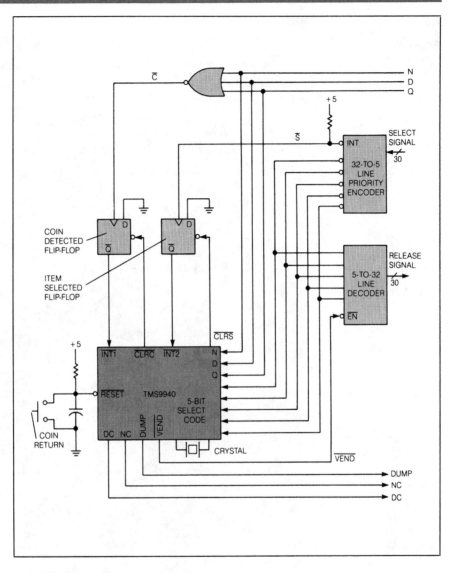

Assembly Language

In an assembly language
program each of the 4
fields of an assembly language statement provide a
certain type of information
about the instruction.

In order to understand a microcomputer program written in assembly
language form, the parts of the assembly language statement must be
understood. An assembly language statement has the following general
format:

Label   Mnemonic   Operand   Comment

The Label and Comment fields are optional. The Mnemonic field is
always required and the Operand field may be required depending on the
instruction. The first instruction of *Figure 5-13* has all four fields.

Figure 5-13.
Vending Machine
Program

An explanation ←

Abbreviation of operation performed →

Label	Mnemonic	Operand	Comment
S0	CLR	R1	Clear TOTAL register
	CLR	R2	Clear VALUE register
	LI	12, >3C0	Set up I/O Base Address
	SBZ	16	Clear SELECT flip-flop
	SBO	16	
S3	SBZ	17	Clear COIN flip-flop
	SBO	17	
	LIIM	3	Activate S ($\overline{S}$) and C ($\overline{C}$) interrupts
S1	IDLE		Wait for interrupt
S2	TB	8	Check for nickel entry
	JEQ	NL	
	TB	9	Test for dime entry
	JEQ	DI	
	TB	10	Test for quarter entry
	JNE	S3	
	JMP	QT	
NL	AI	1, 5	Add 5¢ to TOTAL
	DCA		
	JMP	S3	Go To State 3
DI	AI	1, >10	Add 10¢ to TOTAL
	DCA		
	JMP	S3	Go To State 3
QT	AI	1, >25	Add 25¢ to TOTAL
	DCA		
	JMP	S3	Go To State 3
S4	STCR	3, 5	Get SELECT code
	MOV	VAL(3),2	Get item VALUE from table into R2
	C	2,1	Compare item VALUE to TOTAL
	JLE	VD	Go to VEND if VALUE ≤ TOTAL
	SBO	18	Generate DUMP
	SBZ	18	
	JMP	S0	Go to State 0 (S0) if VALUE > TOTAL
VD	SBZ	19	Generate VEND
	SBO	19	
	JEQ	S0	If VALUE = TOTAL go to State 0 (S0)
S5	S	2,1	else subtract VALUE from TOTAL
	LI	4,1	
	COC	4,1	If difference is odd
	JEQ	NC	go to NC to deliver nickel
DC	SBO	21	else deliver dime
	SBZ	21	by generating DC
D?	LI	3, >10	Subtract 10¢ from difference
	S	3,1	
	DCS		
	JEQ	S0	If 0, go to State 0 (S0)

**Figure 5-13.
Vending Machine
Program (Cont.)**

S6	SBO	21	else deliver another dime
	SBZ	21	
	JMP	S0	go to State 0 (S0)
NC	SBO	20	Deliver nickel by
	SBZ	20	generating NC
	LI	3,>5	Subtract 5¢ from difference
	S	3,1	
	DCS		
	CI	1,0	
	JNE	56	
	JMP	50	Check for need for dime in change

The label is a name of the location of an instruction in the microcomputer memory and is used on any instruction that may be jumped to from another instruction. It also can be used to indicate the start of an important section of a program. For example, in *Figure 5-13* the label of the first instruction is S0 to correspond to state 0 of *Figure 5-8*. Thus, the sequence of instructions beginning at the instruction labeled S0 and ending with the instruction just before the instruction labeled S1 will accomplish the requirements of state S000 of *Figure 5-8*.

The mnemonic is an abbreviation of the instruction operation used to assist a programmer's memory. The operand indicates what is to be operated on. Comment is an explanation in abbreviated English.

The mnemonic is an abbreviation of the operation being performed. In the first instruction of the program of *Figure 5-13*, the mnemonic is CLR, which is an abbreviation for the operation:

CLeaR the contents of the storage location specified in the operand field to all zeros.

The operand field indicates which storage location is involved in the instruction. In the first instruction of *Figure 5-13*, it is the location known as R1. This means Register 1 of the processor workspace register set of which there are 16 registers.

The comment field is simply a verbal explanation for what the instruction is doing. In the first instruction of *Figure 5-13*, the comment is:

Clear TOTAL register

In other words, register 1 has been assigned the function of keeping the coin total and it is being cleared to all zeros by the first instruction in the program. The second instruction of this sequence uses the same mnemonic to clear register 2 (R2) which has been assigned the function of holding the value of the item selected. Thus, the comments of a program are a description of what the program is doing.

A program of the type shown in *Figure 5-13* can be understood from the comments even if the reader is not familiar with the meaning of the instruction mnemonic and operand abbreviations used in the assembly language coding. For example, the reader may not be familiar with the mnemonic SBZ or SBO of the fourth and fifth instructions of *Figure 5-13*, but the comment indicates that these instructions are being used to clear the select flip-flop. Immediately following these in the sixth and seventh instructions is another SBZ and SBO pair which the comment indicates is used to clear the coin flip-flop. These are assigned the label S3. Notice that the program jumps to S3 at other times to clear the coin flip-flop through the jump instructions, JNE and JMP.

The purpose of the SBZ instruction is to set the indicated bit to zero (bit 16 for the select flip-flop and bit 17 for the coin flip-flop) and SB0 is to set the indicated bit to one. This causes a 0 followed by a 1 to be sent to the $\overline{\text{CLR}}$ input of the flip-flop. In other words, a momentary low pulse is delivered to the $\overline{\text{CLR}}$ terminal of the flip-flop to clear the flip-flop, then a high level remains so that the flip-flop can function.

The following explanations of the mnemonics used in *Figure 5-13* should help the reader to understand the basic operation of each of the state sequences S0 through S6. These are listed in alphabetical order.

AI	R, value	Add the value to the contents of register R.
C	R1,R2	Compare the contents of register R1 to the contents of register R2.
CLR	.	Clear the storage location in the operand field to all 0's.
DCA		Make the previous addition correct for decimal (BCD) codes.
IDLE		Wait for an interrupt.
JEQ	Label	Same as JNE only the jump is made if the last result was equal to 0. If the last operation was a TB operation, the jump will occur if the bit tested was a 1.
JMP	Label	Go execute the instruction at Label next.
JNE	Label	If the last result was not equal to 0 (unless it was a TB operation), go execute the instruction at Label next; if not, execute the next instruction after the JNE instruction.
LI	R, value	Place the value into the register R.
LIIM	n	Set the interrupt mask to n; this determines which interrupts will be responded to (levels n or less).
MOV	01,02	Move the contents of location 01 to location 02.
S	R1,R2	Subtract the contents of register R1 from the contents of register R2 and store the results in register R2.
SBO	n	Set bit n to a 1.
SBZ	n	Set bit n to a 0.
STCR	R, n	Input n bits into register R.
TB	n	Test the value of bit number n; place the value in the EQ flip-flop in the microcomputer.

WHAT HAVE WE LEARNED?

1. The troubleshooter must thoroughly understand the sequence of operations of a sequential logic machine to determine the reason for abnormal system behavior.
2. The troubleshooter must understand the detailed operation of all input and output circuits as well as the sequence of operations the controller goes through in response to input signals and past operations.
3. This operational sequence is normally described in a flow chart or in a step-by-step program listing.
4. Deviations from the described normal sequence can be related to problems with state flip-flops or input signal circuits.
5. Once a fault has been isolated to a particular set of input circuits or state flip-flops, it is possible to locate the fault by using the techniques described in previous chapters; that is, voltage, resistance, or current measurement; signal tracing techniques; or component testing techniques.
6. If a microcomputer is used as the controller, in addition to checking the hardware, the program must be analyzed to determine if some flaw exists within the program.

Quiz for Chapter 5

1. A sequential logic system has outputs that depend on:
   a. only the inputs to the system at the current time.
   b. present as well as past inputs.
   c. memory device outputs independent of system inputs.

2. In the vending machine item selection logic *(Figure 5-3)*, a pulse is received on lines S1 and S30. What will be the condition of $\overline{V30}$?
   a. Low
   b. High

3. In the example of problem 3, when VEND is received, what item will be vended?
   a. Item 1
   b. Item 2
   c. Item 30

4. In the example of problem 3, what will be the value V_4 in *Figure 5-4*?
   a. Low
   b. High

5. If a customer enters two nickels and one quarter, what will be the output of the 8-bit register at the time of the $\overline{S}$ signal in *Figure 5-5*?
   a. 35
   b. 00100011
   c. 00110101
   d. 01010011

6. In the controller of *Figure 5-6*, what state will cause an output of low on the $\overline{CLR}$ line?
   a. State 0
   b. State 3
   c. State 7
   d. State 2

7. In the circuit of *Figure 5-6*, what state can cause a VEND signal?
   a. State 4
   b. State 5
   c. State 6
   d. State 7

8. In the circuit of *Figure 5-6*, if the current state is state 3, under what input conditions will the next state be state 4?
   a. T>V is high
   b. CLRCOIN is low
   c. S is high
   d. None

9. Under what conditions could the machine described in *Figure 5-8* go from state 5 to state 7?
   a. Under no conditions.
   b. If in going from state 5 to state 6 the second flip-flop changes faster than the third flip-flop.
   c. If in going from state 5 to state 6 the second flip-flop changes slower than the third flip-flop.
   d. If in going from state 5 to state 0 the first flip-flop changes faster than the third flip-flop.

10. If in the clock circuit of *Figure 5-9a*, the capacitor is changed to 0.5 microfarad, what will be the frequency?
   a. 10 hertz
   b. 20 hertz
   c. 200 hertz
   d. 1,000 hertz

11. The purpose of the control bus in *Figure 5-10* is to:
   a. determine the location in the system to be accessed.
   b. to provide communications from the outside world to the processor.
   c. to determine when memory or inputoutput reads and writes are to occur.
   d. to provide data and instruction codes to the processor.

12. In the program of *Figure 5-12*, the instruction AI represents the hardware component of the:
   a. comparator.
   b. item select logic.
   c. adder.
   d. coin detection logic.

Memory Problems

ABOUT THIS CHAPTER

The basic principles of microcomputer subsystems and system operation were introduced in the last chapter. A microcomputer system such as a special controller or a personal computer may have a large amount of memory that includes read-only memory devices and read-write memory devices which were introduced in Chapter 2. The principles of operation and special methods to find a fault in these memory subsystems that must be understood to troubleshoot modern microcomputer systems will be discussed in this chapter.

READ-WRITE MEMORY

The read-write memory devices, usually called RAM (random access memory), consist of an array of storage cells. A bit can be written into the cell or a bit can be read from the cell. System power must be supplied continually to a RAM to maintain the stored bits in the cells.

The cells consist of either simple R-S flipflops (discussed in Chapter 1) or special charge storage cells consisting of gating transistors and capacitors. In either case, the array is a rectangular structure that has a certain number of rows with each row containing a certain number of columns of storage cells. The RAMs that utilize flip-flop storage cells are called static RAMs since they maintain the stored bits without further action after the flip-flop is set. The RAMs that utilize the charge storage mechanism are called dynamic RAMs (DRAMs). They must be refreshed periodically, usually once every one to two milliseconds, to maintain the stored information. Refresh is necessary to recharge the capacitor because the charge gradually leaks away. Failure to refresh the stored information at the required rate will cause the loss of the stored information. It is the refresh requirement that is the main difference between a static memory and a dynamic memory.

Static Memories

Single Cell

A typical static memory cell is shown in *Figure 6-1*. The cell structure for this memory is the flip-flop formed by the cross-coupled NAND gates, $\overline{GQ}$ and GQ. The stored cell data will be output to the data line if a read operation is being performed ($\overline{S}$ and $\overline{G}$ both low with $\overline{W}$ high). Similarly, data on the data line will be stored into the cell if a write operation is being performed ($\overline{S}$ and $\overline{W}$ both low with $\overline{G}$ high).

Read-write memory is usually a RAM device. Assuming the supply voltage is maintained, static RAMs hold their inputted data indefinitely, but dynamic RAMs must be refreshed every one or two milliseconds.

The data flow to and from the data line is controlled by three-state buffers (BO and BI) which in turn are controlled by gates (GR and GW, respectively) that enable the buffers under the proper $\overline{S}$, $\overline{G}$, and $\overline{W}$ conditions. If a read operation is performed and the cell shown is in the row selected by the address decoder with $\overline{S}$ low, the output of the control gate GR will be low. This, will place BO in the state to pass the value (0 or 1) of Q onto the data line. The outputs of the other seven storage cells in the same row (not shown) will be connected to the other seven data lines to output a complete 8-bit code to the data bus.

If a write operation is performed and the cell shown is in the row selected and $\overline{S}$ is low, the output of the control gate GW will be low. This will place BI in the state to pass the data on the data line to the input to the storage cell (essentially the R and S inputs to the flip-flop). If this condition exists long enough for the flip-flop to respond, the 0 or 1 on the data line will be stored in the cell. At the same time, the data on the other seven data lines will be stored into the other seven cells on the selected row.

For a read, the address decoder enables the three-state buffer to pass the bit status of the memory cell to the bus. For a write, the address decoder enables the three-state buffer to pass the bit status on the bus to the memory cell.

Figure 6-1.
Static Memory Cell

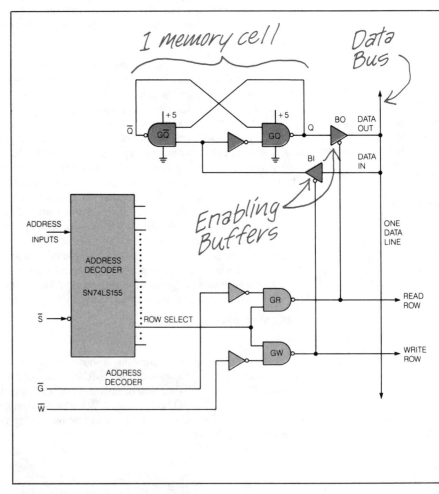

IC RAM

Figure 6-2 shows an integrated circuit TMS4016 static RAM in block diagram form. This circuit has 16,834 cells similar to that of *Figure 6-1*. The cells are organized as 2,048 rows with eight cells per row, thus, each row of cells stores a byte of information. In order to determine which row of storage is read from or written into, the system must provide an 11-bit address code (2^{11} = 2,048) to the circuit. The signals $\overline{G}$ and $\overline{W}$ indicate to the circuit whether a read or write operation is to be performed; however, neither read nor write operation can occur unless a logic 0 is applied to the $\overline{S}$ (Select-not) control input.

To read information from a given row, the 11-bit address must be placed on lines A_0 through A_{10}, the lines $\overline{S}$ and $\overline{G}$ must be brought low (logic 0) while $\overline{W}$ is held high (logic 1). The 8-bit byte will be output on lines D_0 through D_7 (the data bus) as long as *both* $\overline{S}$ and $\overline{G}$ are held low. During this time, the address code on lines A_0 through A_{10} must be held stable and no other device in the system must try to output 1's or 0's onto the data bus.

A similar signal sequence is required to write into the memory. The 11-bit address code is placed on lines A_0 through A_{10} and the data to be stored in the memory is placed on lines D_0 through D_7 by the system processor or other memory control device. Then lines $\overline{S}$ and $\overline{W}$ are brought low while $\overline{G}$ is held high for a long enough time to permit the information to be stored in the selected row of cells. Once this time has expired, the S and W signals are returned to their inactive high levels, the data can be removed from the lines D_0 through D_7, and the address code on lines A_0 through A_{10} may be changed.

To either read into or write from a 2048 word memory, an 11-bit address code locates the desired memory word through an enabled address decoder. To read into memory, $\overline{G}$ is held low; or to write, $\overline{W}$ is held low.

**Figure 6-2.
TMS4016 Static RAM**

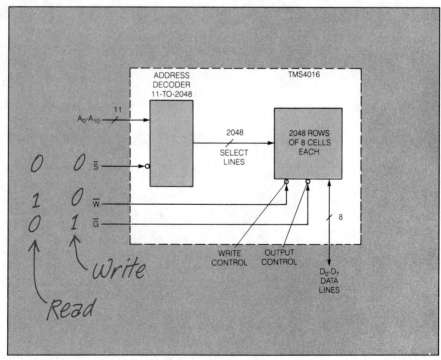

Memory Subsystem

The circuit shown in *Figure 6-3* is an 8,192 byte memory made up of four of the 2,048 byte integrated circuit memory devices of *Figure 6-2*. External circuitry must provide the signals A_0 through A_{10}, $\overline{S}$, $\overline{W}$, and $\overline{G}$. External circuitry also must provide the data on lines D_0 through D_7 during a write operation or receive the data from the memory on lines D_0 through D_7 during a read operation. The microprocessor normally provides these external signals.

The TMS9980 microprocessor in *Figure 6-3* typically provides 14 bits of address code. The least significant 11 of these address bits are connected to the address inputs A_0 through A_{10}. The three most significant address lines and the memory enable ($\overline{\text{MEMEN}}$) signal are connected to the 2-to-4 address decoder to generate the signal $\overline{S}$ to enable a specific memory integrated circuit. The processor also generates read and write control signals to provide the $\overline{G}$ and $\overline{W}$ signals for the memory device.

**Figure 6-3.
Static Memory
Subsystem Comprised
of TMS4016 ICs**

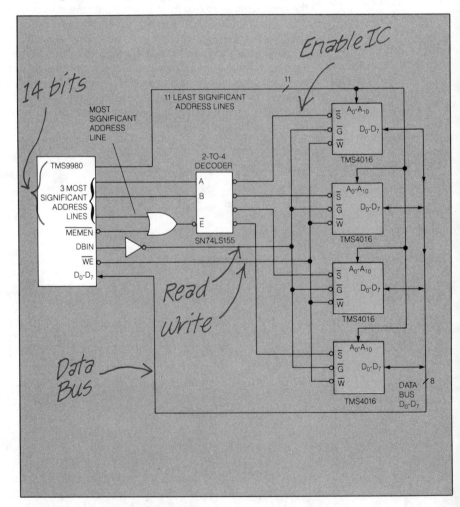

The D_0 through D_7 lines of the memory circuits and the processor are connected together so that data can pass from one to the other. The $\overline{WE}$ (Write Enable Not) line of the processor is connected to the $\overline{W}$ lines of the memory circuits and the DBIN (Data Bus In) signal is connected through an inverter to the $\overline{G}$ inputs of the memory circuits. In the processor shown, DBIN is high for a read operation and $\overline{WE}$ is low for a write operation. $\overline{MEMEN}$ is low for either memory operation. When the $\overline{E}$ input of the decoder is low, one of the output lines of the decoder is low as selected by the high order address lines, thus one (and only one) of the $\overline{S}$ inputs will be at an active low level to enable one particular memory circuit.

The three most significant address bits and $\overline{MEMEN}$ enable the decoder, which activates one of four IC memory packages. The eleven least significant address bits actually select the particular memory word in each package.

In this example, the 14-bit address can select any one byte out of a total memory capacity of 16,384 bytes. Since the memory shown only has 8,192 bytes, the most significant address bit must determine whether the memory is activated or not. Since $\overline{MEMEN}$ and the most significant address bit are sent through a OR gate to the $\overline{E}$ terminal, both must be low to enable the decoder and, in turn, to enable the selected memory circuit. Thus, the binary address code for the 8,192 byte memory must always begin with 0 and the 8,192 byte memory responds to binary addresses 0000 0000 0000 0000 (0000 hexadecimal) through 0001 1111 1111 1111 (1FFF hexadecimal). If the most significant address bit were sent through an inverter before being sent to the OR gate, the memory would be activated only if the most significant address bit were a 1. In that case, the memory would respond to binary addresses 0010 0000 0000 0000 (2000 hexadecimal) through 0011 1111 1111 1111 (3FFF hexadecimal). Thus, it is usually a simple matter to examine the inputs to the decoder to determine the range of the address values to which the memory responds.

Dynamic Memories

Dynamic RAMs serve the same purpose as static RAMs; i.e., to provide storage and retrieval of system data and programs. To operate properly, the dynamic RAM design must include provisions to be periodically refreshed as well as the proper interconnection to the system address, data, and control lines. The refresh requirement is a result of the technique used to provide the binary storage in dynamic memories.

Single Cell

A MOS capacitor, CS, is the heart of the dynamic RAM cell. It controls the gate of a MOS storage transistor TS.

The basic storage cell is shown in *Figure 6-4*. The storage component is the capacitor CS which is part of the MOS transistor TS. The other transistors gate information into and out of the cell for write and read and refresh operations. These transistors are shown as TW, TRD, and TRF, respectively in *Figure 6-4*.

In addition there is gating similar to that used in the static RAM to use the row select, column select, and read/write signals coming into the memory from decoders to determine which storage cell in an array is to be activated. If the decoders select the row and column of the cell in *Figure 6-4*, then the read, write, and refresh NAND gates GRD, GW, and GRF, respectively, will cause the desired action of the selected storage cell. In all cases, both the row and column select lines of all NAND gates must be at their active level (high in the example of *Figure 6-4*), for any action to occur.

If R/$\overline{\text{W}}$ is low, the output of gate GW is low to turn on transistor TW which connects the storage capacitor to the input data line. This allows the capacitor to charge to the 0 or 1 level on the input data line to store the input data. If R/$\overline{\text{W}}$ is high, a read operation occurs and two things happen. First, transistor TRD connects the output of the storage transistor TS to the three-state buffer for a read operation when the cell is selected by the inputs to gate GRD. The capacitor voltage is inverted twice — once by the inverter consisting of TS, TRD, and TL, and once by the three-state buffer which is enabled when R/$\overline{\text{W}}$ is high and $\overline{\text{CS}}$ is low. Thus, the 0 or 1 level output to the data line is the same as that stored in CS.

Capacitive element CS, connected to the data line through a write transistor (TW) when the R/$\overline{\text{W}}$ line is low, charges to the logic level on the data bus for a write function. When R/$\overline{\text{W}}$ is high for a read function, the logic level of CS is outputted to the data bus through an inverter and a 3-state buffer.

Figure 6-4.
Dynamic Memory Cell

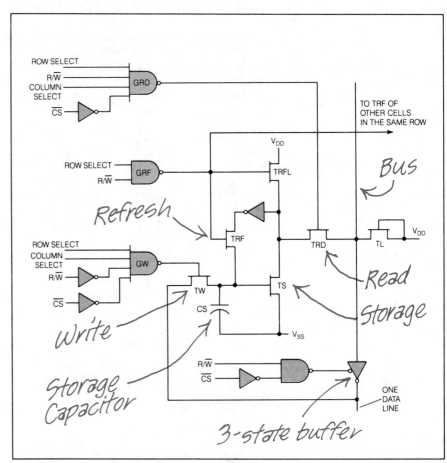

The charge on each capacitance element CS, in a row of cells, is refreshed whenever that row has been chosen for a read function.

At the same time, every cell in the selected row is refreshed by connecting the output of transistor TS through an inverter and transistor TRF to the storage capacitor to renew the charge on the capacitor. This occurs as a result of the low on the output of gate GRF for the selected row during a read operation. Thus, a row of cells is refreshed when a normal read occurs. A row of cells also can be refreshed by a refresh read in which R/$\overline{\text{W}}$ is high, but $\overline{\text{CS}}$ is in its inactive state. Under these conditions, the data from the cell is not delivered to the data line since the three-state buffer is not enabled by $\overline{\text{CS}}$ and the transistor TRD is not turned on. In all cases, transistor TL is permanently turned on to act as a load resistor or pull-up resistor for the storage cells. Transistor TRFL is used to provide the pull-up action for a refresh only operation.

IC DRAM

The single cell of *Figure 6-4* is duplicated over and over in an integrated circuit and the cells are organized in a matrix as indicated in *Figure 6-5*. In this type of structure, the number of rows and columns usually are equal. The product of the number of rows and the number of columns is equal to the number of binary storage cells in the memory. Typically, such circuits have 16,384 or 64,536 storage locations of one bit each. Note that each bit is individually addressable in this IC, but in the static RAM eight bits at a time are addressable.

Figure 6-5.
TMS4116 Dynamic RAM

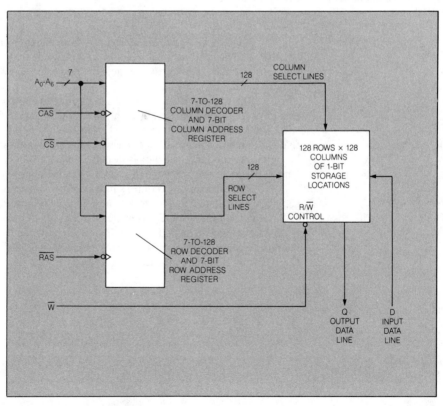

Memory Subsystem

To provide a memory subsystem with eight bits per addressable location, eight such circuits have to be operated in parallel as shown for a 16,384 byte memory in *Figure 6-6* in which eight TMS4116 dynamic RAMs are connected in parallel. Note that all address lines and control lines of all eight ICs are connected together. However, the input and output of each IC is connected to a separate line from D_0 through D_7 of the data bus. The control signal $\overline{WE}$ which goes to the $\overline{W}$ input of the IC determines whether a write or read operation is performed. If $\overline{W}$ is brought low with data on the data lines, the data will be written into the memory. If W is high, the data will be read from the memory.

The example 16 kilobyte memory subsystem, which has a word size of 8 bits per address location, is configured so that all address and control buses are each connected in parallel; therefore they operate simultaneously. The outputs, which are wired independently, each represent one bit in the 8-bit word.

The purposes of the signals $\overline{RAS}$ and $\overline{CAS}$ are not so obvious. The $\overline{RAS}$ signal is used to strobe the row address, usually the least significant seven address bits, into the memory. Of course, the address must be present on the address inputs A_0 through A_6 of the memory circuit at the time $\overline{RAS}$ makes its high to low transition. Then, the next seven more significant address lines must be connected to lines A_0 to A_6 and the $\overline{CAS}$ signal caused to make a high to low transition. Such a transition on $\overline{CAS}$ will cause the selected operation (read or write) to occur. If $\overline{CAS}$ remains high, a refresh will occur for all row cells addressed, but no data will be output because $\overline{CAS}$ enables the three-state output buffer in each IC. Similarly, a write operation will not occur if $\overline{CAS}$ remains high.

Timing

All of these signals must occur in a specific time order for the operations to be successful. The troubleshooter must understand the time relationships of the signals to find faults in memories. Let's look at the timing of a static RAM.

The timing diagram for the TMS4016 read cycle in *Figure 6-7* shows that after the address has stabilized, the data will be available to be read within 250 nanoseconds (ns) for the slowest version of this IC. This is assuming that the $\overline{S}$ and $\overline{G}$ are in their active low states. Data is available 120 ns after $\overline{S}$ is brought low. Similarly, the data is available 100 ns after $\overline{G}$ is brought low. As long as the processor provides this timing, the memory will operate properly.

Write operations require similar timing constraints. The write timing signals are not shown in *Figure 6-7*, but the basic requirements are that $\overline{S}$ and $\overline{W}$ be held low for at least 120 ns while data is applied to the device with stable address signals also applied. These times are easily met by most modern microprocessors. For very fast microprocessors, there are very fast versions of the TMS4016 that are compatible.

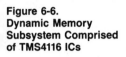

**Figure 6-6.
Dynamic Memory
Subsystem Comprised
of TMS4116 ICs**

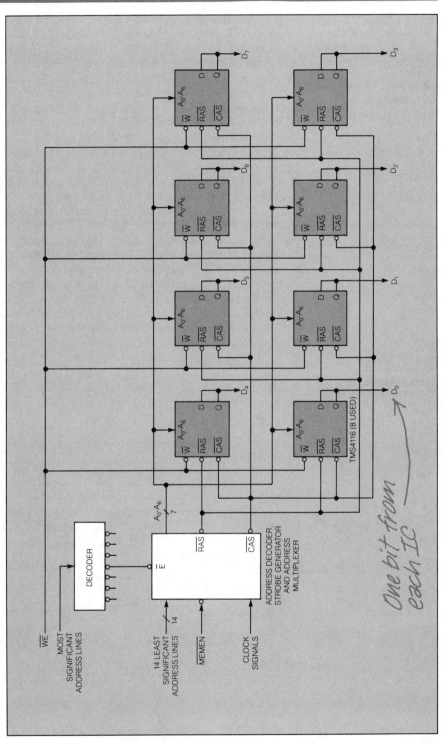

Because digital functions are sequential and interrelated, timing relationships between events, the duration of events, and transitional times between state one and zero, are all critical.

The timing requirements for the TMS4116 dynamic RAM read cycle are shown in *Figure 6-8*. In the slowest version of this device, there must be at least 35 ns between the high-to-low transition of $\overline{RAS}$ to the high-to-low transition of $\overline{CAS}$. Then $\overline{CAS}$ must be held low for at least 165 ns. Once $\overline{CAS}$ has been brought low, the data (DO) will be available within 165 ns. Then $\overline{RAS}$ must be brought back high for at least 150 ns. Similarly, $\overline{CAS}$ must be brought back high for at least 100 ns at the end of a memory cycle. The total memory read operation must take at least 410 ns. These times are met easily even by early microprocessors. Higher speed versions of the TMS4116 are available for the newer (second and third generation) microprocessors that operate at higher speeds (faster clock rates). Similar times must occur for a write operation. Write timing is not shown in *Figure 6-8*, but the write data must be stable and $\overline{W}$ must remain low for at least 75 ns.

The dynamic RAM requires more than just providing the correct read and write control signals and the $\overline{RAS}$ and $\overline{CAS}$ signal sequence for proper operation because the entire memory must be refreshed once every 2 milliseconds (0.002 second). This is done by providing each row address to the memory with an $\overline{RAS}$ signal when the memory is not being accessed by the processor. In the case of the TMS4116, there are 128 rows of 128 columns of 1-bit storage locations; therefore, a 7-bit row address must be presented to the device once every 15.6 microseconds (0.002 second/128 rows = 0.0000156 second or 15.6 microseconds). The row address must be incremented after each refresh so that each refresh will operate on a different row of the memory.

**Figure 6-7.
Timing Diagram for
TMS4016 Read Cycle**

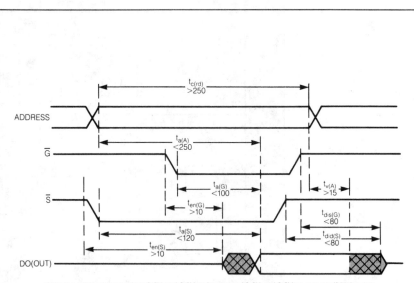

All timing reference points are 0.8V and 2.0V on inputs and 0.6V and 2.2V on outputs (90%) points. Input rise and fall times equal 10 ns. All times are in nanoseconds.

Thus, the refresh will ripple through the 128 rows so that the entire memory will be refreshed every 2 milliseconds. There must be a timer in the refresh controller circuitry so the controller can request access to the memory for a refresh operation every 15 microseconds. During the refresh operation, only $\overline{RAS}$ must be pulsed low (not $\overline{CAS}$) to provide a safe refresh of the memory without destroying or changing any data.

**Figure 6-8.
Timing Diagram for
TMS4116 Read Cycle**

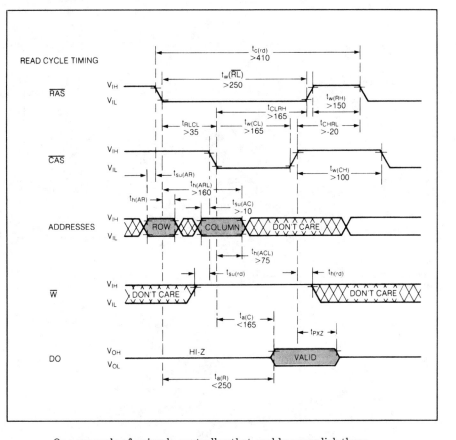

A dynamic RAM requires refreshing every 2 milliseconds. For the example IC memory, the refresh controller must address each row every 15 microseconds to complete the total refresh in 2 milliseconds.

One example of a simple controller that could accomplish these operations is shown in *Figure 6-9*. Since f = 1/T, the 15 microsecond timing is provided by an astable oscillator that produces a 67 KHz square wave. When the square wave oscillator Q_1 terminal changes to a 1, a refresh request signal (RFRQ) is sent to the memory system. The memory system circuit must respond with a refresh grant signal (RFGR) when the memory is not going to be used by the processor for a period of at least 1/3 to 1/2 of a microsecond. The RFGR signal is passed through the AND gate (G1) to the clock terminal of the 1/3 microsecond multivibrator to generate the $\overline{RAS}$ pulse. Notice that during the RFGR pulse, the refresh address counter (a modulo 128 counter) outputs A_0 through A_6 which are gated through the address multiplexer onto the A_0 through A_6 lines of the TMS4116's.

Figure 6-9.
Dynamic RAM Refresh
Controller

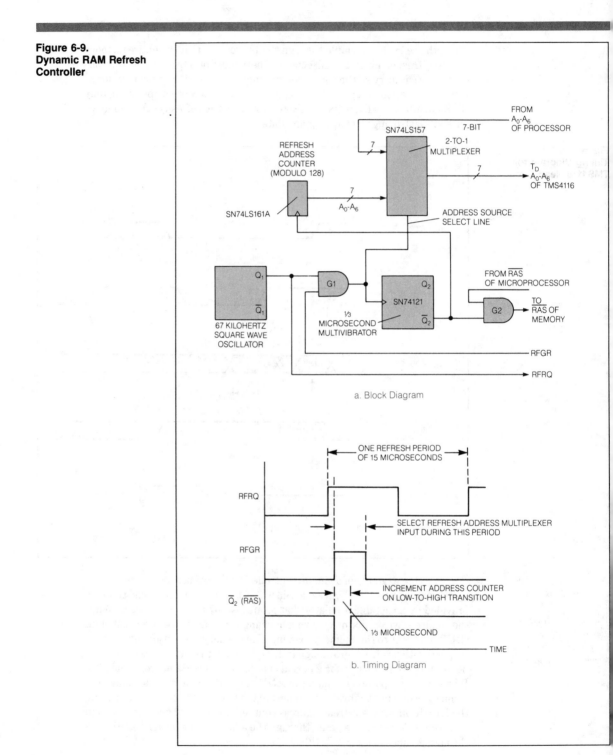

a. Block Diagram

b. Timing Diagram

Then the $\overline{\text{RAS}}$ pulse from the multivibrator is passed through the $\overline{\text{RAS}}$ AND gate (G2) to deliver the $\overline{\text{RAS}}$ signal to the TMS4116's to cause the refresh to occur. Note that no $\overline{\text{CAS}}$ signal is generated. The low-to-high transition of the refresh $\overline{\text{RAS}}$ signal from $\overline{\text{Q}}_2$ is used to increment the address counter to get the next address ready for the next refresh cycle. The address multiplexer is switched back to the processor address lines for normal memory operation when RFGR returns to the low state. This sequence will repeat once every 15 microseconds every time the astable output RFRQ goes high. Since all signals in the circuit of *Figure 6-9* are changing at a rate of around 67 kilohertz, most of the troubleshooting techniques covered in the first chapters of this book would not be sufficient to determine if the refresh controller were operating properly or not.

In fact, most of the techniques discussed thus far in the book would not enable the troubleshooter to verify the timing requirements shown in *Figure 6-7* and *6-8*. However, many of the dc and resistance measurements discussed in earlier chapters would help a troubleshooter to determine if a memory circuit were faulty. For faults involving short or open circuits, the dynamic RAM, static RAM, and read-only memories would be analyzed in similar ways. The main external difference between RAM and ROM is that both the read and write operations of RAMs must be verified, but for ROM, only read operations are examined. More advanced techniques that allow the verification of the timing signals which might be necessary for certain memory problems will be discussed in Chapter 8. Some of these techniques are necessary to determine if a dynamic memory is being refreshed properly.

MEMORY COMPONENT PROBLEMS

Because of the large number of memory storage locations, a computer-based memory excerciser must be used to verify the states of the decoders, gates, and of the memory itself.

The components of a memory subsystem consist of decoders, gates, RAMs, and ROMs. *Figure 6-3* is a typical use of these components in a RAM memory subsystem. Other memories would use these components in a similar manner. In terms of the numbers of different integrated circuits, the memory of *Figure 6-3* is not as complicated as a sequential machine system of the type considered in Chapter 5. What makes the memory more difficult to troubleshoot are the large number of different storage locations whose operation must be verified. A single RAM IC can have from 2,048 to 65,536 internal locations and many memory subsystems have more than one RAM IC. It is an impossible task to manually test and verify the operational status of each location. Thus, if the problem lies within the RAM IC, some type of memory exerciser, probably microcomputer-based, must be used to determine if a given memory circuit is working or not. However, before the memory circuit itself is tested, the simpler combinational circuits (decoders and gates) can be verified relatively simply and quickly.

Combinational Circuit Faults

Defective decoder compo-
nent isolation involves inputting a known logic test
signal sequence and
monitoring the output
with the appropriate test
instrument. For basic gate
devices, the gates are
pulsed and the resultant
output monitored.

In the circuit of *Figure 6-3*, an OR gate generates the enable to a simple 2-to-4 decoder from the signal $\overline{\text{MEMEN}}$ and the most significant address bit. The decoder can be tested by exercising it with signals applied to the three most significant address lines. These signals could come from the system microprocessor or a memory testing instrument. The most significant address line must alternate between zero and one with it at 0 for access to the memory for a read or write. A sufficiently fast test instrument must be available to monitor the signals. (Such an instrument will be discussed in Chapter 8.) With these test signals applied, the output of the OR gate should alternate between zero (memory operation) and one (non-RAM operation). Further, the signals on the decoder select lines should indicate the same 2-bit select code on alternate operations. These tests would indicate the processor-to-decoder circuit is working properly.

If the OR gate output always stays at a 0 or a 1, or if one or more of the select lines always stays at a 0 or a 1, the fault must lie in the path between the processor and the decoder select inputs or OR gate inputs, or in the OR gate itself. The proper operation of these lines and gates can be determined by removing the microprocessor from the system and using signal tracing techniques (logic probe and pulser or voltmeter measurements) along the lines in question. Similarly, the operation of the OR gate can be verified by isolating its input pins and output pin from the processor and decoder and applying known input conditions and checking for proper output operation.

Once the signals into the decoder are working properly, the high speed test equipment should be used to verify that the selected decoder output (and no other) alternates between zero and one. If this does not occur (decoder output stuck at a 0 or 1), either the decoder is faulty or there is a fault in the wiring from the decoder output to the memory chip select inputs. Again, pin isolation and signal tracing techniques can be used to determine the nature of the fault and corrective action taken. Such corrective action will be either to replace the decoder circuit or to repair the wiring. The decoder operation should be verified for all possible select codes (output lines 0 through 3 of the decoder working properly).

Decoder and OR gate op-
eration may be manually
verified by inputting all
combinations of ones and
zeros.

If it is not possible to test the decoder and OR gate operations at normal microprocessor speeds (usually over 1 megahertz), it is possible to verify the operation of these devices with the techniques presented in Chapters 2 through 4. First, the three most significant address lines and $\overline{\text{MEMEN}}$ line to the microprocessor must be isolated or opened. This could be done by removing the microprocessor IC if it is in a socket. Next, place logic 0's on the $\overline{\text{MEMEN}}$ and the three address lines. Voltage measurements should verify logic 0's on all decoder inputs and only on decoder output 0. The other decoder output lines can be exercised by manually placing logic 0 and logic 1 voltages on the select lines of the decoder in all possible combinations while the output of the OR gate is maintained at a 0. If the OR gate or the decoder fails to operate properly, the circuit or wiring at fault can be determined and corrected or replaced.

Of course, none of these tests would be made unless there was a problem suspected or known to exist in the memory subsystem. It is not a simple matter to isolate a microcomputer problem to the memory and it is even more difficult to isolate a particular memory subsystem. Further, even if the fault is known to be in the memory, the techniques discussed thus far in this section would only indicate that the fault is or is not in the combinational section of the memory (the decoder and gates). If it is not in these devices, it is somewhat more difficult to determine which memory circuit is at fault and why. Some of the problems in determining which memory circuit is at fault will be considered in the following section.

Memory Circuit Faults

In normal operation of a memory subsystem, either ROM or RAM, a faulty location may not be accessed until long after the system has been in operation. This is especially true if the problem is in a portion of the RAM circuits. The only indication of such a problem may be an occasional data error in a data processing system, or an occasional error in the position of a machine part in a machine controller system. Such an error could be due to input or output problems or a faulty processor as well as the memory. In fact, any problem with any circuit or wire in the system could cause such a problem.

If a ROM is defective and the system program is stored in that ROM, then the system would not work properly or would stop working altogether. However, erratic response to commands entered on a keyboard could be caused by a faulty keyboard or input problems. So again, it may not be easy to isolate the problem to just the system memory.

Memory Tests

Memory testing requires automation techniques because of the enormous number of locations involved. Automatic testing is performed by test instrumentation or by a built-in program.

Even if it is known that the memory is at fault, there must be some way of automatically testing the memory location by location. Manual testing of 2,000 to 64,000 locations by placing successive address codes and timing signals on the memory and reading the contents of each location would take hundreds to thousands of hours of test time. Obviously, this is not acceptable. Automatic testing of the memory usually is done by connecting a special test instrument or by the system processor executing a memory test program. In fact, in some systems, a memory test program is run automatically every time the system is turned on. Usually, the results of an automatic testing sequence are displayed on a CRT or printed out with a printer to inform the operator which circuit is at fault and why.

A faulty memory cell may be isolated by inputting to the memory, at periodic intervals, the complete sequence of addresses and detecting a given stored pattern of data. The address signals may be generated by counters or a microprocessor.

If such testing instruments or programs are not included in the system, there are some simple techniques that can be used to determine a faulty circuit if the processor can be forced to provide address signals that step in order through successive locations of memory and a sufficiently fast test instrument is available. An example technique is shown in *Figure 6-10*. The processor is replaced with a counter that generates address signals for successive addresses. A two-position switch permits either of two ways to be used to increment the address. In the manual position, the address is advanced only when the pushbutton switch is depressed. Each depression of the button advances the address by one. In the automatic position, the oscillator output provides a very slow clock so the address is continually advanced by one about every half second. The control inputs are manually set to enable the memory circuit that is to be tested for a read operation. The address input and the data outputs of the memory are monitored by LEDs in the test circuit of *Figure 6-10* so that the 0 and 1 levels of all memory outputs can be monitored simultaneously.

Figure 6-10.
Simple Memory Tester

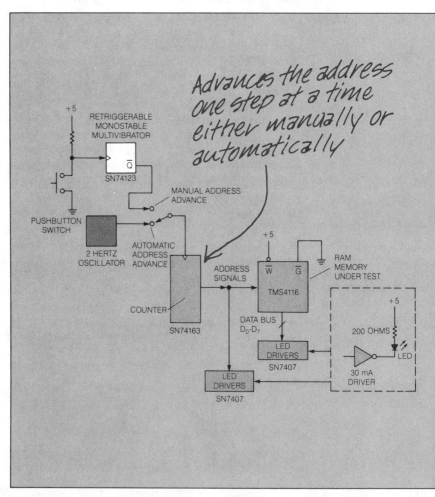

In the example tester, the LED display will show only major memory defects by the pattern of light that is displayed during the test sequence.

If a given memory has a stuck-at-0 or a stuck-at-1 condition in a given output position (one or more output positions), it will be indicated by an LED that remains on or off all the time while the LEDs on the other outputs and on the address lines change. The address LEDs will show a binary counting pattern while the LEDs on the output of the memory should alternate off and on in some random fashion. If any output LED should remain off or on through all addresses, the RAM is faulty internally for that data output or there is a fault in the wiring or connections. This sequence of tests should be performed on each of the other ROMs or RAMs in the memory subsystem.

This test will detect only the most gross defects, but it can be made with a relatively inexpensive test circuit. If the counter is incrementing at a 2 hertz rate so that addresses are changed once every ½ second, it would take 4,096 seconds (over an hour) to test an 8,192 byte memory. A memory can be tested at a 1 megahertz rate if a processor-controlled instrument can be used or if the system has a memory self-test feature built into its system program. At this 1 MHz rate, an 8,192 byte memory could be tested in less than 9 milliseconds, which would be unnoticeable to a human operator. Even a 64K byte memory could be tested in less than 66 milliseconds, compared to 9 hours using the techniques of *Figure 6-10*. Automatic memory tests will be considered in the next section.

TESTING PROCEDURES

The basic concept of testing memory is to be able to verify that each cell location is able to store and to read a 1 or 0 state. The test instrumentation must be able to isolate the defective area and inform the technician.

The objective of a RAM testing program is to exercise all storage cells in the system for the ability to store and read 0's and 1's. The test instrument or program simply has to write a 0 to each cell and read that cell to verify the 0 condition, then write a 1 to each cell and again read each cell to verify the 1 condition. The basic objective of a ROM testing program is to verify that the desired code sequences are stored in the ROM. The desired code sequence also must be available to the test instrument so that the code read from each location in the ROM under test can be compared to the desired code. If a location within a ROM or RAM is found faulty, the test instrument must notify the user which circuit is faulty and what the problem is. It could do this by printing a message on a printer or a CRT display or it could turn on an LED near the faulty chip. The faulty circuit should be replaced or tested further by the previously described techniques to detect faulty decoders and control gates.

Static RAM Testing

The basic RAM test program for a TMS9980 processor along with an explanation of the operation of each instruction is shown in *Figure 6-11*. In the first case, this program would reside in the memory of the system under test.

The test program could
originate either in the
computer's memory or in
the test instrument.

The program could be executed when the system is first turned on to verify memory operation or it could be executed in response to a memory test command. For the second case, the program would be in the memory of a processor-driven test instrument that is connected to the system. It would disable the system's processor and the test instrument would control the address, timing, and data lines. In either case, the memory test program would perform a sequence of tests to test a 2,048 byte RAM such as the first RAM in *Figure 6-3*.

Before the main program calls the TEST subroutine of *Figure 6-11*, it must clear register 1 to 0, initialize registers 6 and 7 to the proper beginning addresses for the FAULT tables, and clear the location named FLAG to zero. With this done, the main program calls the TEST subroutine.

The first instruction of the TEST subroutine clears register 2 to all 0's so the beginning address of the test is 0000 hexadecimal. Then the test code of alternating ones and zeros, 0101 0101 0101 0101 binary (5555 hexadecimal) is loaded into register 3. The value 2,048 is loaded into register 4 which serves as a counter. As each memory byte is tested, its value is decremented by 1; thus, when its value is zero, all 2,048 bytes have been addressed. Next, the MOV instruction copies the 5555 hexadecimal data in register 3 to the memory address specified in register 2, then increments the address in register 2 to the next location. This loop continues writing the 5555 code until register 4 (the counter) is zero which indicates all 2,048 locations have been filled with the test pattern.

The actual test is performed in the second sequence of read instructions beginning with CLR 2. Again the address of 0000 hexadecimal is loaded into register 2 and a count value of 2,048 is loaded into register 4. The memory location is read and the contents placed into register 5. The contents of register 5 are compared to the contents of register 3 (which holds the test code) to see if the bit pattern is identical. The comparison is performed with an exclusive-OR (XOR) instruction which will place all 0's in register 5 if the correct code has been read from the memory location. If the result is all 0's, the testing continues normally. If the result is not all 0's, the program jumps to the instruction labeled FAULT.

In the FAULT sequence, the location named FLAG is set to all 1's. Then the address in register 2, which is the address of the faulty memory location, is stored in a table addressed by register 6. Next, the contents of register 5, which contains a 1 in each bit position that did not match, is stored in a table addressed by register 7. After the fault conditions are recorded in the tables, testing is continued by jumping back to the instruction labeled CONT. The end of this test sequence occurs when the counter in register 4 is decremented to zero.

**Figure 6-11.
RAM Test Program**

```
TEST        CLR 2           Set R2 to first address of memory under test.
            LI 3,>5555      Set R3 to alternating zeros and ones.
            LI 4,2048       Set R4 to count 2048.
LOOP        MOV 3,*2 +      Write test code to RAM (See note).
            DEC 4           Decrement byte counter.
            JNE LOOP        If all RAM not written, continue writing at loop.
            CLR 2           Else again set R2 to first address of memory under test.
            LI 4,2048       Again load counter to 2048.
LOP         MOV *2 +,5      Read memory.
            XOR 3,5         Check if bits read are same as bits stored.
            JNZ FAULT       If not, go to fault.
CONT        DEC 4           Else decrement counter.
            JNZ LOP         If counter not zero, continue testing at loop.
            JMP NEXT        Else go to next.
FAULT       SETO FLAG       If there is a fault, set flag to all ones.
            MOV 2,*6 +      Store address of fault.
            MOV 5,*7 +      Store bad bit pattern.
            JMP CONT        Continue testing.
NEXT        CI 1,1          Has memory been fully tested?
            JEQ OUT         If so, go to out.
            INC 1           Else indicate last pass of tests.
            INV 3           Swap zeros and ones positions in test code.
            CLR 2           Again set R2 to first address of memory under test.
            LI 4,2048       Again load counter to 2048.
            JMP LOOP        Continue testing at loop with new test code.
OUT         RTWP            Return
```

Note: The + after the register indicates the address will be incremented to point to the next location to be accessed after this operation.

This RAM Test program performs the operations required to run a complete memory test.

At this time, a jump to the instruction labeled NEXT occurs and the register 1 contents are compared to the number 1. If register 1 contains 1, the tests are finished and a jump to instruction OUT is performed to return from the TEST subroutine to the main program. If register 1 still contains 0, the tests are not finished; therefore, register 1 is incremented to 1 and the test code is changed to 1010 1010 1010 1010 (AAAA hexadecimal) by the INV 3 instruction. Notice that this pattern still is alternating ones and zeros, but the 0 and 1 positions are swapped from those of the first test code. Register 2 is again cleared to 0000, register 4 (the counter) is again loaded with 2,048 and a jump to the instrucion labeled LOOP is made to begin the new test. When the TEST subroutine has completed execution as indicated by 1 in register 1, the main program will check location FLAG.

If FLAG is all 0's, the memory circuit is working properly and the main program can send a message to the printer or the CRT display that "RAM 0 is working properly". Then it can go on to execute similar programs for the next three RAMs of *Figure 6-3*. In fact, the subroutine TEST could test all RAMs if the main program passed the starting address of the RAM to be tested into register 2 through the variable START. Of course, the CLR 2 instructions would be changed to LI2, START.

The diagnostic printout may inform the troubleshooter which memory package has a fault and should be replaced. It could also provide actual diagnostic information to isolate the word and the location that is at fault.

If, after execution of the TEST subroutine, location FLAG contains all 1's, the main program will execute a program sequence to print the message "RAM 0 is faulty and should be replaced". It also could print out the contents of the fault tables addressed by registers 6 and 7 with a sequence of messages of the form: "Location (contents of table addressed by R6) is faulty in bit position (contents of table addressed by R7)" for each entry in the two tables. Such a print-out would enable the user to pinpoint which locations are in error and which data lines for those locations (the bit positions containing a 1) are in error. If only positions that should have stored a 0 are at fault, the storage position is stuck at 1. Similarly, if only positions that should have stored a 1 are faulty, the storage position is stuck at 0. This would allow the troubleshooter to use pin isolation techniques to determine if the external wiring is shorting to the plus line of the power supply or to ground before replacing a memory circuit that may be operating properly.

Instructions could be added to the program so it could determine if a pin is stuck at 0 or stuck at 1 only for certain memory locations (addresses) or for all memory locations. If only certain locations are stuck at 0 or 1, then most likely the circuit is faulty. If all locations in one RAM show the same pin stuck at a 0 or a 1, most likely there is a short or open in the external wiring, although a faulty RAM could cause the problem. Thus, if more instructions are added to the diagnostic program so that it performs more tests in more detail, the computer or test instrument can collect a lot of data which it can analyze to determine the problem. Then it can print out a detailed report for the troubleshooter. Such a program could do almost everything except the actual physical repair.

ROM Testing

The program codes or other codes that are supposed to be stored in the ROM to be tested have to be duplicated in a test instrument. The test instrument compares its reference code with the ROM code. A complete match would indicate that the tested ROM is working properly while any deviation from a match would indicate a faulty ROM or wiring.

ROM, PROM and EPROM memory can be tested the same as RAM.

Figure 6-3 could be converted to an EPROM version by directly replacing all the TMS4016s with the EPROM equivalent, the TMS2516. Then, a test microcomputer system would be connected to disable and replace the processor in the system of *Figure 6-3* so the test instrument would completely control the EPROM subsystem. A copy of the codes stored in the 8,192 byte EPROM subsystem and a test program of the type shown in *Figure 6-12* would have to be stored in the test instrument memory. Assume that the code to be compared is placed in the test instrument memory from locations 8000 through 9FFF hexadecimal and the program to control the testing sequence (*Figure 6-12*) is placed in locations beginning at A000 hexadecimal. The test instrument then can access the EPROM of the modified *Figure 6-3* as if it occupied

UNDERSTANDING DIGITAL TROUBLESHOOTING

locations 0000 through 1FFF hexadecimal in the test instrument memory space. Under these conditions, the testing program of *Figure 6-12* would be able to perform the desired test.

In the program of *Figure 6-12*, registers 6 and 7 again will hold the addresses of tables to store the addresses of faulty memory locations and the positions of the faulty bits. Register 4 again is the counter, but in this program it is loaded with 8,192 to test the full range of 8,192 bytes. Register 2 again holds the address of the byte in the memory to be tested, thus, it is initialized to 0000. The use of register 3 is different in this program; it holds the address of the byte of the reference code in the test instrument memory that is to be compared with the byte of EPROM code addressed by register 2. Thus, register 3 is initialized with the address 8000 hexadecimal.

Then, beginning with the instruction labeled LOOP, the reference byte is moved to register 5 and the byte from the EPROM memory under test is exclusive-ORed (XOR) with this reference byte. A result of all 0's indicates the test memory is alright and the test continues at the instruction labeled CONT. A 1 in any bit position in register 5 after the XOR indicates an error in the EPROM under test and a jump is made to the instruction labeled FAULT. This sequence is exactly like the one in *Figure 6-12*.

After the fault conditions are recorded, the test sequence continues at the instruction labeled CONT. At this point in the program, the counter in register 4 is decremented and the count checked for zero to see if all 8,192 bytes have been tested. If not, the test is continued at LOOP. If all bytes have been tested, a return is made to the main system program. The way the main program calls the ROMTEST subroutine and handles the error conditions is like that explained for *Figure 6-11*.

**Figure 6-12.
ROM Test Program**

```
ROMTEST    LI 4,8192      Set counter to 8192.
           LI 3,>8000     Set reference file address to 8000.
           CLR 2          Set address of memory under test to all zeros.
LOOP       MOV *3+,5      Read reference code to R5 (see note).
           XOR *2+,5      Read ROM under test and compare to reference code.
           JNZ FAULT      If not equal, go to fault,
CONT       DEC 4          Else decrement counter.
           JNZ LOOP       If counter not 0, continue testing,
           RTWP           Else return.
FAULT      SETO FLAG      If fault, set flag to all ones.
           MOV 2,*6+      Store address of fault.
           MOV 5,*7+      Store bad bit pattern.
           JMP CONT       Continue testing.
```

Note: The + after the register indicates the address will be incremented to point to the next location to be accessed after this operation.

Dynamic RAM Testing

The DRAM, although having similar testing requirements as the RAM, has several important differences, which include cell organization, cell refresh requirements, and timing and control signal relationships.

Testing of a dynamic RAM is similar to that for a static RAM. The main differences are the refresh requirements of the DRAM and the different cell organizations. The static RAM often is organized in bytes so that a certain number of complete bytes can be stored in one integrated circuit while the DRAM typically is organized in bits so that it has a certain number of locations with each one storing 1 bit. This means that one 8-bit byte is spread across eight ICs operated in parallel instead of being totally contained in one IC. This changes the analysis of the test results. A line stuck at a 0 or stuck at a 1 in a static RAM will either have to be caused by the output buffer in that bit position in the RAM integrated circuit or in the wiring on that line. In the case of the DRAM, the failure of a single IC (a problem in its input decoder or timing buffer circuits) would cause the bit position assigned to it to be at fault for all memory locations within the dynamic memory address range. Thus, it may be possible to even more quickly determine which circuit is faulty since generally the same bit will then be in error for all addresses tested. Of course, the problem could be in the wiring to that circuit, just as it could be for the ROM or static RAM.

Testing of the refresh operation of the DRAM requires different techniques which will be covered in a later chapter. The other aspect of DRAM testing is that the particular timing and control signal relationships (*Figure 6-8*) makes a special tester of the type shown in *Figure 6-10* somewhat difficult to build. It is much more convenient and cost effective to use automatic testing programs of the type shown in *Figure 6-11* for this purpose. The testing program could be in a microprocessor-based test instrument or as part of the system turn-on diagnostic sequence. More will be said of such system self-diagnostics in the last chapter.

WHAT HAVE WE LEARNED?

1. Semiconductor memory subsystems consist of storage circuits along with decoders and gates.
2. The testing of static RAM, dynamic RAM and ROM is similar.
3. The combinational logic portion of the memory can be tested by using the techniques presented in earlier chapters, particularly Chapter 4.
4. Testing the storage devices is somewhat more complicated because usually many thousands of locations must be tested and a complete summary of thousands of such tests maintained.
5. It is possible to do the testing manually with a simple test instrument; however, testing a memory of many thousands of locations could take hours.
6. A microprocessor and special test program can determine quickly and easily if system RAM and ROM are working properly.
7. Automatic testing can provide detailed test results and analysis to help the troubleshooter locate the fault quickly.

Quiz for Chapter 6

1. A static memory will store information:
   a. even when power is not applied to the memory.
   b. as long as power is applied to the memory.
   c. as long as power is applied and the memory is refreshed periodically.

2. A dynamic memory will store information:
   a. even when power is not applied to the memory.
   b. as long as power is applied to the memory.
   c. as long as power is applied and the memory is refreshed periodically.

3. The typical number of bits in a static memory location is:
   a. 1
   b. 2
   c. 8
   d. 16

4. The typical number of bits per dynamic memory location is:
   a. 1
   b. 2
   c. 8
   d. 16

5. A static memory generally contains:
   a. no decoders.
   b. row decoders.
   c. column decoders.
   d. both row and column decoders.

6. A dynamic memory generally contains:
   a. no decoders.
   b. row decoders.
   c. column decoders.
   d. both row and column decoders.

7. If, in *Figure 6-3*, the processor provided 16 address bits, how many memory circuits would be required to provide a memory that would utilize all possible addresses?
   a. 4
   b. 8
   c. 16
   d. 32

8. In the case of problem 7, if the structure of *Figure 6-3* is used with the most significant address bits sent to a $\overline{\text{NAND}}$ gate to generate the enable signal $\overline{E}$ for the decoder, what would be the address of the first location in the top memory circuit?
   a. 0000
   b. 2000
   c. A000
   d. E000
   e. F000

9. If, in *Figure 6-6*, the signal $\overline{E}$ is generated when the most significant address lines contain the code 10_2, what would be the address of the last location of the memory shown?
   a. 0000
   b. 4FFF
   c. 8000
   d. 8FFF
   e. BFFF

10. If the memory test circuit shown in *Figure 6-10* is able to test one location per second, how many hours would it take to verify the operation of the memory shown in *Figure 6-3*?
    a. 0.4
    b. 2.22
    c. 133.3
    d. 8000

11. If each instruction in *Figure 6-11* takes 2 microseconds to execute, approximately how many seconds would it take to test a good memory of the form of *Figure 6-3*?
    a. 0.006
    b. 0.06
    c. 0.6
    d. 6
    e. 60

12. If the dynamic memory refresh controller of *Figure 6-9* is used with a 64K memory circuit, what would be the refresh interval in microseconds?
    a. 2
    b. 4
    c. 8
    d. 16
    e. 32

13. In the case of problem 12, what would be the number of row address bits out of the counter and the multiplexer?

a. 7
b. 8
c. 9
d. 10
e. 16

14. If, in the system of *Figure 6-3*, none of the memory responds to a memory access by the processor, the most likely fault is·

a. faulty line 0 output of the decoder.
b. faulty memory devices.
c. faulty decoder.
d. faulty enable gate.
e. c or d above.

15. If, in the memory system of *Figure 6-6*, bit D_3 is always 0, the most likely error is:

a. faulty decoder.
b. faulty $\overline{RAS}$ generator.
c. faulty memory circuit in the D_3 position.
d. faulty $\overline{CAS}$ generator.

16. If a memory consists of four rows of circuits of the type shown in *Figure 6-6* with a 2-to-4 decoder and it is observed that the memory in address range 0000 through 3FFF is faulty, the most likely problem is:

a. fault in the output 0 line of the decoder.
b. faulty decoder.
c. faulty $\overline{CAS}$ generator.
d. faulty row of memory circuits in first row of memory.

17. For a memory of the type of problem 16, if the fault is that D_3 is wrong when accessing the address from 8000 through BFFF, the fault is most likely to be:

a. faulty decoder.
b. open in one of the decoder output lines.
c. faulty $\overline{RAS}$ generator.
d. bad memory circuit in the third row, D_3 column.
e. bad memory circuit in the second row, D_3 column.

18. If the entire memory described in problem 16 is faulty, the most likely problem is:

a. faulty decoder.
b. open in one of the decoder output lines.
c. faulty $\overline{RAS}$ generator.
d. bad memory circuit in the third row, D_3 column.
e. bad memory circuit in the second row, D_3 column.

19. In the test program of *Figure 6-11*, the strategy is to:

a. send alternate 1's and 0's to each memory location and read these locations for correct storage, then repeat the test with the 1 and 0 pattern inverted.
b. send all 0's to each memory location and verify the ability to store 0's, then repeat the test with an all 1 pattern.
c. neither of the above.

20. If the strategy of the test program of *Figure 6-11* is changed from 19a to 19b or vice-versa, what instruction must be changed?

a. LI 3, 5555
b. INV 3
c. XOR 3,5
d. CLR 2

Input/Output Problems

ABOUT THIS CHAPTER

In the last chapter, the basic operation and problems associated with microcomputer memories were discussed. The principle purposes of the input and output subsystem were introduced in the first part of Chapter 5. In this chapter, the types of input and output designs and interfacing techniques encountered in microcomputer designs will be considered along with some typical faults and the techniques for fault detection in such systems.

TYPES OF I/O COMPONENTS AND PROBLEMS

In a microcomputer system, the input and output circuits are controlled by the microprocessor through the address and control bus lines. Information is transferred between the processor and the input and output devices along the data bus lines. The types of information transfer and the circuits coupling the processor and the buses will be considered in this section.

Three access methods to I/O devices commonly used in microcomputer systems are: memory mapped, I/O mapped multiple-bit transfers, and bit-mapped I/O transfers.

There are several ways that can be used to control input and output devices in a microcomputer. Generally these devices consist of registers and three-state buffers, though decoders, encoders and multiplexers also are used. The three commonly used ways to control access to these input and output devices are: (1) memory-mapped I/O, (2) I/O-mapped multiple-bit transfers, and (3) bit-mapped I/O transfers. Every processor does not use all of these ways, but all processors do allow the memory-mapped method. When the memory-mapped method is used, the I/O device is assigned a memory address, as if it were a location in the memory. Then the I/O device is connected to the address bus and control bus signals in the same way as a memory device. Recall that these were discussed in the previous chapter.

Some processors also will work with the I/O-mapped method. When this method is used, the I/O registers and three-state buffers have an address that is valid only as an I/O address. They will not respond to a memory address. Transfers to and from the I/O devices occur on the system data bus; therefore, they are either 8-bit parallel transfers or 16-bit parallel transfers, depending upon the microprocessor. Most 16-bit microprocessors that have a 16-bit data bus offer the alternatives of 8-bit or 16-bit transfers to and from registers and three-state buffers.

A few processors further support transfers to and from single addressable bits in the system along a single-bit input and output set of lines. All of these I/O alternatives will be considered in this section along with problems that may occur in the operation of such circuits.

Bit-Mapped Output

The first example that will be considered is the bit-mapped output circuit shown in *Figure 7-1*. In this case, the microprocessor is the TMS9980 which is a 16-bit processor with an 8-bit data bus. This processor has the capability of addressing 2,048 individual input and output bits. The bit transfers occur on the lines CRUIN (bit input line) and CRUOUT (bit output line). The processor also outputs a signal CRUCLK to indicate when valid data is appearing on the CRUOUT line.

The output select device in *Figure 7-1* is an addressable octal latch. The address lines corresponding to the least significant 3 bits of the address are connected to the three select code lines to select the output line. The CRUCLK signal is used to enable the circuit to latch the bit on CRUOUT onto the selected output line. Therefore, when CRUCLK makes a high-to-low transition, the flip-flop inside the device that receives the 0 or 1 on CRUOUT will be determined by the 3-bit select code. The bit can be stored into the selected flip-flop only when the device enable signal is in its active state.

As shown in *Figure 7-1*, the addressable octal latch can be thought of as a 3-to-8 decoder whose outputs are sent to the latch (clock) inputs of eight D-type flip-flops. The latch line is selected by the input code of the 3-to-8 decoder and enabled by the signals that are gated into the decoder enable terminal. The CRUOUT signal is sent to the D input of all eight flip-flops, but is stored only in the flip-flop receiving the latch pulse. The latch pulse on the selected line is an inverted copy of the CRUCLK signal.

Notice in *Figure 7-1* that the eight most significant address lines are sent to a NAND gate along with the CRUCLK signal. Thus, when all of these signals are high, the NAND gate output will go low, enabling the decoder and the entire addressable octal latch. Therefore, the octal latch will be enabled only when the address code is:

111 1111 1XXX

where XXX is the 3-bit flip-flop select code. The complete address of the top flip-flop (FF1) in *Figure 7-1* would be 7F8 hexadecimal because XXX = 000. The complete address of the bottom flip-flop (FF8) would be 7FF hexadecimal beçause XXX = 111. This is the general way to determine the address for any specific bit in the bit-mapped I/O subsystem.

> *NOTE: Hexadecimal is usually abbreviated HEX, (H), or H. For the remainder of this book, an H (as in 7FFH) will be used for the word hexadecimal.*

To send a 0 to such a bit using the instructions of the TMS9980 microprocessor, one would program the instruction:

SBZ n

to set the bit indicated by n to a 0. The bit receiving the 0 is identified by the address code obtained by adding the value of n from the instruction to the base address contained in register 12 (R12) in the processor. Thus, if R12 contains

In the output bit-mapping example, one flip-flop of an addressable octal latch has its latch signal activated by the output of a 3 to 8 decoder to capture data sent to all flip-flops.

the base address 7F0H and the instruction SBZ 8 is executed, the bit address will be 7F0H plus 8 or 7F8H. The bit at address 7F8H would be cleared to 0. In other words, the top flip-flop (FF1) of *Figure 7-1* would receive a 0 on the CRUOUT line.

Similarly, the instruction:

SBO n

would set the addressed bit to a 1. Thus, if R12 contains the base address 7F0H and the instruction SBO 15 is executed, the bit at address 7FFH (7F0 + F) would be set to 1. In other words, the bottom flip-flop (FF8) of *Figure 7-1* would be set to 1.

**Figure 7-1.
Bit-Mapped Output
Circuit**

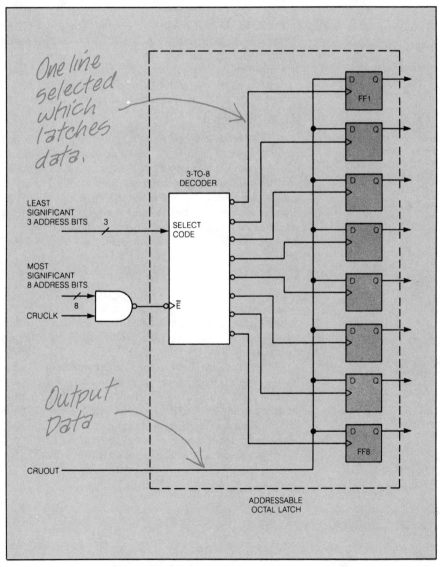

Troubleshooting

The most common flip-flop
faults are those where one
or more of the flip-flops
are stuck at either level. If
all of the flip-flops fail to
respond, the cause is
something common to all
of them.

From a troubleshooting viewpoint, the operation of the circuit of
Figure 7-1 is relatively simple. The most likely problem is that the flip-flops do
not receive either a 0 or 1, but are stuck at a 0 or a 1 level. If all flip-flops do not
respond to output instructions, then the fault is not with the flip-flops, but is
located in some portion of the circuit that is common to all flip-flops. The
problem would have to be in the enable input or in the D input line. An open in
either line would cause the circuit to fail to respond to a 0 or 1 output
instruction. The enable fault could be due to a fault in the NAND gate that is
decoding the most significant address lines and passing CRUCLK through to
the enable pin.

If all but one flip-flop operates normally in response to an output
instruction, the fault could be in one of three places: (1) in the decoder which
generates the latch to the flip-flop, (2) in the line connecting the CRUOUT
signal to the flip-flop input, or (3) in the line connecting the decoder output to
the flip-flop latch input. In an addressable octal latch, any of these would
indicate a component failure inside the integrated circuit. In any case, the fault
can be found relatively easily with simple measurement techniques.

Bit-Mapped Input

In the input bit-mapped
input example, an 8 to 1
multiplexer decoder se-
lects the one input line, of
eight, that is to be passed
to the CRUIN line.

The bit-mapped input circuit of *Figure 7-2* is very similar to the
output circuit of *Figure 7-1*. The input selection device is an 8-line to 1-line
multiplexer. In this example, the enabling gate again is a NAND gate and the
multiplexer has the same address range (7F8H-7FFH) as that of the output
circuit of *Figure 7-1*. There is no CRUCLK input to the NAND gate since the
input is enabled only by the eight most significant address bits. The gating of
the input to the microprocessor is controlled at the microprocessor input
register. The least significant three address bits are used to select which one of
the eight inputs is passed to the CRUIN line.

The instruction that inputs the 0 or 1 on one of the eight input lines is:

$$TB\ n$$

where again n is added to the base address in register 12 of the processor to
obtain the address of the selected bit. For example, if the base address in
register 12 is 7F8H and bit 7 is to be input, the instruction TB 7 would be
required to obtain the address 7FFH (7F8 + 7 = 7FF).

Problems that can occur in this circuit are limited to multiplexer
failure, NAND gate failure, or an open or short in one of the lines in the circuit.
If none of the bits can be input to line CRUIN, the fault is in the enabling
connection and gate. If the input on only one line can't be passed to CRUIN,
the fault is in the connection of that line to the multiplexer or in the multiplexer
itself. A failure of two inputs would be due to a fault in one of the select lines
which is causing a bit of the select code to be stuck at a 0 or at a 1.

Figure 7-2.
Bit-Mapped Input Circuit

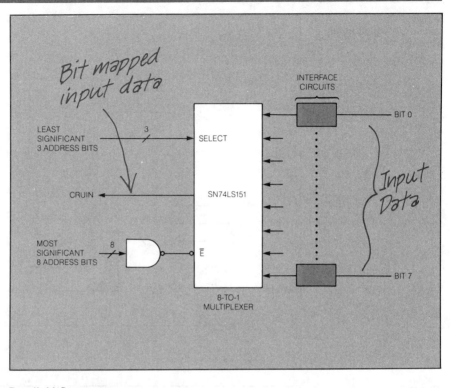

Parallel I/O

The parallel I/O (I/O mapped multiple-bit transfers) method is different from the bit-mapped method because the parallel I/O transfers occur on the data bus of the microprocessor like memory transfers. The difference is that the parallel I/O responds to an I/O enable signal, but the memory-mapped I/O responds to a memory enable signal.

Memory-Mapped I/O

In the memory-mapped I/O system, the input I/O register and output I/O register are addressed just like memory. A control signal determines that the address is for I/O and not for memory.

The basic structure for a memory-mapped input register is shown in *Figure 7-3* for a TMS9980 processor. *Figure 7-4* shows the basic structure for the memory-mapped output register. Both the input and output registers are assigned the memory addresses 1000H through 1007H. There also may be a memory circuit with addresses 1000H through 1007H, but the memory circuit must be disabled when these addresses are used in an I/O operation. That is the purpose of the memory disable ($\overline{\text{MDIS}}$) line in *Figures 7-3* and *7-4*.

In the input circuit in *Figure 7-3*, the decoder responds with a low on one of its output lines to enable an input register when all the following conditions are true: (1) a memory address between 1000H and 1007H is addressed, (2) the memory enable signal (MEMEN) is active, (3) the input transfer enable signal DBIN is active, and (4) the most significant address lines are active. Thus, the input register will deliver its data to the data bus for transfer to one of the processor registers or one of the memory locations when an input instruction is executed.

Figure 7-3.
Memory-Mapped Input
Circuit

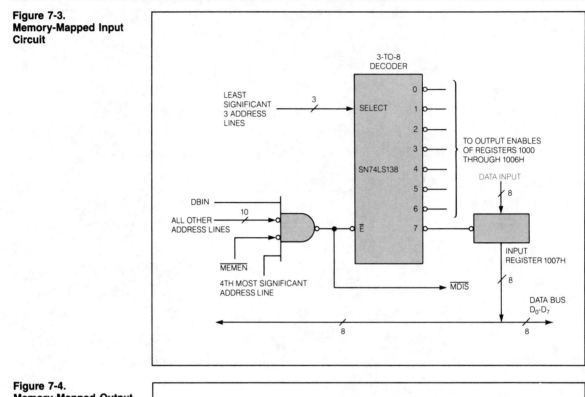

Figure 7-4.
Memory-Mapped Output
Circuit

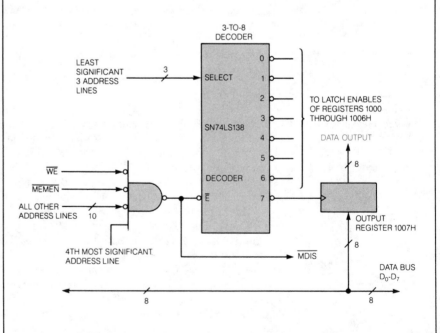

In *Figure 7-4*, the decoder controlling the output registers is enabled under the same conditions except the write enable signal $\overline{WE}$ is used instead of DBIN. The processor will deliver data to the data bus and the selected output register will store this data when an output instruction is executed.

For example, to input the data from the external register at 1002H to the memory location 2000H would require the execution of the instruction:

```
MOV @ > 1002, @ > 2000
```

To output data from processor register 2 to the output register at location 1007H would require the execution of the instruction:

```
MOV 2, @ > 1007
```

thus, it is a relatively simple matter to relate the instruction to the input or output transfer operation.

Interface circuits convert digital signals to signal levels used by other systems. Control circuits convert outputs to physical action.

Regardless of which input or output method is used, it allows the microprocessor to receive or send a single signal or a sequence of digital signals from or to another system or a control device. To make these signals useful for control or communications, the voltage levels of the digital signals must be changed to other voltage levels. The circuits between the input/output registers and the other system that do this voltage change or otherwise modify the signals are called interface circuits. The circuits that use the output signals to cause a physical operation (such as turning on a motor) are called control circuits. Both interface circuits and control circuits may be the source of system failures; therefore, these circuits and their operation must be understood.

Control Circuit

A common control circuit is a relay energized by a computer output logic 1, whose contacts control a high-current or high-voltage circuit.

Figure 7-5 illustrates a type of output circuit that is encountered often in systems that must control high power loads such as heaters or motors. The high current relay driver responds to digital voltage levels at its input and provides a large current flow in the output circuit when a logic 1 is present at the input. This current can be used to energize the coil of a 24 to 28 Vdc relay to cause the relay contacts to close. This switches on the ac power to the heater, motor or other load being controlled to provide the desired action. The diode is placed in parallel with the coil to prevent damage to the relay driver by large voltages that occur when the coil current is switched off. The polarity of this voltage is opposite to the supply voltage, so the diode conducts and dissipates the energy.

By choosing a relay with sufficient voltage and current rating on its contacts, almost any power level load can be controlled by the microcomputer. Similar circuits using a SCR or TRIAC in place of the relay with a pulse transformer or optical coupler to provide isolation for the computer also are used to control high power loads. These are somewhat more complicated than the circuit of *Figure 7-5*, but they have a similar function and similar failure modes.

Figure 7-5.
AC Power Control Circuit

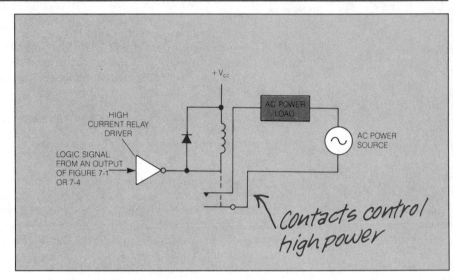

Contacts control high power

Troubleshooting the Control Circuit

In a relay circuit, a defective coil, contacts, or solid-state driver are the most likely sources of failure.

In a circuit of the type shown in *Figure 7-5*, the most likely cause of failure is an open in the relay winding, faulty relay contacts, or a bad relay driver. These can be checked by disconnecting the relay driver input from the microcomputer and applying a 0 level voltage to the input of the driver. The current flow in the coil should be zero and the relay contacts should indicate an open circuit (no current flow in the power circuit). There should be V_{cc} volts at the output of the relay driver.

If the relay driver output is at 0 volts and the relay is closed, there is a short in the driver output circuit and the driver should be replaced. The driver failure may have been caused by an open diode across the relay coil; therefore, the diode should be disconnected and tested with an ohmmeter before replacing the driver. The diode should have low resistance with the negative lead connected to the cathode (bar) and the positive lead connected to the anode (arrowhead). (Remember that some ohmmeters have the black lead positive in the ohmmeter function.) When the connections are reversed, a high resistance (at least 100 times the low resistance) should be indicated. If not, the diode is defective.

If the driver output is V_{cc} when a 0 is applied to its input, then a 1 level should be applied to the driver input. This should cause current to flow through the relay coil, the voltage at the output of the driver to be near 0, and the relay contacts to close. If the voltage at the driver output is V_{cc}, the relay coil may be open or the output of the driver circuit may be open in which case the driver is faulty and should be replaced. However, before replacing the coil or the driver, check the diode. It must work properly to prevent damage to the driver. If the driver is operating properly, but the relay contacts are not closed, then there is probably a fault in the relay coil or its contacts, or the diode is shorted. After the defective part is replaced, again check the circuit for proper operation before reconnecting the driver input to the microcomputer output.

Sensor Circuit

Figure 7-6 illustrates a type of input circuit for sensing an analog signal. A non-electrical signal such as temperature is converted to an electrical voltage through the use of a sensor and a resistive voltage divider circuit. Since the current flow through the sensing circuit is controlled by the variable (temperature or other quantity) being sensed, the voltage into the + input of the operational amplifier is controlled by the variable. Thus, the output of the amplifier is some function of the sensed variable.

> A common sensor circuit uses an operational amplifier as a comparator to detect the level of an input analog voltage compared to a threshold level.

In *Figure 7-6*, the operational amplifier is actually used as a comparator. If the + voltage is more positive than the − voltage, the output of the device is a logic 1 level which is read by the microprocessor through one of its inputs. Similarly, if the + input is less positive than the − input voltage level, the output of the comparator will be a 0 voltage level. Thus, the circuit of *Figure 7-6* tells the microprocessor when the sensed variable is above or below a reference level. This is the simplest way to convert an analog signal to a digital signal.

Troubleshooting the Sensor Circuit

> The sensor circuit may be checked by measuring voltages, establishing certain input logic conditions, and checking for shorts with an ohmmeter.

The most likely faults that might occur in the circuit of *Figure 7-6* are a faulty sensor, a faulty amplifier, and an open or shorted resistor. These can be found by simple component isolation and testing techniques and by resistance measurements. The + and − voltages can be measured with the sensor in place. If either is 0 volts, there is a short to ground at the test point or an open between the test point and the V_{CC} supply. If either is at V_{CC} volts, there is a short in R1 or R2, or there is an open in the sensor or R3.

The comparator operation can be checked by placing a ground on the − terminal and some positive voltage on the + terminal, then verifying the output is a TTL 1 level. Similarly, placing a 0 on the + terminal with the positive reference voltage on the − terminal should produce a TTL 0 output.

**Figure 7-6.
Sensor Threshhold
Detector Circuit**

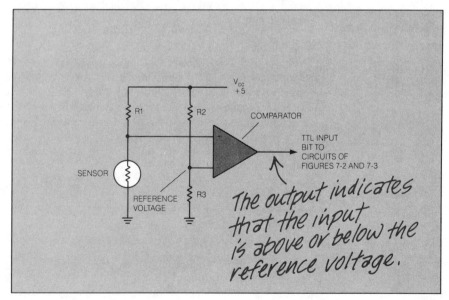

I/O TERMINALS

The basic input and output circuits considered in *Figures 7-1* through *7-6* are used for sensing input signals and controlling output actions within a computer system, but they are not the kind normally used for communication with a computer. The most common I/O device for computer communications is the computer terminal. It normally consists of a typewriter-type keyboard and a CRT (cathode ray tube) that presents a television-type screen display. (Some terminals have a keyboard and printer combination so all information is displayed on the printer.) Information in the form of characters and numbers (alphanumeric) is displayed on the CRT screen while commands and text information are entered into the computer through the keyboard. Usually the connection between the computer and the terminal is through a serial data connection using a standard arrangement of signal logic levels and timing known as an RS232 interface. The operation of a CRT terminal with an RS232 interface and keyboard will be discussed next.

Serial Data Communication

In serial data transfer, the binary signal is placed on a single line and the variation of the signal with time provides the transmission of the binary codes of a desired length. A commonly used serial data format for asynchronous data transmission is shown in *Figure 7-7*.

Serial data transfer has data bits framed by added start and stop bits, reproduced for each character in sequence.

The signal pattern begins with a change in the line voltage from a logic 1 level to a logic 0 level. The receiver detects this as the start bit transition. At a certain time later, the line voltage is checked again by the receiver to confirm that the voltage is still zero. If it is, the receiver has detected a valid start bit generated by the transmitter. From this point on, both the transmitter and receiver must agree that once every n seconds there will be a stable data bit of either a 0 or 1 where n is the reciprocal of the transmission rate in bits per second. In the example of *Figure 7-7*, the bit rate is 300 bits per second (usually called 300 baud) so that n is 3.333 milliseconds (1/300).

The least significant bit (LSB) of the code is sent first and the most significant bit (MSB) is sent last so that the 8-bit code being transmitted in the example of *Figure 7-7* is 0000 1011 binary or 0BH. (Remember that the LSB is normally written as the rightmost bit.) The 8-bit code must be followed by one or more n intervals with the line held at the logic 1 level. Each of these n intervals is called a stop bit. In the example of *Figure 7-7*, the line is held high for at least one n interval, thus, one stop bit is used. Therefore, the 8-bit data code requires 10 bits for each character when the start and stop bits are included. Baud rate differs from bit rate in many cases because start and stop bits are included in baud rate.

Figure 7-7.
Asynchronous Serial
Data Transmission

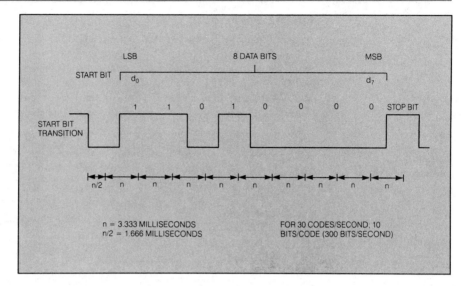

Parity

A parity bit is added at transmission to detect errors. For even parity its value is a 1, when necessary, to make the 1's present in the word even. For odd parity the total would be odd.

It also is common to use a parity bit as a simple error checking method. Parity means that information is added to the code to help detect if the transmitted code has been received correctly. In this case, another bit is added to the code. This is called single-bit parity. Either even or odd parity may be used as long as the transmitter and receiver agree. For even parity, the added parity bit is made a 0 or 1 so that an even number of ones is present in the code. As each character code is made ready to transmit, special circuits in the transmitter add the parity bit so there is always an even number of 1's in the character code that is transmitted. For odd parity, the added parity bit is made a 0 or 1 by the special circuits so that an odd number of ones is present in the transmitted character code. If the received parity does not agree, the receiver knows that there is probably an error in the data.

For reliable serial communication, the transmitter and receiver must use the same format (data bits per word, parity condition, number of stop bits, and baud rate), and the character and control code must also be identical.

To establish reliable communications using the serial data format of *Figure 7-7*, both the transmitter and receiver must use the same number of data bits, the same parity condition (even, odd, or none), the same number of stop bits, and the same baud rate. The data usually is transmitted in the form of typewriter character and control codes using the American Standard Code for Information Interchange (ASCII). This 7-bit binary code is summarized in table form in *Figure 7-8* with bit 7 as the most significant. If eight bits are transmitted, bit 8 is always zero (unless it is used for some other purpose), thus the code for the capital letter A is 01000001 or 41H. Similarly, the code for the carriage return (CR) control key is 00001101 or 0DH. The reader should look up these codes in the table of *Figure 7-8* as an exercise.

Other formats and codes are used in data communications; however, the basic concepts are the same as those discussed above. In addition to standards for codes, there must be standards for signal levels and time relationships of the signals. A commonly used standard, called a protocol, is the EIA RS232 standard.

EIA RS232 Standard

The Electronics Industries Association (EIA) established the RS232 standard for use between units of a computer system. Most importantly, the standard defines a logic 0 as voltages more negative than -3 (but not more negative than -15 volts) and a logic 1 as a voltage more positive than $+3$ volts (but not more positive than $+15$ volts). It also limits the resistance that may be placed on a line and specifies the connector pin for each signal.

Figure 7-8.
American Standard Code
for Information
Interchange (ASCII)

BIT POSITIONS:												
6 →					0	0	0	0	1	1	1	1
5 →					0	0	1	1	0	0	1	1
4 →					0	1	0	1	0	1	0	1
3	2	1	0									
0	0	0	0	NUL	DLE	SP	0	@	P		p
0	0	0	1	SOH	DC1	!	1	A	Q	a	q
0	0	1	1	STX	DC2	"	2	B	R	b	r
0	0	1	1	ETX	DC3	#	3	C	S	c	s
0	1	0	0	EOT	DC4	$	4	D	T	d	t
0	1	0	1	ENQ	NAK	%	5	E	U	e	u
0	1	1	0	ACK	SYN	&	6	F	V	f	v
0	1	1	1	BEL	ETB	'	7	G	W	g	w
1	0	0	0	BS	CAN	(	8	H	X	h	x
1	0	0	1	HT	EM	)	9	I	Y	i	y
1	0	1	0	LF	SUB	*	:	J	Z	j	z
1	0	1	1	VT	ESC	+	;	K	[	k	{
1	1	0	0	FF	FS	,	<	L	\	l	|
1	1	0	1	CR	GS	–	=	M	]	m	}
1	1	1	0	SO	RS	.	>	N	^	n	~
1	1	1	1	S1	US	/	?	O	—	o	DEL

Example Circuit

Commonly available interface circuits, known as RS232 line drivers and line receivers, are used to convert the digital signals of the computer equipment to the RS232 signal conditions. The basic interconnection between a computer terminal and a computer board using the RS232 interface circuits is shown in *Figure 7-9*. This figure also shows the circuit interface from a microprocessor to the serial data line using a special purpose controller called an asynchronous communications controller (ACC).

Transmit

Commonly, data is transmitted from one digital system to another in an RS232 format by using an asynchronous communications controller.

The ACC accepts data from the microprocessor a byte at a time in parallel form, or a bit at a time in serial form until it has a byte available for transmission. In the example of *Figure 7-9*, the data is transferred from the microprocessor to the ACC a bit at a time since this processor uses a bit-mapped I/O subsystem (recall *Figures 7-1 and 7-2*). Once the byte is inside the ACC ready to be sent, the ACC generates the signal sequence of the type shown in *Figure 7-7* on the line XOUT. This is sent through an RS232 line driver to the data terminal through pin 3 on the RS232 interface.

Receive

At the receiver, after a byte of data is received and parity bit is checked as O.K., the data is sent to the microprocessor.

The data terminal sends an RS232 serial signal through pin 2 of the DB25 interface to the computer. The signal is converted to digital signal levels by the receiver (75189 in *Figure 7-9*), and the digital signal is sent to the RIN line of the ACC. The ACC receives this data one bit at a time in accordance with the format of *Figure 7-7* until it accumulates a byte of data as indicated by receipt of the stop bit. It also checks for errors in the start bit, stop bit(s) and parity bit (if any). Once a byte is received, the processor is notified through the interrupt line. At this time, the processor can send a signal to ask the ACC to determine if errors were found in the transmission. If not, it sends a signal to the ACC to tell the ACC to send the data to the processor.

In addition to the normal serial input (RIN) and output (XOUT) lines, there are other protocol signals such as RTS (request to send) and CTS (clear to send) which are not shown in *Figure 7-9*. One such signal which is shown in the ACC block in *Figure 7-9* is the $\overline{\text{DSR}}$ (Data Set Ready Not) signal which notifies the ACC that the data terminal is on-line and ready to exchange information.

While the circuitry represented by the blocks in *Figure 7-9* may be very complex internally, the connections between them are relatively simple. This simplifies troubleshooting as the following example will illustrate.

Figure 7-9.
Interface to a 743
Data Terminal with a
TMS9902 ACC

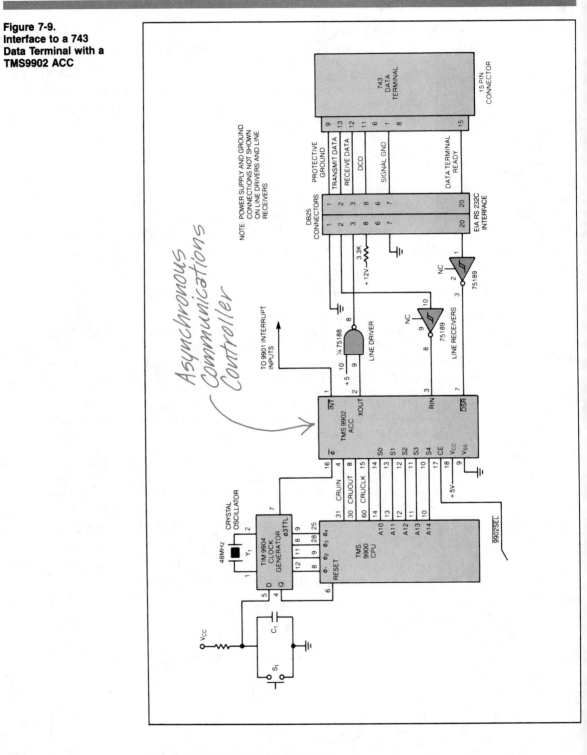

Basic Terminal Problems

The communications between a computer and a terminal can fail due to one of three general problems:

1. The terminal may be faulty in which case the troubleshooting efforts must be directed to the circuitry within the terminal. This can be a very complicated troubleshooting effort.
2. The computer circuits such as the ACC, the line drivers or receivers, or even the processor may be faulty, in which case the troubleshooting methods discussed for the circuits of *Figure 7-1* through *7-6* will have to be used.
3. The wiring between the terminal and the computer may be faulty. In this case, the simple resistance measurement techniques of Chapter 3 may be sufficient to locate and correct the problem.

As an example problem, the configuration of *Figure 7-10* will be considered. This actual case history will review the basic approaches for troubleshooting any problem, including those involving relatively complex digital equipment. Three offices were wired so that a terminal in each office could be connected to a single cable running to a central computer located some distance away. Whenever any office wanted to access the computer, the central cable plug was plugged into the receptacle for the cable going to that office. At the other end of each office cable was an RS232 DB25 connector mounted in a connector box in each office. A mating RS232 connector and cable made the connection from this connector box to the RS232 connector on the terminal. The terminal was a CRT display unit with a RS232 interface, and a separate keyboard unit which was connected to the display unit by a parallel data interface cable.

Possible wiring problems in terminals, in many cases, can be isolated by substituting terminals.

After the wiring and terminals had been installed, it was discovered that the terminal in office 3 would power-up, but would not communicate with the computer. The terminals in offices 1 and 2 worked properly and would transmit and receive data from the central computer when their lines were connected to the central line. The terminal in office 3 was moved into office 2 and connected and the terminal worked satisfactorily. Then the terminal from office 2 was tried in office 3 and it didn't work. Thus, the wiring from office 3 to the receptacle for the central line had to be faulty in some way.

An ohmmeter was used to check the continuity of each connection from the central plug to the end of the RS232 cable and to check for shorts between wires. The four wires involved in the connection (see *Figure 7-9*) were SIGNAL GND, TRANSMIT DATA, RECEIVE DATA, and DATA TERMINAL READY. However, all connections were continuous and no shorts were found.

**Figure 7-10.
Terminal
Troubleshooting
Example**

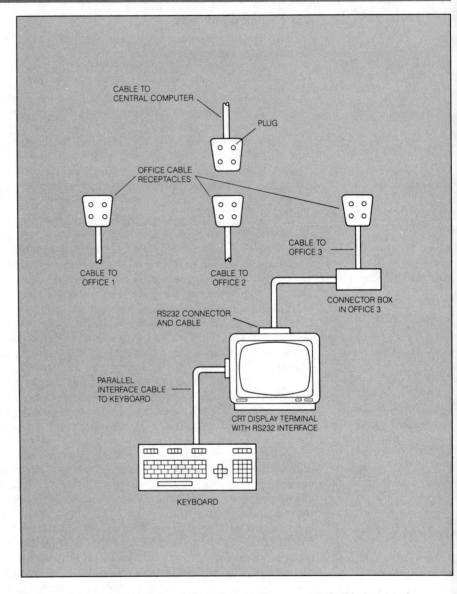

At this point, it seemed that all system components had been tested and were satisfactory; however, a terminal still would not communicate with the central computer from office 3. There seemed to be no other test that could be used to determine the fault, yet there had to be some reason why a terminal would not work in office 3. What would you do?

It was clear that the problem must be in the wiring and either the faulty connection had to be found or all the wiring to office 3 had to be replaced. The troubleshooter remembered that the continuity and short circuit were made with the dc voltage of the ohmmeter, but the data signal was a pulse signal of 1,200 bits per second. Since the pulse rate was high and the 0 to 1 and 1 to 0 transitions occurred at a high rate, it was reasoned that a high resistance connection might cause the problem.

In an attempt to locate the faulty connection, the ohmmeter checks on the wiring were made again, but this time the actual resistance readings were noted. All connections except one had a resistance in the 1 to 2 ohm range; that one exception had 25 ohms. It was in the line from the TRANSMIT DATA OUT driver output to the connection box terminal. While a direct current resistance of 25 ohms should make no difference in the system under test, the resistance could be much higher at high frequencies. After all the connections in the high resistance line were resoldered, the resistance of this line was in the 1 to 2 ohm range; therefore, a change had been effected. The terminal was connected and it worked properly.

Thus, a poor solder joint was preventing a $600 piece of equipment from working properly. The solder joint problem was detected because it had a slightly different resistance from the other connections in the cable. It might not have been found if the troubleshooter had not thought about possible causes of the problem and rechecked the wiring.

If the fault had been inside the terminal, then the most common action would be to take the terminal to a repair shop that had experienced technicians and the test equipment to properly repair it. However, some simple problems can be found even with limited equipment if the troubleshooter understands the operation of the video display and the terminal keyboard. Some terminals may use a printer as the only display device, or a printer may be used in conjunction with the video display. Printers have operational problems that are different from those encountered in a video display device. Some of the problems encountered in keyboards, video displays and printers will be considered in the remainder of this chapter.

In the example, a poorly soldered connection was preventing a very expensive piece of equipment from operating.

KEYBOARD OPERATION AND PROBLEMS

Keyboards are made up of switches and the switch is the component most likely to fail. *Figure 7-11* shows the basic switch construction and the schematic symbol. In its simplest and least expensive form, the switch consists of a fixed metallic contact on a printed circuit board and a movable metallic contact that provides a spring action to the key. The second contact could be printed on a plastic sheet (membrane keyboard) or could be a metallic spring built into a key. In either case, pressing a key completes the electric circuit between the fixed contact and the movable contact. The flow of current in the circuit causes an action in an interface circuit or is sensed by a scanning circuit.

**Figure 7-11.
Basic Keyboard Switch**

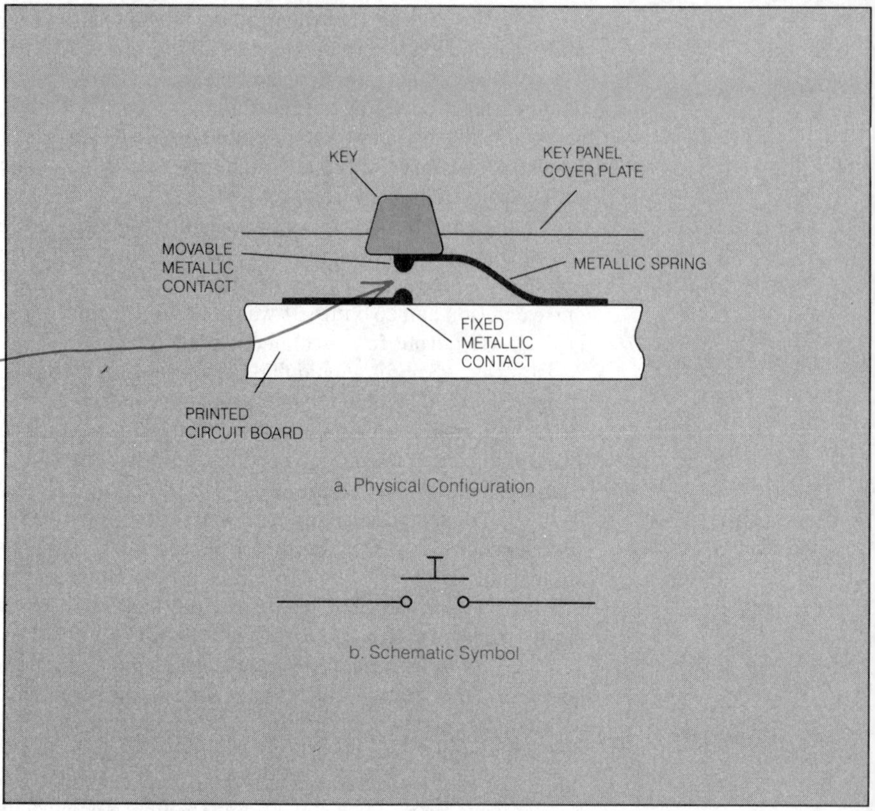

KEY

KEY PANEL
COVER PLATE

MOVABLE
METALLIC
CONTACT

METALLIC SPRING

FIXED
METALLIC
CONTACT

PRINTED
CIRCUIT BOARD

a. Physical Configuration

b. Schematic Symbol

Input indicated by closing contacts.

Keyboards are an array of fixed metallic contacts on a printed circuit board with spring-action. Common problems include misalignment, oxidation, and conductor breakage.

Common problems in a keyboard switch are misalignment of the conducting material, oxidation of the surface of the conductive material, or a break in one of the metallic pieces. A break or misalignment should be obvious upon visual inspection. It may be possible to repair the break with a jumper wire or the mechanical misalignment may be corrected by bending one of the contacts with needlenose pliers.

The oxidation problem may not be as obvious by visual inspection. As a metal is exposed to oxygen and moisture or other more corrosive chemical vapors, the metal at the surface is converted to a metallic oxide which is an insulator. Low voltage like that used in semiconductor circuits cannot cause current to flow through the oxide, thus, no connection can be made by the switch. If the contacts are easy to reach, the oxide can be removed with sandpaper, a file, or a sharp knife.

CAUTION: *Emery cloth should not be used to clean electrical contacts because the emery particles are conductive and could cause a short circuit.*

Of course, the most reliable repair, whatever the cause of failure, is to replace the switch. Unfortunately, single switches sometimes cannot be replaced because of the way the keyboard is made.

So far, the assumption has been that the system does not respond at all when a key is depressed; however, in some cases, a system response can be obtained by pressing very hard on the key. In such a case, the system may respond as if the key had been depressed rapidly several times instead of only once due to contact bounce caused by the excessive force. If this response is observed, the keyboard should be taken apart to expose the metallic contacts for examination and correction.

Misalignment Example

An actual case history of such a problem is a calculator whose keyboard operated intermittently. The calculator worked properly except it did not respond correctly to the number 8 key. Depressing this key usually would cause no response, but striking the key hard would cause several 8's to appear on the display. This was very frustrating when adding numbers because the no-8 or multiple-8 entries caused errors and required that the entire string of numbers be re-entered.

Improper alignment of the contacts can cause erratic operation.

The keyboard was taken apart by removing several screws and lifting the key buttons off of the metal spring switch matrix. There was no corrosion or breaks in the metal components of the switch matrix and there were no horizontal misalignments (in the plane of the printed circuit board). However, close examination revealed that the bottom contact of the number 8 switch was lower than the bottom contacts of other switches as shown in *Figure 7-12*. Only if the upper metal of the bad switch was forced all the way down to the printed circuit board could contact be made, and that was very unreliable due to the location of the contact buttons. Only a small depression of the upper contact was required for proper operation of the good switches. The remedy was clear; the bottom contact had to be brought up to the normal position. This was accomplished by using a fine needle probe to carefully bend the problem contact to the proper position. The keyboard was reassembled and the 8 key worked normally; it continued to work properly for the life of the calculator.

Corrosion Example

Contact oxidation requires that the keyboard operator depress the keys abnormally hard.

Another actual case history shows a problem that can be caused by contact corrosion. A typewriter-type keyboard had certain keys which had to be struck several times, often quite hard, to get a character display on the CRT screen. The key cover was removed and visual inspection revealed that the contacts had a tan to slightly bronze coloration. By scraping the contact surface with a sharp knife and buffing the surface with a small piece of sandpaper, the metallic shine was restored. The keyboard worked normally after reassembly. Every several weeks, the contacts had to be cleaned in this manner to keep this particular keyboard operating satisfactorily. It was a relatively inexpensive one that did not have non-corrosive contact points. More expensive keyboards prevent this problem by using gold-plated contact points.

**Figure 7-12.
Calculator Keyboard
Troubleshooting
Example**

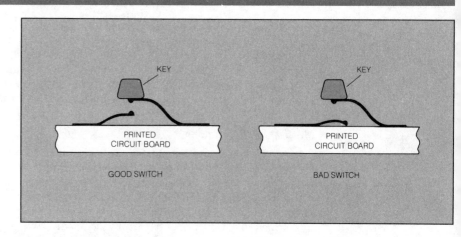

Electrical connectors such as printed circuit board connectors or cable connectors that don't have plated contacts also can have intermittent connections or high resistance connections. These connector problems can be analyzed and repaired in much the same way as the keyboard contacts. For most cleaning operations, a commercial solvent is available and should be used for contacts, cable connectors and printed circuit board edge connectors.

Circuit Example

Faulty key switch contacts are not the only problem that can cause keyboard failure. The connections between the key switch matrix and the encoding circuitry can be faulty or the encoding circuit itself can be defective. One example of such a problem that was encountered by the author involved a peculiar symptom. Sometimes the keys on the left side of the keyboard would cause incorrect characters to be displayed on the CRT while the right side of the keyboard always worked properly. More than one key would cause this problem so there had to be some fault common to the left side keys. In an attempt to detect the fault pattern, a sampling of good and bad keys were depressed and the resulting CRT display and ASCII codes were tabulated as shown in *Figure 7-13*.

**Figure 7-13.
Computer Keyboard
Troubleshooting
Example**

Bad Key	ASCII (Hex)	Actual Display	ASCII (Hex)		Good Key	ASCII (Hex)
1	31	9	39		Z	5A
5	35	;	3B		H	48
T	54	\	5C		Y	59
G	47	O	4F		N	4E

Examination of the ASCII codes for the good keys indicated that they all share the common feature that the least significant hex digit of the code was 8 or more. For all the faulty keys, the least significant hex digit of the desired character was less than 8, but the system was interpreting the key closure as an ASCII value that was 8 more than the correct code. The only fault that could have caused this condition was for the binary digit D_3 (if D_0 is the least significant bit of the code) to be stuck at 1. The reader can verify this analysis by using the ASCII table in *Figure 7-8*. Thus, a small amount of detective work and reasoning reduced the area of the fault to a specific line in the output of the encoder circuit.

In this particular keyboard, the encoding was performed by a read-only memory. Its inputs were the row and column code for the depressed key and its output the appropriate ASCII code. The circuit is shown in *Figure 7-14*. A scanning circuit places a 0 on successive rows of an 8 row by 8 column key switch matrix until a switch is closed. At that time, a 0 occurs on the row line and on the column line containing the closed switch. All of the other row and column lines have a 1 on them. The 8 row and 8 column lines go to separate 8-to-3 priority encoders whose 3-bit output is a code that represents the row and column lines of the closed switch. Thus, the 6-bit code into the PROM is a 6-bit address. The byte stored in the PROM at that address is the ASCII code for the depressed key.

Since it was suspected that output D_3 of the PROM was stuck at 1, it was necessary to verify this and to determine what was causing this condition. The proper operation of the encoder and scanning circuits was verified by holding a key down and observing the voltage patterns on the inputs and outputs of the encoders. This was done for several different keys to exercise several rows and columns of the switch matrix.

As shown in the example of *Figure 7-14*, a key in the second row and third column was held down. Measurements confirmed a 0 on row 2 and column 3 of the matrix. Measurements also confirmed the correct 3-bit binary codes out of the encoder into the PROM. Thus, the scanning circuit and encoders were working properly. However, measurements at the PROM output indicated that line D_3 was stuck at 1. Thus, either the output circuit on line D_3 of the PROM was faulty or the wiring for D_3 was shorted to the $+5$ volt power supply.

The fact that the observed problem during operation was intermittent would make one think that the fault was in the D_3 wiring or connections, not the PROM. However, isolating the PROM output pin for D_3 from the D_3 wiring caused the 1 to be removed from the line, but the voltage on the PROM output pin for D_3 was still stuck at 1 which indicated the PROM was bad. Replacement of the PROM restored normal operation of the keyboard.

**Figure 7-14.
Example Keyboard
Interface Circuit**

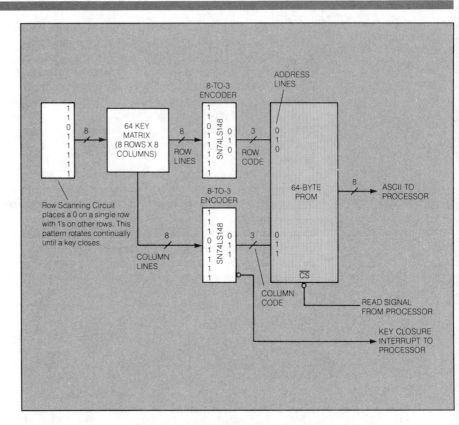

The examples covered in this section are taken from true case histories and represent the most common problems that occur in keyboards. Usually it is reasonable to suspect bad contacts or wiring faults since these are much more likely to occur than component failures. However, as the last example indicated, components do fail and complete testing must be done to detect such failures. Fortunately, replacement of faulty components is a simple procedure that can quickly restore normal operation to the system.

CRT OPERATION AND PROBLEMS

The CRT display unit of a terminal is a complex piece of equipment that normally should be repaired by professionals. Some of the circuits have critical adjustments and the high voltage on the CRT presents a danger to both people and test equipment. However, some troubleshooting and repair can be accomplished by a non-professional. Caution must be used to prevent striking or scratching the glass envelope.

Basically, the CRT display unit is like a monochrome television set without the circuits that select channels and demodulate the carrier. The CRT display unit has circuits that generate characters in response to the ASCII code from a keyboard. The character generation circuits also generate characters when an ASCII code is received from another source, such as a computer.

Much of the basic functional analysis that was introduced in Chapter 3 would apply to the analysis of a CRT terminal display. The basic components of such a display, including the interface to a keyboard and RS232 serial data link, are shown in *Figure 7-15*. The horizontal and vertical oscillators and amplifiers generate the beam deflection waveforms that move the electron beam to trace horizontal line after horizontal line across the CRT screen. The video amplifier controls the intensity of the electron beam in the CRT, but unlike the gray scale variations from black to white that occur in a television receiver, the beam is either on or off. Since the beam is always off except when a particular character is displayed, the CRT screen is dark if nothing is displayed rather than totally white as it is in many TV receivers.

The on or off state of the beam depends on the patterns of 0's and 1's shifted out of the video shift register. This register is loaded for each row of each character from the ROM containing the dot display patterns for the character. The entire display is controlled by the video timer controller (VTC) and the contents of the display (video) RAM. The display RAM contains an ASCII code for each position on the screen. If it is the space character, that position is dark; otherwise, the character whose code is in the RAM is displayed.

A video timer controller controls a video display by providing addresses to a RAM and ROM for character and timing data, and blanking and sync pulses for the CRT.

The VTC keeps track of which row of which character position is being displayed. It provides this location information to the RAM through the location code and to the character ROM through the character row code. The RAM in turn provides the character ROM with the ASCII code for the next character to be displayed. The VTC also determines when the display is in a horizontal retrace or vertical retrace operation and provides the appropriate blanking and synchronization pulses to the vertical and horizontal oscillators.

The microprocessor obtains characters from the keyboard and sends them to the computer through the RS232 interface. Characters from the computer to the microprocessor return on the RS232 lines and update the contents of the display RAM at what's called the cursor position. The VTC continues displaying old information while new information is obtained from the keyboard or the external computer. However, when the screen is full, old information scrolls (moves) off the screen as new information is added.

The high voltage supply provides the CRT anode voltage. If it fails, the screen will be dark and no characters can be displayed. If the vertical oscillator fails, the screen will display a single white horizontal line (or a narrow band of lines). If the horizontal oscillator fails, the screen will be totally dark or possibly display a vertical bar of compressed raster information. If the entire screen can be uniformly illuminated by turning up the brightness, but contains no character information, there is a fault in the VTC, processor, keyboard, RAM, ROM, or dot register. If data cannot be entered onto the screen via the keyboard, there is a fault in the processor-to-RAM interface or in the keyboard-to-processor interface. If wrong characters are displayed when a key is depressed, there is a fault in the keyboard circuitry (as discussed earlier) or the character ROM circuitry is faulty.

**Figure 7-15.
Functional Block
Diagram of a
CRT Display**

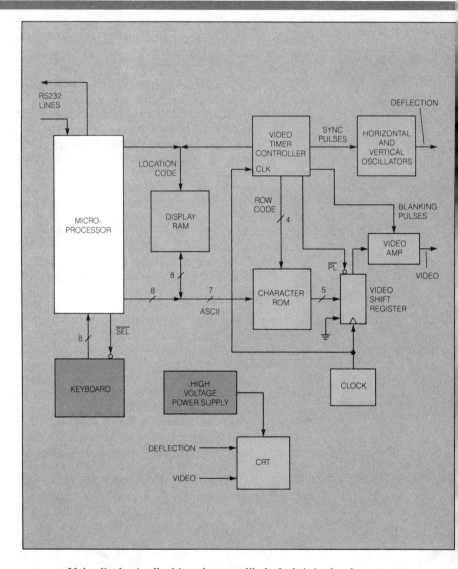

If no characters appear at
all on the screen but the
screen is white, a common
problem could be the
ROM.

If the display is all white, the most likely fault is in the character ROM to register connection or in the register to video amplifier circuitry. It is unlikely (but possible) that the RAM contains an ASCII code for an all white rectangle in every RAM location. Further, it would seem likely that the VTC is operating properly. If the ROM is disabled it would float its lines (having no voltage level applied) or force them to all 1's. This would produce all white in the character display areas, but the columns and lines between character positions would be black. Thus, the display would have a certain number of rows and columns of white rectangles. If the output of the video shift register were stuck at 1, or if the video amplifier output is shorted to the + supply, then all dots would be on and the entire screen would be white.

Which of these three conditions is present can be identified by the nature of the display (all white or white rectangles at all character positions) and by controlling the input to the video amplifier circuitry. If the display consists of all white rectangles where characters would normally be displayed, the ROM is continually disabled (possibly an open in the ground connection to $\overline{CS}$) or the register does not latch information properly (possibly an open in the connection to the parallel load terminal $\overline{PL}$).

If the display is totally white, then the output of the shift register should be disconnected from the input to the video amplifier. When ground is applied to the input of the video amplifier, the screen should go totally black; if it doesn't, there is a fault in the video amplifier. (The entire video amplifier may be in one module that can be replaced to repair this fault.) If the display does go black when the input to the video amplifier is grounded, the output line of the shift register is stuck at 1. This output line should be examined to determine if it is shorted to the + supply. If it isn't, the register itself should be examined for a fault. A similar sequence of troubleshooting and analysis could be used if the screen is all black, but also remember the previously mentioned conditions that can cause the screen to be totally black.

PRINTER OPERATION AND PROBLEMS

By controlling the voltage level of certain lines, the printer can communicate to the computer its status, permitting the computer to know when it may send data.

A printer can be a very simple system or a very complex system depending upon its features and its control electronics. A diagram of a simple and inexpensive printer is shown in *Figure 7-16*. The control electronics consists of a single chip microcomputer (TMS9940) and the interface circuits required to drive the electromechanical and thermal elements of the printer mechanism, and to receive sensor inputs. Most of the operational features of the system are stored in the microcomputer program contained inside the TMS9940. Communications between the printer and the computer or terminal consist of an 8-bit parallel bus for data codes, a signal indicating data is present ($\overline{DS}$ in *Figure 7-16*) and a signal from the printer that indicates when the printer is ready for the next character to be sent ($\overline{BUSY}$ in *Figure 7-16*).

The control signals $\overline{BUSY}$ and $\overline{DS}$ are active low signals and typically their transitions are related. The data is placed on the 8 data lines by the computer and $\overline{DS}$ is pulsed low for a minimum period of time. Within a specified period of time, the printer controller will pull $\overline{BUSY}$ low to indicate to the computer that the printer is ready to accept the character. The computer must maintain the data on the 8 input lines until $\overline{BUSY}$ goes back high. By this time, the character has been accepted and stored within a buffer within the printer to prepare for printing. Then, the computer may place new data on the lines and initiate another transfer with a $\overline{DS}$ pulse.

**Figure 7-16.
Block Diagram of a
Simple Printer**

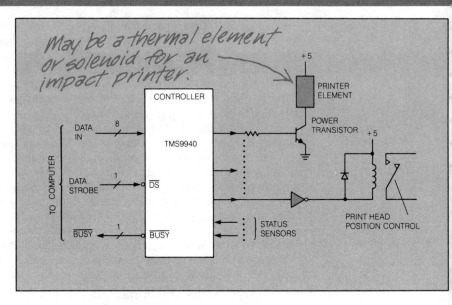

**Figure 7-16.
Block Diagram of a
Simple Printer**

The TMS9940 controller in the example of *Figure 7-16* also generates
TTL signals to control the printer element through current driver gates or
transistors. The printer element may be solenoids for an impact printer or
heaters for a thermal printer. The controller also controls the paper movement
and printer head position mechanisms through relay drivers or SCR circuits. It
receives status signals from sensors such as OUT-OF-PAPER and PRINTER
NOT READY. The program memory of the 9940 contains the dot pattern to be
used in the printing of each character as well as the memory for the position of
each character in a line. It keeps track of buffer status, times for each
operation (such as carriage return or line feed) and makes sure these times are
maintained at correct values.

Troubleshooting the Printer

Some printers have a self-test feature that checks the basic printer
operation; if this test is successful, the problem probably is in the interface
circuit or the computer.

If a self-test is not available, the operation of the printer can be
checked manually. Eight switches can be connected to the eight printer data
lines. These switches can be set to produce any ASCII code. Then $\overline{DS}$ can be
generated by depressing a push button switch that causes an external
monostable multivibrator to generate the proper pulse. If the printer prints
the character set by the eight switches, then the problem is with the computer,
the wiring or the software.

Once it is known whether the problem lies in the computer or the
printer, then the techniques discussed previously can be used to isolate the
fault. If the fault is in the computer, then analyzing circuits of the types shown
in *Figure 7-1* through *7-6* would be required. If the fault is in the printer, then it
would be necessary to reason through the operation of the printer as described
next.

Printers have either built-
in diagnostics or manual
checks. If a fault occurs
and the printer's inter-
nally-generated test
characters do print out,
the problem is probably in
the computer.

Printer Faults

Most printer faults can be isolated quickly. For example, if the print head stays in one position, there must be a stuck-at-0 or stuck-at-1 condition in the control circuit, or the relay or print head advance motor is faulty. If the line feed fails to occur on a carriage return so that all characters are overprinted on just one line, there would be a similar condition on the control circuit driving the paper advance solenoid or motor, or a faulty solenoid or motor.

Each element can be individually tested using component isolation techniques. For example, the input to the driver can be isolated and a 1 applied to its input to energize the relay. If the relay doesn't operate, the output of the driver can be isolated and ground applied directly to the relay coil. If the relay still doesn't energize, there must be a faulty relay coil. If the relay does energize, then the driver is probably stuck at 1 in its output circuit. If the relay coil and driver are working and the relay contacts close (which can be determined with a continuity check), there must be a fault in the solenoid or motor circuit. This could be checked by shorting across the relay contacts to see if the correct action occurs. If not, there is a problem in the wiring or in the motor or solenoid itself.

In a dot matrix printer, each character is formed by a particular arrangement of dots. Each dot in the vertical direction is controlled individually. If the solenoid or the solenoid control circuit is faulty for a particular dot, this dot won't print in any character. The result will be a printed line that has a thin white line through it. The only situation that can cause this is for the circuit between the 9940 and the printing element for that dot to be inoperative. One of the driver transistors, the print element, or the 9940 output could be faulty. These can be checked individually by using isolation techniques described previously. Thus, by reasoning through the operation, it is generally possible to pinpoint a portion of the circuit of *Figure 7-16* that is likely to be at fault. Then it is possible to proceed with some simple tests and experiments to determine precisely what the problem is.

Troubleshooting the printer involves determining whether the problem is in the mechanics or electronics. If the mechanics check out, the problem is likely in the drive and control circuits.

WHAT HAVE WE LEARNED?

1. The troubleshooting of input and output circuits is not significantly different from troubleshooting other digital subsystems once the operation of I/O circuits is understood.
2. This is also true of the I/O peripheral devices such as CRT terminals and printers.
3. Generally the basic techniques of visual inspection, continuity checks, voltage checks, checks for short circuits, and component substitution will find the cause of a problem.
4. For some problems, the particular signal shape and timing are critical so these signal characteristics must be checked. This requires different test techniques and equipment which will be discussed in following chapters.

Quiz for Chapter 7

1. In a bit-mapped I/O system each:
   a. bit occupies its own memory location address.
   b. byte is assigned a memory address.
   c. bit is assigned an I/O address.
   d. byte is assigned an I/O address.

2. In a memory-mapped I/O system each:
   a. bit occupies its own memory location address.
   b. byte is assigned a memory address.
   c. bit is assigned an I/O address.
   d. byte is assigned an I/O address.

3. In an I/O mapped system each:
   a. bit occupies its own memory location address.
   b. byte is assigned a memory address.
   c. bit is assigned an I/O address.
   d. byte is assigned an I/O address.

4. In the example of *Figure 7-1*, the fourth flip-flop corresponds to bit address:
   a. F0H
   b. 7F3H
   c. 7F4H
   d. 7F8H
   e. 7FBH
   f. 7FCH

5. In the example of *Figure 7-1*, the data will be latched into the selected flip-flop when the:
   a. data is available from the processor.
   b. address lines are at the appropriate code.
   c. CRUCLK makes a low-to-high transition.
   d. CRUCLK makes a high-to-low transition.

6. In the example of *Figure 7-3*, the register occupies the addresses:
   a. memory address 1007H.
   b. register address 1007H.
   c. bit addresses 1007H through 100FH.

7. In the circuit of *Figure 7-5*, the purpose of the diode is to:
   a. increase the switching time of the relay.
   b. decrease the switching time of the relay.
   c. protect the relay coil from a voltage of improper polarity.
   d. protect the gate from a high voltage.

8. If bit D_4 of an ASCII encoded keyboard is stuck at a 0, what would be transmitted when the H key is depressed:
   a. H
   b. X
   c. 8
   d. @

9. If bit D_4 of an ASCII encoded keyboard is stuck at a 1, what would be transmitted when the H key is depressed?
   a. H
   b. X
   c. 8
   d. @

10. If in *Figure 7-5* the relay contacts do not close when the output bit is at a 0:
   a. the current driver circuit is faulty.
   b. the relay coil is open.
   c. the diode is shorted.
   d. all of the above are equally likely.
   e. the circuit is working normally.

Basic Timing Problems

ABOUT THIS CHAPTER

Most of the problems that have been examined up to this point have been due to shorts or opens in the wiring of a digital system or in one of its components. Such faults can be determined with simple voltage and resistance measurements or by using signal-tracing techniques. There is another very important operating characteristic which must be considered. It is classified as timing. That is, a circuit does not operate, a signal does not pass through a gate, nor does data get stored unless it is triggered by a signal to tell it when to operate — a timing signal. This chapter will consider such timing and control functions. To determine timing faults, the details of the signals and their effects on the operation of the system must be known. The timing and control signals of synchronous systems will be examined first.

TIMING IN DIGITAL SYSTEMS

Pulse timing and pulse shape are both important in digital transmission and processing.

The timing signals in a digital system must have certain characteristics if the system is to operate properly. Generally, these characteristics concern the time at which the signals occur in relation to other signals in the system. However, the shape of the signal as a function of time must also be considered. In synchronous systems, all timing signals are derived from a central timing generator — the system clock.

Single-Phase Clocks

Some digital systems use a single-phase clock signal from which all of its other timing signals are derived. Other digital systems use a multi-phase clock where two or more inter-related clock signals are used to determine the master timing of the system. The voltage versus time of a single-phase clock is plotted in *Figure 8-1*.

The clock output waveform should have a low to high transition (rise time) and a high to low transition (fall time) as nearly square as possible vertically.

Recall from Chapter 1 that the time for the signal to make the transition from the low to the high level is called the rise time of the signal. Similarly, the time it takes for the signal to make the transition from the high to the low level is called the fall time. As shown in *Figure 8-1*, these times are measured from the 10% (of the amplitude) point on the waveform to the 90% point on the waveform or vice versa. These times are listed in the specifications for each digital component. In typical operation, factors such as the length of the wiring coupling signals together, or the number of like circuits that an output must drive affect the rise and fall times of any given component.

The clock frequency
generated by a crystal-
controlled oscillation (so
the frequency is stable),
must not be too low or the
DRAMs lose their data.

Another important time for the clock signal is its frequency or period. Recall that the period T is the time between like points on the waveform as shown in *Figure 8-1*. It is equal to 1/f; therefore, frequency is the reciprocal of the period (f = 1/T). The period of the clock waveform is determined by the clock generator circuit and is often controlled very precisely by a crystal oscillator. The crystal oscillator vibrates at a high frequency and generates the pulses which the clock generator uses to create the system clock. Timing signals must occur within a certain period of time, otherwise circuits in the system will not operate properly. The period must not be too long, otherwise components such as dynamic storage circuits (recall the refresh requirement of dynamic RAMs from Chapter 6) will lose their information. On the other hand, the period must not be too short, otherwise circuits in the system with slow response do not have time to respond to the clock signal. Digital integrated circuits such as flip-flops, registers, and counters all have a minimum and maximum operating frequency which, in turn, determine the acceptable clock pulse-width.

**Figure 8-1.
Single-Phase Clock**

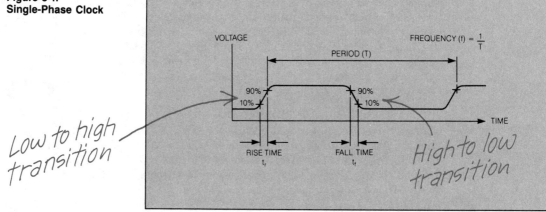
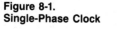

Multi-phase Clocks

Microcomputer digital systems usually require a two
or four phase clock signal.
The periods must be iden-
tical, but the phases are
different by a fixed and
stable amount.

Some digital systems, particularly microprocessors and microcomputers, require a two- or four-phase clock signal. Example waveforms for a two-phase clock are shown in *Figure 8-2*. The main characteristics of such waveforms is that they have the same period or frequency, but the phase 1 voltage is not at the 1 level at the same time as the phase 2 voltage. Each has a certain rise and fall time as well as a fixed delay between one waveform and the other. Some microprocessors or microcomputers require a four-phase clock, which would have waveforms similar to those shown in *Figure 8-3*.

In some microprocessor or microcomputer integrated circuits, clock signals are generated internally. In other cases, an external clock generator sold by the microprocessor manufacturer provide the clock signals. Multi-phase clock generators, whether internal or external to a microprocessor, usually are crystal controlled so the clock generator will be stable and the timing signals occur with little variation.

Figure 8-2.
Two-Phase Clock

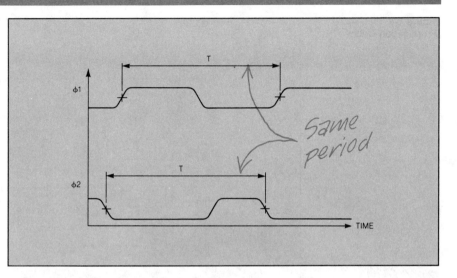

Figure 8-3.
Four-Phase Clock
(Source: W. D. Simpson,
Gerald Luecke, D. L. Cannon
and D. H. Clemens, 9900
Family System Design, Texas
Instruments Incorporated,
Copyright © 1978)

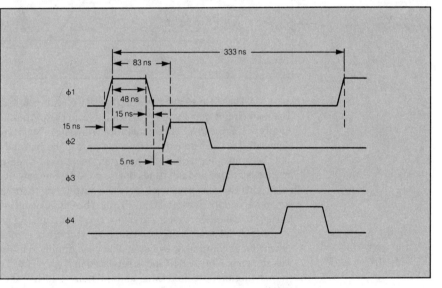

Timing Signals

When a logic pulse passes through a gate or buffer, it is delayed in time (the propagation delay) and rise and fall times usually are modified, especially by increased loading.

The timing signals in a synchronous (clocked) digital system may be simply a copy of the clock waveform or one of the clock pulses sent through a logic gate. The effect of sending a signal through a digital gate or buffer driver is shown in *Figure 8-4*. The input waveform, which could be a clock signal, is shown in time relation to the waveform at the output of the buffer. Notice that the propagation delay causes a difference in the time that the two 1 levels occur. (Recall that propagation delay was explained in Chapter 1.) Also the rise and fall times of the output waveform may be different from those of the input waveform.

Figure 8-4.
Propagation Delay

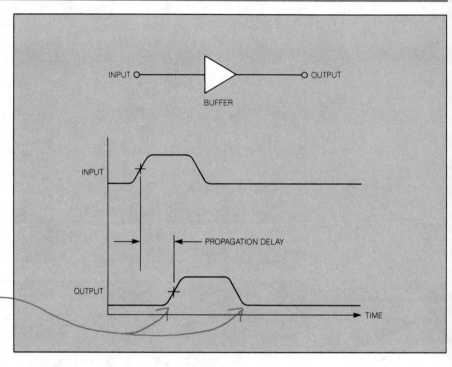

Rise and fall
times
may be
different
than input.

Propagation delays may
cause an upset in overall
timing relationships be-
tween signals at various
circuit points, resulting in
a loss of data integrity.

These times are measured with a circuit coupled to a particular load.
The load circuit may include resistance from the output line to the positive
supply voltage and a load capacitance from the output line to ground.
Generally, as the load capacitance increases, the rise and fall times increase
and the propagation delay of the circuit increases. Excessive propagation delay
or excessive rise and fall times due to a faulty component or unusual load
conditions (large capacitance from the output line to ground) can delay the
signal beyond its expected time. Thus, the signal could arrive at its destination
too late to cause the system to take a correct action.

A delayed signal may cause the storage of erroneous data into a
synchronous flip-flop or register. The basic timing required by such devices
was shown in *Figure 1-10* and is repeated in *Figure 8-5*. The principal times are
the set-up time, the hold time, and the pulse-width of the clock. In the example
in *Figure 8-5*, the triggering or latching edge of the clock is the low- to high-
transition. The set-up time is the time the input data must have stabilized at its
0 or 1 level before the triggering edge of the clock. The hold time is the time the
data must remain stable after the triggering edge of the clock to ensure
accurate storage of the input data. Many circuits have a minimum clock pulse-
width that is necessary for proper operation. As shown in *Figure 8-5*, this is
the time from the 1.5 volt point on one side of the clock pulse to the 1.5 volt
point on the other side of the pulse. (Some manufacturers may specify the time
from the 90% voltage point on the leading edge to the 90% voltage point on the
falling edge to determine the pulse-width, though most data books seem to be
using the 50% voltage point at this time.)

Figure 8-5.
Timing Requirements for
Synchronous Storage
Device

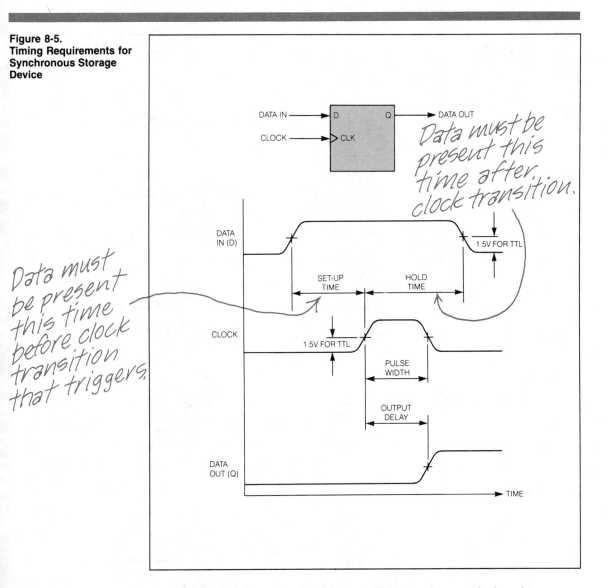

Data must be present this time after clock transition.

Data must be present this time before clock transition that triggers.

Clock delay may result in an inadequate hold time or set-up time for data being stored in a flip-flop.

Generally, once the clock generator is adjusted to provide the pulse-width and rise and fall times required by a given logic family, the pulse-width requirements are not a problem. However, it is possible that the delay of a clock pulse through gating or buffer driver logic may cause the clock pulse to arrive late enough that the hold time requirements for reliable data storage is no longer met. In this case, reliable operation of the device is no longer assured. The result of this delayed clock pulse is illustrated by the dashed line clock pulse in *Figure 8-6.* The output data line tries to hold at the 1 level but fails to do so.

**Figure 8-6.
Effect of Delayed Clock
Pulse on Output Data
Signal**

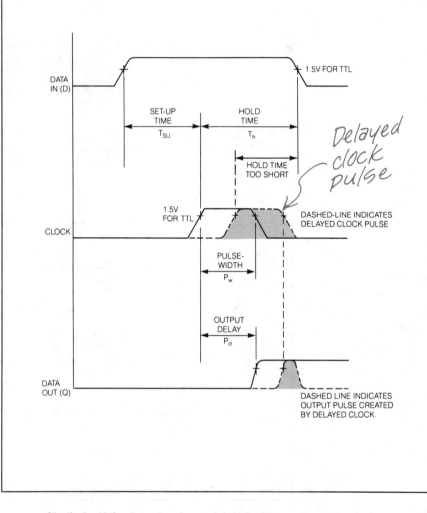

Similarly, if the data signals are delayed with respect to the clock pulse, the set-up time requirements may no longer be met, again causing unreliable storage of the data. This effect is illustrated by the dashed line signal in *Figure 8-7*. The cross-hatched area in the DATA OUT signal indicates that the starting edge of DATA OUT could occur anywhere in that area, if the pulse transitions at all. These problems are often difficult to detect and their effect difficult to observe. Special measurement techniques are often required to observe the effects.

**Figure 8-7.
Effect of Delayed Data
Input Signal**

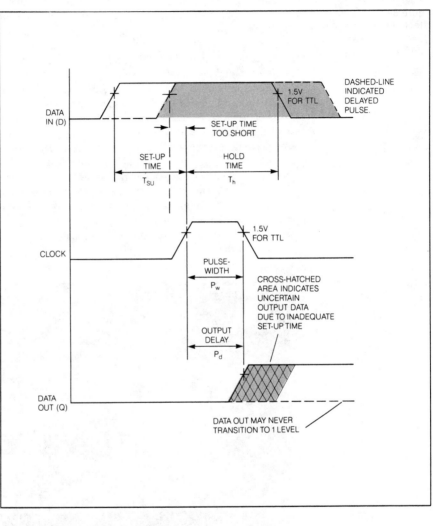

MEASUREMENT TECHNIQUES

The oscilloscope is widely used to display and measure digital system signals.

To determine timing related problems, one must first be able to define the shape of the clock pulse and its relationship to other signals in the system. These clock pulses are very fast and occur for only a brief instant of time. Typical clock frequencies for microcomputers are in the range of 1 to 10 megahertz with time periods in the range of 1,000 to 100 nanoseconds. Rise, fall, set-up, hold and propagation delay times are all in the 10 to 20 nanosecond range. Thus, an instrument is needed that will display signal voltage variations versus time over these very short periods. As mentioned in Chapter 1, one instrument capable of performing such measurements is the oscilloscope. The basic operation of the oscilloscope is discussed in Appendix A.

A multi-channel os-
cilloscope is required to
compare the time rela-
tionships between two or
more signals.

A single-channel oscilloscope can display only one signal at a time.
This is satisfactory for measuring the shape, time characteristics and voltage
levels of a clock signal or a single pulse, but it would not be sufficient for
measuring the time relationship between two or more signals. With such a
single-channel instrument, it would not be possible to examine the set-up, hold,
or propagation delay times of two signals. To perform these measurements, the
oscilloscope must be capable of displaying two signals at the same time. This
type of oscilloscope, called a dual-channel oscilloscope, provides two separate
signal inputs and two separate vertical calibration controls. Also available are
four-channel scopes that are needed to display signals of the type shown in
Figure 8-3. Using a multi-channel instrument, the critical time relationships
between signals can be examined to see if they are at the correct time to cause
correct system operation. A typical multi-channel oscilloscope is shown in
Figure 8-8. The sample waveforms displayed on the screen are typical of those
the troubleshooter might see when using an oscilloscope to isolate a fault. With
this type of instrument, the timing relationships that may be causing faults in
system operation can be detected.

Figure 8-8.
Multi-Channel
Oscilloscope
(Courtesy of Tektronix, Inc.)

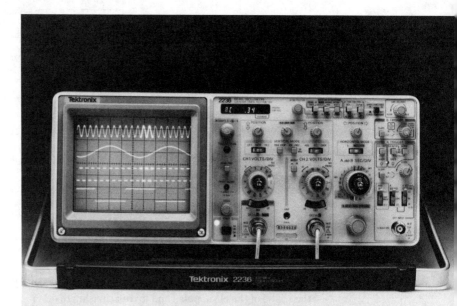

TIMING PROBLEMS IN SEQUENTIAL SYSTEMS

Improper timing relationships in a system are often difficult to find without detailed signal measurements using the oscilloscope. Generally, timing problems are not as severe in a synchronous system as they are in a non-synchronous (asynchronous) system, unless the synchronous system is operating very near the high frequency limits of its components. However, it is possible for timing faults to occur in systems of low frequency if components designed for high frequency operation are used.

The effects of timing problems in a sequential system can be illustrated through the vending machine example in Chapter 5. The basic circuit diagram for the controller is in *Figure 5-6* and the associated input and output circuits are shown in *Figures 5-3* through *5-5* and *5-7*. The important starting point for analysis of possible effects of timing problems is the sequence control program or flow chart. The program for this example is given in *Figure 5-8*. Basically, in a clocked (synchronous) system, timing problems in the state flip-flops or in the clock signal would be the most likely cause of system faults. The system is protected from transitions that may occur between clock edges (leading edges in the case of *Figure 5-6*), since the state flip-flops, and thus their outputs, change only with the arrival of a clock leading edge. Only if the input to a flip-flop is changing at the same time that the clock edge occurred would there be any problems. Noise spikes that might erroneously indicate a coin entry, item selection, or a momentarily unexpected output would be a problem, but these are not normally considered timing problems. Further, if the clock frequency is low enough, the output signals will be present long enough to cause the desired operation. In the vending machine, the VEND, DUMP and CHANGE signals must exist long enough to satisfy the requirements of the relatively slow-operating electro-mechanical components they are driving.

Faulty Clock Generator

One simple problem that might cause unacceptable system operation would be a faulty clock generator. For example, in the clock circuit shown in *Figure 5-10a*, if an open occurs in the capacitor that determines the timing for the generator, the circuit would oscillate at its maximum frequency instead of at 100 hertz as desired. This fault could be easily detected on an oscilloscope because the CRT would display the excessively high clock frequency. The observed system operation that might lead one to suspect a faulty clock generator could be similar to the operation caused by other faults that were discussed in Chapter 5. Therefore, just from a limited amount of information it is difficult to definitely say the clock is causing a particular problem. More investigation is needed.

Timing problems in asynchronous systems may be more difficult to isolate than synchronous systems unless the synchronous systems are operating near their frequency limit.

One effect the very high frequency clock signal could have in the system in *Figure 5-6* is that the state flip-flops and other components in the circuit may not be able to respond to such a signal. If the pulse-width of the faulty clock signal is too short for proper operation of the flip-flops, they would never respond to their inputs and the machine would never change from state 0.

Even if the flip-flops were able to make the transition from one state to another, the transitions would happen so fast that the entire sequence would occur in less than 100 nanoseconds. The vending machine output devices could not possibly respond in such a short period of time, thus, there would be no change delivered, no coins dumped, no items vended.

In either case, the vending machine would act as though it were turned off; however, this would also be the case when it is stuck in state 0 or 1. Therefore, interconnection wiring and clock faults would have to be considered.

Once it is determined that the clock circuit is the cause of the machine's actions (or lack of action), the problem could be located easily. For example, if the clock is outputting a square wave signal, but at a very high frequency, one could verify the open capacitor problem. This could be done by temporarily inserting a 5 microfarad capacitor in parallel with the existing one. The oscilloscope would show the clock frequency in the 100 hertz range if an open original clock capacitor is the fault.

Incorrect Transition From State 1 to State 2

Even if the clock circuit is operating properly in the vending machine example, improper operation still can occur due to circuit timing. A problem can occur, for example, when the next-state code differs from the present-state code in more than one bit position such as the transition from state 1 (001) to state 2 (010). In this case, as shown in *Figure 5-6*, both the Q_0 and the Q_1 outputs of flip-flops FF3 and FF2, respectively, must change in response to the leading edge of the clock. If Q_0 changes faster than Q_1, there would be a momentary state of 000 between the state 1 and state 2 conditions. This is shown in *Figure 8-9* along with its effect on the system signals.

For some reason, Q_0 of flip-flop FF3 starts changing from a 1 to a 0 before Q_1 of FF2 starts changing from a 0 to a 1. This may be due to a fault in FF2 that causes it to slow down, or it may be due to a fault in the input or output circuitry of FF2. In any case, the flip-flop outputs are at 000 for a brief time, shown as about 20 ns in *Figure 8-9*. This would cause an output on the $\overline{CLR}$ line which, for that time, might be long enough to clear the coin total register (*Figure 5-5*). Thus, when the machine does get to the 010 state, the total value is zero. It's as if no coin signal had ever been present. A problem of this type could not occur in going from state 2 to 3 or from state 3 to 1 since, in these transitions, only one flip-flop is changing so it doesn't matter how long it takes.

If a fault occurs and the clock operates at a high frequency, both appear as if the machine were stuck in state 0 or 1.

Particular timing problems can occur when two flip-flops are changing at the same time.

**Figure 8-9.
Synchronous System
Timing Problem**

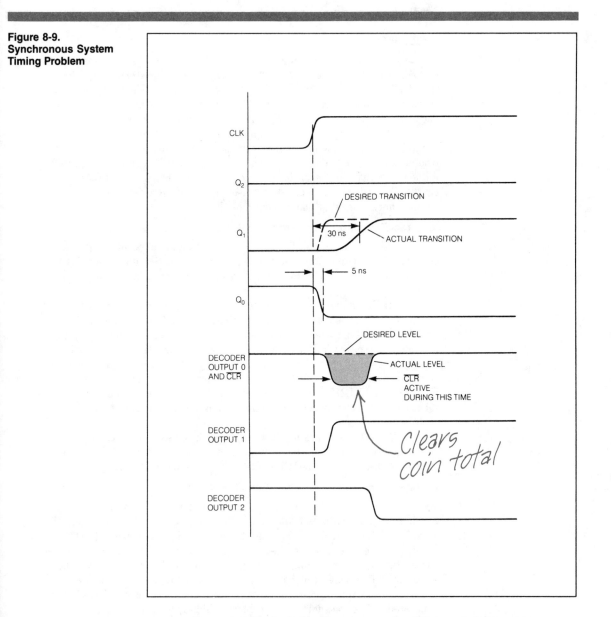

However, when both flip-flops change, the difference in timing must
not be too large, otherwise, misoperation will occur. In this case, the coin total
register is cleared. The damage has been done. In *Figure 5-6*, when signal S is
true, the contents of the total register is 0 so that the total is less than the item
value and all coins would be dumped.

Open Line

The observed machine operation is the same as when there is an open in the line labeled C so that states 2 and 3 are never entered. However, the troubleshooter can determine which of these two faults is causing the improper operation by looking at the outputs of the three state flip-flops and the $\overline{\text{CLR}}$ line at the same time on a four-channel oscilloscope. Observation of the incorrect momentary 0 on the $\overline{\text{CLR}}$ line and the delay in the transition of FF2 would indicate a timing problem rather than an open circuit problem. Next the troubleshooter would have to determine whether the slow action of the flip-flop is due to a faulty flip-flop or due to excessive loading of its input or output circuit. Excessive loading could be caused by a leakage resistance to ground or a capacitance to ground that shouldn't be there.

Incorrect Transition From State 1 to State 4

Another example of a timing problem that might occur during state transition is the transition from state 1 to state 4 when S is at a 1 level. In this case, state flip-flops FF3 and FF1 in *Figure 5-6* both are changing at the same time.

If FF3 is significantly faster than FF1, the machine could go through a momentary state 0 condition before it reaches state 4. The momentary state 0 would have the same effect on the coin total and item flip-flops as a reset; thus, it would clear these flip-flops and cause signal S to transition to state 0. Then the machine would act as if neither coin entry nor item selection had occurred. Item value would equal coin total; therefore, no coins would be returned. Further, when VEND is generated, with all item selection flip-flops cleared, no release signal would be generated and no item would be delivered to the customer.

If FF1 is significantly faster than FF3, the state will change briefly to state 5 before it finally reaches state 4. Although this signal probably would be present for too short a time, CHANGE could be generated.

Other Possible Incorrect State Transitions

The state 4 to state 5 transition does not have a potential timing problem since only FF3 in *Figure 5-6* is changing from a 0 to a 1. However, the state 5-to-6, the state 6-to-0, and the state 5-to-0 transitions may cause timing problems since, in each case, two state flip-flops are changing at the same time. In the state 5-to-6 transition, Q_0 and Q_1 of FF3 and FF2 are changing at the same time. If FF3 is faster than FF2, then a momentary state 4 will occur before state 6. Probably this would not cause a problem since the VEND signal generated will be too short to cause another item to be delivered. If FF2 changes before FF3, a momentary state 7 would occur before state 6. Since there is no activity assigned to state 7, this would not be a problem.

In going from state 6-to-0, either a momentary state 4 or a momentary state 2 could occur. Again, any short pulse output on the VEND line in state 4 would cause no action and a momentary state 2 would have no important effect.

In the state 5-to-0 transition, there could be a momentary state 4 or momentary state 1. Neither of these would have any significant effect on the operation of the machine. Thus, the only critical timing problems in the vending machine would be the state 1 to state 2 transition and the state 1 to state 4 transition. In both cases, a short pulse could occur on the $\overline{CLR}$ line which would cause a system fault. Either of these conditions could be checked quickly with a four-channel oscilloscope.

Design Considerations

Many timing problems could be avoided by involving only one flip-flop in a state transition, or by using a second set of flip-flops as a generator for all system control and output signals.

All of these timing problems could have been avoided altogether had the machine been designed more carefully. By making all transitions from one state to another involve a change by only one flip-flop, none of these timing problems could occur. Another set of state flip-flops would also eliminate problems. By using this second set of flip-flops to generate all system control and output signals, momentary state changes occurring in FF1, FF2, and FF3 would never have any effect on the machine's operation. However, it is possible that even the best synchronous sequential machine may still have some potential timing related problems. This is also true of microcomputer-based sequential systems. Let's look at some of these.

TIMING PROBLEMS IN COMPUTERS

In computer systems, the timing relationships are all based on the clock. All of the events must occur within a certain time relationship.

A computer is a sequential digital system, but its structure tends to isolate timing problems to a particular subsystem. It is also a synchronous system so that all timing signals are in some known relationship to the system clock or clocks. Of course, these relationships must be maintained if the system is to work properly. Another characteristic of computers is the large number of binary signals that occur at the same time (in parallel). To properly observe the timing relationship between these signals, multi-channel oscilloscopes are a necessity and special purpose instruments called logic analyzers may be needed to completely analyze the operation of a computer system. The operation and application of logic analyzers will be covered in the next chapter.

Input/Output Timing Problems

The simplest input and output devices that are used in a computer system are registers and flip-flops. Circuits will generate a reliable data output when the correct input and timing signals are provided by the processor. The timing relationships described in *Figure 8-5* apply to these types of input and output devices.

In a microcomputer, the data for an output operation is present for only a brief time with respect to a clock signal. Similarly, the data for an input operation must be available for the processor at a specified time.

Figures 7-1 and *7-2* are examples of simple input and output circuits. These bit-mapped input and output circuits are representative of many synchronously latched circuits.

The basic timing of the output circuit is shown in *Figure 8-10*. The data is output on the CRUOUT line at the same time the address signals are output by the processor. These outputs are shown in *Figure 8-10* as a 1 level. A little later in the cycle, the CRUCLK signal is sent out by the processor. Usually, the data is latched on the trailing edge of this clock pulse. The data and addresses have been present for about 500 nanoseconds by the time this trailing edge occurs. This time is much greater than the approximately 20 ns normal set-up time requirement for registers and flip-flops. The data and addresses remain on the output devices for about 160 nanoseconds after the clock trailing edge occurs. This, too, is far more than the typical 5 nanoseconds hold time required for registers and flip-flops.

Delayed Signals

Delays in signals are particularly bothersome. If the signal is an address, a wrong bit will be transferred. If the signal is data, a wrong level is transferred.

Even with these relatively generous time allowances, there still could be timing problems. An example problem is shown in *Figure 8-11*. For some reason, either the data signal or one or more of the address signals is delayed by 500 nanoseconds or more. Due to this delay, the signal has not reached the 1 level by the time the trailing edge of CRUCLK occurs. If the delayed signal is an address bit, an incorrect address will be on the lines; therefore, the wrong bit will be transferred. If the delayed signal is an output bit, a zero will be output instead of a one. This, of course, will produce incorrect results. For example, an external device that should be turned on by a 1 bit will not be turned on. If the delayed signal is an input bit, the processor would take its next action on the basis of incorrect information.

Figure 8-10.
9900 Family Bit-Mapped
Output Timing

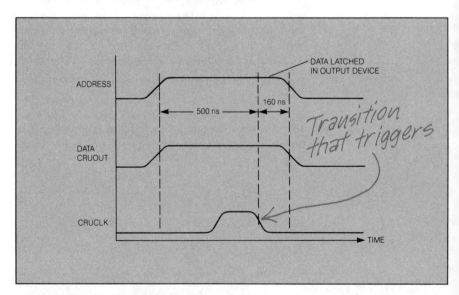

**Figure 8-11.
Fault in Address or Data
Line of Bit-Mapped
I/O Transfer**

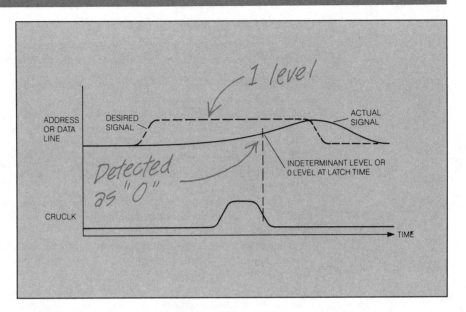

A multi-channel oscilloscope helps locate timing problems. It would show the excessively delayed rise time of the data or address signal.

This problem can be found by placing the data, address and CRUCLK signals on a multi-channel oscilloscope and observing the excessively long build up (rise time) of one of the address or data signals. If it is possible to insert a test instruction in the processor, a LOOP sequence could be written which would keep the selected I/O bit turning on and off continually.

Once this LOOP sequence were operating, it would continually address a selected I/O bit so that the address and data signals could be examined.

If the wrong I/O bit is selected, then there is a problem with an address line. For example, suppose the base address for the output operation is 080H, but the output at address 000H is selected while the output at address 080H is never transferred to the output lines. This means that the bit that was supposed to be a 1 in the address code (the eighth address bit) is remaining at a 0. Thus, the desired address code of 0000 1000 0000 is always occurring as 0000 0000 0000. With this information, the suspected address line is easily found with the oscilloscope.

If a signal actually is occurring on the correct output, the address lines and CRUCLK are operating properly. However, there must be a problem with the data signal and its timing should be measured in relation to CRUCLK and the address lines. Close observation and careful measurement may reveal that, although a signal is output, it is actually the complement of what it should be. This means that the output would be a 0 when it should be a 1 and vice versa. This would point to a problem with the data line which can be examined to find the physical problem in the circuit. Of course, if the output is stuck at a 0 or a 1, the problem is related to timing only if the CRUCLK signal has been delayed or has deteriorated in some way. If the CRUCLK signal is normal, then the stuck-at-0 or 1 condition is caused by a faulty circuit or wire as discussed in previous chapters.

Memory Timing Problems

Whether or not a memory device can respond fast enough to meet the timing requirements of a processor depends upon its timing features.

Write Timing

The characteristics of the memory control signals for a typical 9900 family processor write operation is shown in *Figure 8-12*. The sequence of operation is as follows: The data and address are sent to the memory subsystem at the beginning of a memory cycle and the write control signal $\overline{\text{WE}}$ is sent a short time later. The data and address signals are present for a total of about 667 nanoseconds while $\overline{\text{WE}}$ is at its active low level for about 333 nanoseconds.

For the memory write to occur successfully, the memory decoder must have selected the addressed memory location. The address and data must be available for a minimum time, $t_{c(wr)}$, called the write cycle. Once the memory location is addressed, the data must be present long enough for it to be stored in memory after $\overline{\text{WE}}$ transitions low. More importantly, address and data must be available during the time, t_w, when the write enable signal $\overline{\text{WE}}$ is present. In these memory integrated circuits, the data is not latched into the memory device on the leading edge of the write enable, but is gated into an asynchronous storage device such as an R-S flip-flop or, in the case of a dynamic memory, a capacitor. The write operation will not be successful if:

1. The write enable and address signals are not present long enough while the data is present.
2. The write enable pulse is delayed so much that the address and data signals are removed before the write enable occurs.
3. The address signal is delayed so much that the desired location cannot be selected by the device in the time period.
4. The data signal is delayed so much that the data is not present long enough.

Read Timing

The memory read timing is simpler because the address and the memory read control signal (DBIN) are sent at, or near, the same time. They will arrive at the memory at the beginning of a read cycle and both are present for the full 667 nanoseconds. In order for the processor to receive the data, the memory must hold the data on the data bus to provide sufficient set-up (t_{su}) and hold (t_h) times. This will allow the processor to store the data in an internal register until it is ready to use it. If the processor requirements of 40 nanoseconds set-up time and 10 nanoseconds hold time are not met, a data error will occur.

A successful memory operation depends upon the proper time relationship of the application of address signals, the write or read enable, and the data.

A successful read operation depends upon the memory being able to keep the data on the bus long enough for it to enter the appropriate storage register in the processor.

Figure 8-12.
Basic Memory Timing in
a 9900 Family
Microprocessor

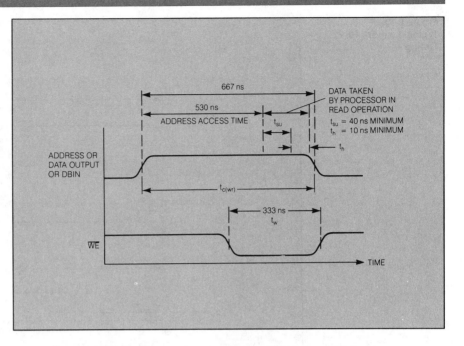

The timing of the signal for a read operation for a typical memory subsystem is shown in *Figure 8-13*. The minimum total read cycle time, $t_{c(rd)}$, is specified for each type of memory integrated circuit as well as its access times. The notation $t_{a(ad)}$ is the time it takes the memory to output data on the data bus after it has been addressed by the processor. Similarly, the access time $t_{a(cs)}$, is the time from the arrival of chip select ($\overline{CS}$) or output enable ($\overline{OE}$), until the data is put on the line. The data must be on the data bus a certain amount of time before the processor will latch it into its data register. This is the setup time identified as $t_{(su)}$ in *Figure 8-13*. Similarly, the data must remain stable on the data bus a minimum time after the processor generates a data latch signal. This holding time, identified as t_h, allows time for the data register flip-flops to store the data.

Causes of Timing Delays

Some timing problems are specific to performing a read or write operation.

In a reliable design, maximum address access time of a processor should exceed the memory access time to provide a design margin for component deterioration.

Let's refer to *Figure 8-12*. The maximum address access time ($t_{a(ad)}$) that could be considered for use with the processor would be 530 nanoseconds. If a memory device is selected whose address access time is 500 nanoseconds, there would be a 30 nanosecond safety margin for component aging. If a fault occurs in one of the address or chip select lines that exceeds this built-in safety margin, the memory read operation will not yield reliable data or instruction transfers to the processor. The problem can be detected only by very careful measurements of the address and data waveforms at the pins of a memory circuit. Such measurements would verify that the access times specified in the data sheet for the circuit are being met.

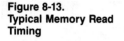

**Figure 8-13.
Typical Memory Read
Timing**

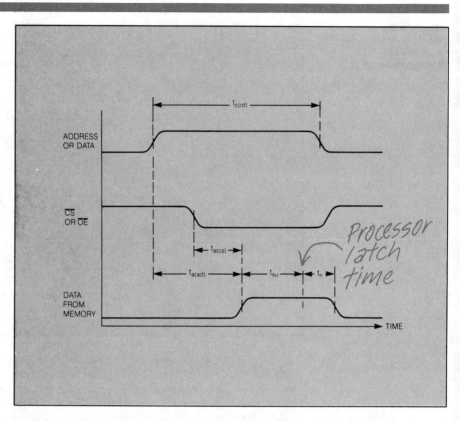

In some systems, a relatively slow memory may have been coupled with a fast processor so that the write enable active time is only marginally sufficient for the memory device. Then, as the components deteriorate with age and delay times increase, errors may occur during write operations.

Some memory and timing problems are the same whether the operation is a read or write.

Some timing problems are the same whether a memory subsystem read or a write operation is being performed. The basic reasons for timing problems are summarized in *Figure 8-14*, and the components that can cause the problems are shown in *Figure 8-14a*. The circuits are simplified by representing them with general equivalent circuits. The current source, I_D, represents the circuit that forces the signal voltage (V_C) to a 0 or 1. The output of the current source circuit is a 0 or 1 logic level. It could be a circuit inside the memory, if the operation is a memory read, or it could be a circuit inside the processor if the operation is a memory write. The resistor and capacitor, drawn in the dashed-line box, represent the load circuit receiving the signal. This load circuit can cause changes in the shape of the output signal.

The output circuit must charge or discharge the capacitor (C) while maintaining the current flow through the resistor. The current (I_C) available for charging or discharging the capacitor is the output circuit current, I_D, minus the resistor current, I_L ($I_C = I_D - I_L$). This I_C causes the voltage, V_C, to rise to a 1 or fall to a 0 level at a rate proportional to the value of I_C, and inversely proportional to the value of the capacitance.

At any given time, even for a constant I_D, the value of I_C may vary. This is because the value of I_L is proportional to V_C. This means that if V_C changes, I_L changes. In a typical circuit receiving the output signal, the resistor is very large so that I_L stays at a very small value. In this case, I_C is maintained at or very near the value of I_D. Depending upon the nature of the output circuit, I_D may vary, and, as a result, I_C would vary with it. Even with a varying I_D, the capacitor voltage will charge to a 1 level or discharge to a 0 level relatively quickly. The result would be the solid-line waveform of *Figure 8-14b* (large R, small C). The rise, fall, and delay times are very short and would cause no problems in a properly designed circuit.

When the value of capacitance increases significantly due to a problem in layout or wiring, it takes a much longer time for V_C to reach its desired 0 or 1 level. The result would be the dotted-line waveform shown in *Figure 8-14b* (large R, large C). The rise, fall, and delay times are now large which may cause errors in the read or the write operations, or both. It will depend upon whether the large capacitance occurs on an address, data, or control line.

Usually, the capacitance on a line does not change significantly with time, so the above problem does not occur in properly designed systems. If, after a system is designed, it ends up with very little safety margin in the memory access, read, and write times; then even relatively small changes in line or component capacitances could cause a problem. The fault could be detected easily by examining the data, address, and control line waveforms and measuring the access and other timing relationships.

Distributed capacitances from component positioning, lead positioning, or length may affect rise and fall time and cause pulse delays.

Figure 8-14.
Effect of Faults in Circuits Connected to a Bus Driver

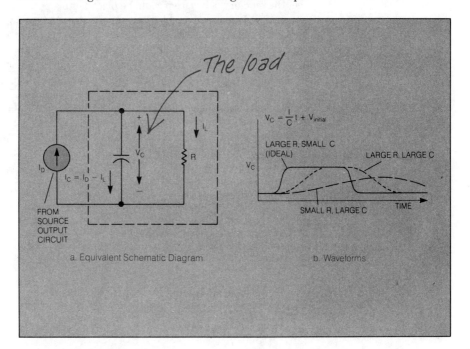

The load

$$V_C = \frac{1}{C}t + V_{initial}$$

LARGE R, SMALL C (IDEAL)

LARGE R, LARGE C

V_C

$I_C = I_D - I_L$

I_D

I_L

V_C

R

FROM SOURCE OUTPUT CIRCUIT

SMALL R, LARGE C

TIME

a. Equivalent Schematic Diagram

b. Waveforms

In a circuit where the load is represented by a resistor in parallel with a capacitor, a low resistance path in parallel with the capacitor would reduce the rise time of the voltage across the load significantly.

The most severe and most common problem is that a low resistance path develops across the capacitance. A low resistive path could develop due to changes in the input circuit receiving the signal, or it could be due to a conductive particle across circuit conductors. Such a conductive particle (not the same as a short) would provide a current leakage path around the resistor. In either case, the amount of current available for charging the capacitor is significantly reduced. This greatly increases the time required to charge the capacitor voltage to a 1 level. In fact, it may not even reach the 1 level before I_D changes and starts discharging the capacitor to a 0 level. This effect is shown by the dashed-line waveform in *Figure 8-14b* (small R, large C).

Effect of Timing Delays

Let's look at what happens if such a waveform (small R, large C) appears on the address, data, or control line. If such a signal appears on an address line, data will be read from or written into the wrong location in the system because the address code would not be recognized properly. If such a signal appears on one of the data lines, the proper location would be accessed, but it would not be possible to reliably write a 1 into that location for that bit position.

If the problem occurred on a control line enabling read or write, it would not be possible to either read or write (depending upon the control line affected) into the devices in the system. Even if the signal does reach a logic 1 at some time, it would not reach the level in time to provide proper read or write operations. For example, if the problem occurred on the write enable line, the memory subsystem could be placed into a permanent write condition. If it occurred on a read enable line, it could place the memory subsystem into a permanent read condition.

By monitoring a known repetitive read or write operation, the oscilloscope would show if a line is slow in changing levels.

The waveforms could be observed easily on an oscilloscope by monitoring the address, data, and control lines during a known repetitive read or write operation. If, during the course of such a measurement, one of the signals shows a very slow variation from the 0-to-1 level or back, that line would be suspect. If, at times, a data or address line indicated a 1 when it should be a 0 or vice versa, but at other times indicated the correct value, an intermittent fault would be indicated. Intermittent faults are harder to find. The troubleshooter must use every clue he has to determine if the cause of the intermittent is either a short or an open. With good usage of the oscilloscope and careful examination of all connections and components in the suspected area, the fault can be located.

Troubleshooting Timing Delays

One technique to find the cause of timing delay problems, is to isolate all loads from the line showing the fault and observe the line's signal. If the incorrect condition is still observed, the fault is in the device generating the signal or in the wire that provides the connection of the signal to the other components.

Pulse signal injection techniques will help to determine whether the waveform deterioration is caused by a component or by interconnections to the component.

One possibility is to isolate the line carrying the output signal and drive the line with a square wave from a signal generator and observe the waveform. A signal generator is used to create a known signal whose frequency, pulse-width and period are programmable by the user. If the waveform still has fast rise and fall times, then the device providing the output signal must be bad. If the waveform shows relatively long rise and fall times, there is a low resistance to ground on the line or an unexpectedly large value of capacitance to ground on the line. Once the symptoms of the fault are known, a visual examination may be the fastest way to locate the cause of the fault. Another technique would be to isolate selected portions of the line and observe the waveform at different locations along the line.

If the device output signal is correct when all loads are removed from the line, one of the inputs might be defective. By reconnecting the inputs one at a time until the deterioration in the signal is observed again, the faulty circuit can be found.

This procedure would work regardless if the fault were on an address, data, or control line. If the source of the faulty signal is a memory read or I/O input, the output of the memory or I/O circuit would be isolated first. Actually, if the memory write works satisfactorily, the data line itself must be alright. Therefore, if the memory read or I/O input doesn't work correctly, the most likely cause of the problem would be either the output circuit of the memory, the subsystem generating the I/O read (such as a keyboard or cassette tape reader), or the input circuit of the processor.

WHAT HAVE WE LEARNED?

1. Many of the troubleshooting techniques used in isolating faults that relate to level problems in steady state or slowly changing signal lines also can be used to locate the faults in fast changing signal lines or faults that are related to the timing or shape of digital signals.
2. The oscilloscope must be used instead of simple voltmeters and logic probes to measure the voltage level characteristics of fast changing signals or to measure time characteristics.
3. The improper operation of a system or subsystem often can be traced to a signal arriving too late.
4. A signal can arrive late due to either: (a) insufficient drive current from the circuit generating the signal, (b) excessive line loading due to faulty lines or input circuits, or (c) devices that have excessive propagation delay in their output circuits.

Quiz for Chapter 8

1. The rise time of a signal is the time:
   a. to make a transition from a low level to a high level.
   b. to make a transition from a high level to a low level.
   c. for the output signal to start making a transition to a high level from the time an input signal causes the transition to occur.
   d. between midpoints of a square wave signal.

2. Rise and fall times are measured from:
   a. 50% points on a waveform.
   b. 0 voltage level time to 1 voltage level time.
   c. 10% to 90% points on the voltage transition.
   d. the input signal to the output signal.

3. The hold time for a D-type flip-flop is the time the:
   a. data will be held on the output after a clock signal.
   b. data must be held on the input after a clock edge.
   c. clock must be high.
   d. clock must be low.
   e. data must be stable prior to a clock edge.

4. The set-up time for a D-type flip-flop is the time that the:
   a. data will be held on the output after a clock signal.
   b. data must be held on the input after a clock edge.
   c. clock must be high.
   d. clock must be low.
   e. data must be stable prior to a clock edge.

5. The pulse-width of an active high clock pulse is the time the:
   a. data will be held on the output after a clock signal.
   b. data must be held on the input after a clock edge.
   c. clock must be high.
   d. clock must be low.
   e. data must be stable prior to a clock edge.

6. Clock periods are measured from:
   a. similar points on the clock waveform.
   b. from the low level to the high level.
   c. from the high level to the low level.
   d. from the time the clock pulse is at 50% of its low-to-high transission until it is at 50% of its high-to-low transition.

7. If a clock frequency is 1,000 hertz, what is its period in milliseconds?
   a. 0.001
   b. 1
   c. 1,000
   d. 10,000

8. An oscilloscope with the signal input grounded and the sweep internally triggered automatically, will display what on the face of the screen?
   a. a dot
   b. a vertical line
   c. a horizontal line
   d. a blank screen

9. If a memory device has an address access time of 500 ns, what would be the minimum memory cycle time in ns required for using the device with a processor that had a 100 ns set-up time and a 25 ns hold time?
   a. 500
   b. 600
   c. 625
   d. 750

10. If the line voltage rise time is 20 ns when a line capacitance of 150 pf is charged with a constant current I_D, what will be the approximate rise time in ns if the line capacitance is increased to 300 pf?
    a. 10
    b. 20
    c. 30
    d. 40

Advanced Techniques

ABOUT THIS CHAPTER

For most of the techniques covered to this point, time relationships have not been critical for system operations. As the system operating speed increases, time relationships between signals become more critical and advanced measurement techniques using multi-channel oscilloscopes or other high-speed multi-channel equipment must be used to identify that proper time relationships are being maintained. In addition, as the integrated circuits in systems become more complex, different techniques are required. As the number of memory storage locations increases, or the number and types of input and output functions increase, the troubleshooting techniques must become more sophisticated and, in many cases, totally automated. This chapter will consider some of the more advanced techniques that must be used in such complex digital systems.

LARGE SCALE MEMORY PROBLEMS

For testing large-scale memory, the power-up period does not allow for adequate time to perform a complete self-test sequence using only the more basic techniques.

As the size of a system memory increases above 64,000 locations, the range of practical troubleshooting techniques becomes more and more limited. One approach, as mentioned in Chapter 6, is to provide a system test program that automatically exercises the entire memory to determine the addresses where errors occur. Once an error has been located, it will print a message to guide the troubleshooting action. The problem with this method is the test time. If there are a million locations in the system memory and it takes several microseconds to exercise each location, the diagnostic software may take up to several minutes to complete the memory test. This could be unacceptable during a power-up or self-test sequence. Therefore, let's consider a method in which built-in hardware automatically tests each memory location each time the location is used during routine operation.

Self-Diagnostic Memory Structure

One technique that is used in large capacity memories is shown in *Figures 9-1* through *9-3*. The memory structure, shown in *Figure 9-1*, is a dynamic RAM using devices similar to those discussed in Chapter 6. Each device shown in *Figure 9-1* stores 65,536 single bits of information; that is, one bit per location. By using 16 such devices per row of the memory, 65,536 words of 16 bits each can be stored. (In Chapter 6, each row was designed to store one 8-bit byte; in *Figure 9-1* each row stores two 8-bit bytes or one 16-bit word.) Also in *Figure 9-1*, there are 16 rows of 16 devices which provide a total storage of 1,024,000 16-bit words using a total of 256 circuits.

This memory requires 20 bits for the complete address. The least significant 16 bits go to the memory circuit inputs A_0 through A_7 (multiplexed 8 bits at a time for a total of 16 bits) and the next four higher bits go to the four row select inputs of the 4-to-16 decoder.

The decoder is enabled with the appropriate combination of the remaining address lines (if any) and a memory enable ($\overline{\text{MEMEN}}$) signal from the processor. The signals that provide for a memory write ($\overline{\text{W}}$) and row and column strobes ($\overline{\text{RAS}}$ and $\overline{\text{CAS}}$, respectively) are sent to the corresponding inputs on each memory circuit. Finally, the read enable signal (DBIN or R/$\overline{\text{W}}$) is sent to the output enable of the error correction circuit and the write enable signal ($\overline{\text{WE}}$ or R/$\overline{\text{W}}$) is sent to the output enable of the parity generator.

It is these buffer circuits along with the additional circuits that provide the signals P_1 through P_6 that make the memory self-troubleshooting. The additional circuits are the parity generator circuit, the memory locations that store the parity signals P_1 through P_6 for each row of data storage, and the error correction circuit. These circuits provide automatic error detection, indication, and possible error correction. Although these circuits increase the cost of the memory by approximately 40%, they provide more reliable memory operation and decrease troubleshooting time and costs.

Parity Generation

Extra parity bits are added to each row in order to provide data for error detection and correction circuits, which tend to make the memory example self-testing.

To understand how the parity generators and error correction and detection circuits are designed and how they work, the information contained in *Figures 9-2* through *9-4* must be examined. The basic idea is that as information is written into the 16 left-most columns (D_0 - D_{15}) of a given row or bank of memory circuits, a parity code (P_1 - P_6) is written into the right-most 6 circuits of that same bank or row of circuits.

The parity code is entered into the parity bits (P_1 through P_6) to provide odd parity for selected data bits as shown in *Figure 9-2*. Since odd parity is generated, the bit placed in a particular parity bit storage location makes the number of data bits that are a 1 plus the parity bit be an odd number. Thus, parity bit P_1, which contains the parity of data bits D_0 through D_8, will be a one if the memory circuits storing D_0 through D_8 contain an even number of ones. For example, if the data in the location being accessed is:

$$\text{FOF3H} = 1111\ 0000\ \underline{1111\ 0011}$$

then the underlined bits, D_0 through D_8, contain six ones, an even number of ones. As a result, the parity generator circuit will store a one in bit P_1 to make seven ones, an odd number of ones. Parity bit P_2 checks data bits D_{15}, D_{13}, D_{11}, D_9, D_8, D_7, D_5, D_3, and D_1 which are the bits underlined as follows:

$$\underline{11}11\ \underline{0}0\underline{0}0\ \underline{11}1\underline{1}\ 0\underline{0}1\underline{1}$$

**Figure 9-1.
Large Capacity Dynamic
RAM Memory with
Automatic Error
Detection and Correction**

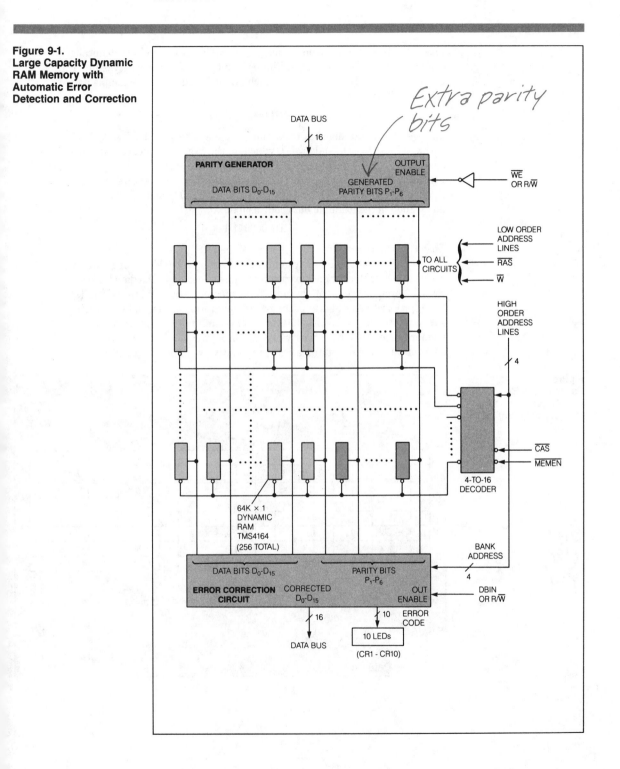

This set of bits contains 5 ones; thus a zero will be stored in P_2 to maintain the odd number of ones that exists. Similarly, bit P_3 checks the parity of bits D_{15}, D_{14}, D_{11}, D_{10}, D_7, D_6, D_3, and D_2, which are underlined in the example data word as follows:

<u>1111</u> 0000 <u>11</u>11 00<u>11</u>

This set of bits contains four ones; thus, a one will be stored in P_3. P_4 checks the parity of bits D_{15} - D_{12} and D_7 - D_4 which, in the example code, contain eight ones; thus, a one will be stored in P_4. P_5 checks the parity of bits D_{15} - D_8 and D_0 which, in the example, contains 5 ones so that a zero will be stored in P_5. Finally, P_6 checks bits D_{15}, D_{12}, D_{10}, D_9, D_7, D_4, D_2, D_1, and D_0. These bits are underlined in the example data code as follows:

<u>111</u>1 0<u>0</u>0<u>0</u> 1<u>0</u>1<u>1</u> 00<u>11</u>

They contain 6 ones; thus, P_6 will store a one.

Generally, the parity generator is simply a bank of 10 or 11 two-input exclusive-OR gates for each parity bit that is generated. The data lines are routed through three-state buffers to the memory array and to the inputs of the appropriate XOR gates of the parity generator. The output of the XOR gate circuits are routed through three-state buffers to the portion of the memory reserved for the parity bits (P_1 through P_6). Thus, the parity generation is handled automatically by relatively simple circuits.

Parity bit generation is accomplished by a series of XOR gates.

Figure 9-2.
Parity Check Bit
Generation Table for
Memory of Figure 9-1

Stream of parallel data bits.

D_{15} thru D_0

Data Bit																Check** Bit	
15	14	13	12	11	10	9	8	7	6	5	4	3	2	1	0		
							X	X	X	X	X	X*	X	X	X	P1	1
X		X		X	X	X		X		X		X*		X		P2	0
X	X		X	X			X	X			X*	X			P3	1
X	X	X	X				X	X	X	X					P4	1
X	X	X	X	X	X	X	X							X	P5	0
X		X		X	X		X			X		X	X	X	P6	1

*Bits P_1, P_2 and P_3 mismatched indicates data bit 3 in error.

**Each check bit is odd parity for those data bits marked with X in the corresponding row.

Error Detection and Correction

A single data bit error results in three to five parity bit errors. By checking the parity bits in error, the data bit in error can be isolated.

The error detection and correction is based on the fact that any given data bit in error will affect certain parity bits, but not necessarily all other parity bits. Notice in *Figure 9-2* that the pattern of parity bits affected by any given data bit error is unique for each data bit position. For example, data bit D_3 affects only parity bits P_1, P_2, and P_3. Thus, if D_3 is in error, parity bits P_1, P_2, and P_3 will be wrong and the other parity bits (P_4, P_5, and P_6) will be correct in a memory read and parity check. In the example data code used above, the full 22-bit code read from the memory for a correct data code would be:

$$1111\ 0000\ 1111\ 0011\ 10\ 1101$$

Now, if D_3 is in error due to a bad memory circuit in the addressed row or bank of memory circuits, the received code along with the generated parity code in the output bus would be:

$$1111\ 0000\ 1111\ \underline{1}011\ \underline{01}\ 0101$$

Note that the underlined bits are changed from what was stored. By comparing the parity pattern read from memory, 10 1101, with the parity pattern generated from the memory data code (01 0101), the error correction circuitry (bottom block of *Figure 9-1*) would know to correct bit D_3, changing its level before sending it to the processor data. Thus, the automatic error detection and correction returns data to the processor in its corrected form so that processing continues normally.

If two or more memory circuits in one row become faulty (two errors per data code), or if one of the parity circuits becomes faulty, automatic error correction is not possible. If that should happen the memory would have to signal the processor that it must be repaired immediately for reliable operation. The existence of more than one bit error in the entire 22-bit data plus parity code is detected by checking the parity of the entire 22-bit code. If this parity is correct, an even number of errors has occurred; no correction can occur and repair must be made. If the 22-bit parity is incorrect, an odd number of errors has occurred, but the circuit usually is designed on the relatively safe assumption that only 1 error has occurred (rather than three, five, etc.) because it is extremely unlikely that three or more circuits in a given row of circuits will fail at the same time.

The entire 22-bit code is checked for correct parity by comparing bit P_6 to the parity of the 22-bit code. If these do not agree, the parity is incorrect. In the example code with the assumed error in bit D_3,

$$1111\ 0000\ 1111\ 1011$$

the parity of the 22-bit code with the assumed error is a 0 since there are an even number of 1's in it. Since bit P_6 is a 1 (as determined for the correct code), there is one error somewhere in the 22-bit code. The error correction circuit would detect the error as being in line D_3.

Error Indication

The error display indicates in binary code which row of a particular IC is faulty.

The basic display circuit using LEDs is illustrated in *Figure 9-3*. If no error has occurred, the LED signaling NO ERROR is turned on. When the parity checking circuit determines that one error has occurred, the display LED signaling ERROR is turned on and latches the row code into the 4-bit register. The latch occurs on the rising edge of $\overline{\text{CAS}}$. The output of the register is connected through current drivers to four LEDs. The light pattern of these LEDs indicates in binary code the number of the row in which the error occurred. If one error has occurred, the 4-bit output of the parity decoder in the error display circuit provides the binary code for the number of the column containing the faulty circuit. The column could be one of the data columns D_0 through D_{15} or one of the parity bit columns P_1 through P_6. Monitoring the LED pattern will enable the troubleshooter to determine which integrated circuit is faulty.

**Figure 9-3.
Typical Error Display
Circuit**

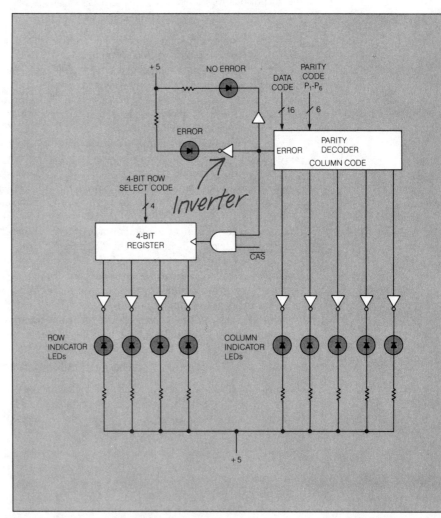

Troubleshooting

If more than one memory circuit is faulty, a check of the row in question using a simple software routine should enable the system to pinpoint which circuits in the row are faulty. The routine would be similar to that discussed in Chapter 6. Since only 64,000 locations are involved in one row, this test would take less than a second of computer time, assuming that the system being tested is a computer. If all circuits in an entire row are indicated faulty by such a test, then the most likely problem is a faulty decoder or a wiring fault in the row select line. This could be detected by low frequency tests of the decoder and the row select wiring using logic probe and logic pulsers or voltmeter measurements as described in Chapter 6.

Decoder Fault

If the entire memory array is indicated faulty, then: (1) the decoder must be at fault, (2) the decoder enable line must be defective, (3) the memory is not being refreshed properly and the fault is in the refresh $\overline{RAS}$ generator, or (4) power to the memory could be defective. Any of these faults can be checked using logic probes or voltmeter measurements.

Refresh Controller Fault

The easiest way to test for a fault in the refresh control circuit is to use an oscilloscope. The address counter, row addresses, and refresh oscillator are likely points of failure.

The testing of the refresh control circuit involves testing the system $\overline{RAS}$ lines in an idle state; that is, the processor is not performing any operation requiring the use of the memory. The $\overline{RAS}$ pulse should be occurring 256 times every 2 milliseconds or approximately once every 8 microseconds. This test can be done by placing an oscilloscope probe on the $\overline{RAS}$ line and also examining the least significant three address lines. A rapidly changing pattern on the address lines and a $\overline{RAS}$ pulse train of approximately 125 kilohertz in frequency should be observed. Similarly, probing the most significant address lines should indicate a signal that changes once every millisecond. Of course, these measurements will show only general activity except for the uniformly repetitive $\overline{RAS}$ pulse train.

If these signals are not observed, the refresh controller should be examined for the fault. Either a refresh cycle is not initiated once every 8 microseconds (an astable multivibrator or oscillator has quit operating) or the address counter is not cycling through a modulo 256 count (possibly an open in the counter clock input or a fault in the counter itself). It may be that there is an open in the line from the refresh circuit $\overline{RAS}$ line to the $\overline{RAS}$ input to the memory bank. Many of these faults can be checked by simple continuity checks using voltmeters or logic probes. The refresh oscillator output can be observed with an oscilloscope capable of measuring a 125 kilohertz square wave. Similarly, the counter output can be observed with a multi-channel oscilloscope capable of measuring square waves in the 1 to 125 kilohertz range, depending upon which of the eight counter outputs are monitored at a given time. The basic refresh circuit components and circuit structure were discussed in Chapter 6.

SIGNATURE ANALYSIS TECHNIQUES

The simple logic probe discussed in earlier chapters is limited in its testing capability to low speed combinational or sequential logic function and continuity tests. With microcomputers, the signals on a given line may be changing at a rate of up to several megahertz and catching a 1 or a 0 at any given instance with a probe is not meaningful.

A signature analyzer instrument permits the analysis of long sequences of bits. It compares the sequence in question to a known standard.

A more sophisticated probing instrument is required that will determine if a long sequence of bits on a line under test is correct or not. This implies that a sequence of bits must be stored and compared to the known good or standard sequence or it must be compressed. In this way it can provide a number code of a fixed length for comparison to a known good code. This is the basic strategy of a test instrument known as a signature analyzer or signature multimeter. An example of such an instrument is shown in *Figure 9-4*. This is a Hewlett Packard 5004A signature analyzer which can be used to detect and localize errors or faults in a microcomputer or any digital equipment.

Figure 9-4.
Signature Analyzer
(Courtesy of
Hewlett Packard Co.)

Error Detection

The basic operation performed by the signature analyzer is to compute the division of a binary bit stream by a known polynomial. The polynomial is generated based on the make-up of the bit stream to generate a 16-bit binary code which is then displayed on four 7-segment LED display devices. The division is performed by using a 16-bit shift left register coupled with a modulo 2 input adder.

This is the same basic strategy used to detect errors in communication data streams or in fields read from floppy disk storage units. The technique, as applied to floppy disk data error detection, is known as a cyclic redundancy check (CRC). When data is written to the disk, a 16-bit CRC code is computed and is written at the end of each disk storage field. The CRC number is computed again when the field is read from the disk and the computed number is compared with the one stored at the end of the field. If the two CRC numbers are not the same, one or more errors exist in the data as read from the disk.

The signature analyzer uses the same cyclic redundancy check technique to detect errors in memory as is used in data communications transmission.

The same approach is used in *Figure 9-5* in which the shift register inputs the next bit from the data stream at the time specified by a clock pulse. This occurs when a start pulse arrives and continues until the arrival of a stop pulse. Thus, a fixed number of bits are shifted into the register and the 16-bit code generated in the register is unique for the bit sequence received. If one or more of the bits are in error, the number stored in the register (and displayed on the instrument LED devices) will be different from that observed in a series of bits with no errors. Thus, by knowing the proper 16-bit number and observing the number in a system under test, the correct operation of a line or a system can be verified. All that is required is that the numbers for each line of a good system are known and that the faulty system is exercised in exactly the same way as the good system. Then, by having the correct number code for each line in the system, the lines in a system under test can be probed and their operational status determined.

Reading the Display

In *Figure 9-5* the display indicates some nexadecimal characters (753) and one digit that is not one of the standard hex characters. In this case it is an H. This is because the 7-segment displays cannot reliably display some of the hex characters (for example, a B looks like an 8). In fact, the indicator does not necessarily display the digits as their corresponding hex value. The table in *Figure 9-6* shows the hexadecimal code and its relative display character. Since the four digit (or character) display does not represent a specific instruction code, but is simply a reference pattern, the assignment of a character to a hex code is not important and may vary with different manufacturers. This is why the display in *Figure 9-5* is H753, which corresponds to the code 1101 0111 0101 0011 in the shift register.

Figure 9-5.
Basic Operation of
Signature Analyzer

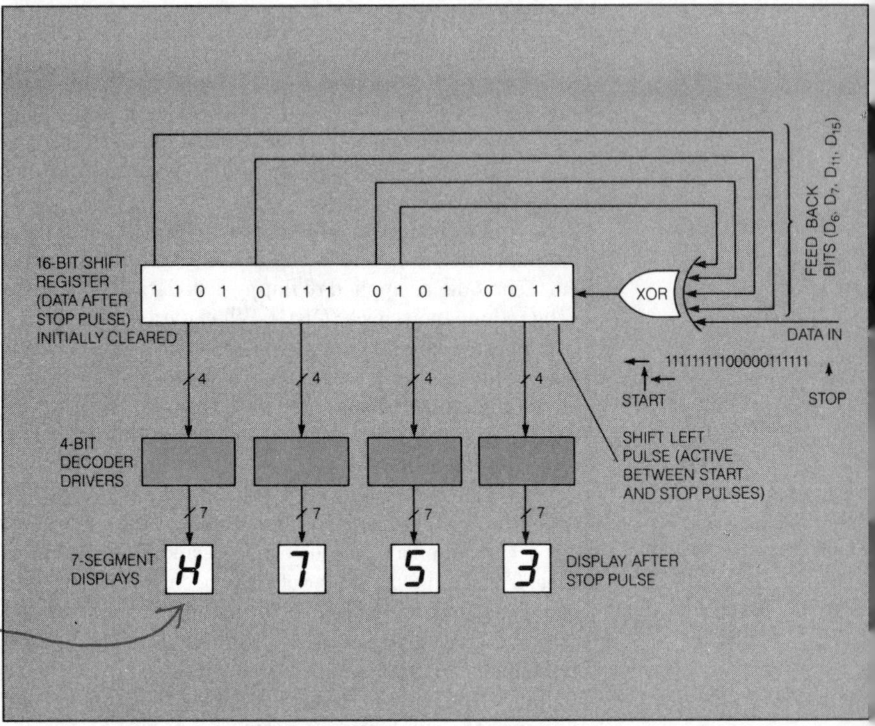

Display code different than a hexadecimal code. (handwritten annotation)

Figure 9-6.
Signature Analyzer
Display Code
(Source: Gary Gordon and Horns Nordig, Electronics, March 3, 1977.)

4-Bit Group to be Displayed	Character Displayed
0000	0
0001	1
0010	2
0011	3
0100	4
0101	5
0110	6
0111	7
1000	8
1001	9
1010	A
1011	C
1100	F
1101	H
1110	P
1111	U

Troubleshooting with the Signature Analyzer

To use an instrument of the type shown in *Figure 9-4*, there are two common test procedures available; the "software-driven" mode and the "free-running" mode.

Software Driven Mode

The software-driven mode uses a test program stored in a portion of the microcomputer's ROM that can be executed to provide known bit sequences on the lines connected to RAM and I/O devices.

Free-Running Mode

In the free-running mode the processor data lines are disconnected from the system data bus. This can be done either with jumpers designed into the hardware, a special microprocessor plug fixture, or using pin isolation techniques. The ROM outputs are similarly isolated from the system data bus and a single byte (8 bits) or word (16 bits) is placed onto the processor data bus. Usually the instruction is a NOP (for No Operation) which does nothing. The processor acts as if it has fetched a NOP at each address in memory so it increments the instruction address and performs another fetch. It continues this (as shown in *Figure 9-7*) to provide all possible address codes on the bus until power is removed from the system.

The processor clock or memory read pulse can be provided to the signature analyzer as the clock input and the 1 to 0 transition on the most significant address line can be used as the start or stop signal. A known or fixed sequence of bits will then appear on each of the address lines and on the outputs of each pin of the ROMs (when the ROMs are enabled). The codes that would appear on the signature analyzer for an 8-bit processor are shown in *Figure 9-8*. By comparing the codes observed on each address line with the codes in *Figure 9-8*, the operation of the processor and address bus can be verified.

Now, by changing the start and stop signals to the decoder output (that drives the chip select of a given ROM) and testing the sequence out of each ROM, the displays for each ROM line can be tested. By comparing these outputs to the standard code listed in a test manual for the equipment under test or obtained from a unit of the same type, the operation of all of the system ROMs can be verified. Similarly, the outputs of all decoders can be verified while the processor is sequencing through all the address codes. Once the free-running test has been completed; the processor, address bus, address decoders, and ROMs all will be verified as to their status and the troubleshooter will know which component or set of lines are faulty and need repair.

A signature analyzer can be used to test ROM memories of a system. The ROM outputs are isolated from the data bus. Then, output data codes are compared to known codes from a good working unit. Any differences are analyzed to identify the specific location of the fault.

**Figure 9-7.
Free Running Signature
Analysis Circuit
Configuration**

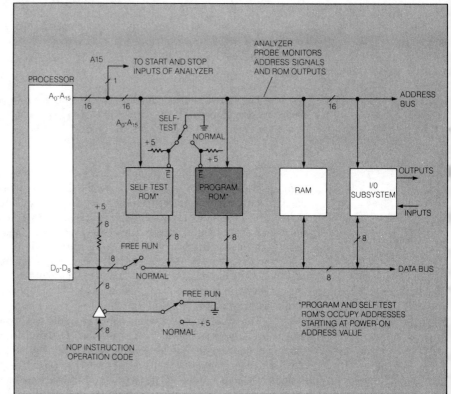

**Figure 9-8.
Signature for Properly
Operating
Address Signals for
16-Bit Processors**
*(Source: Andrew Stefanski,
EDN, Feb. 5, 1979)*

Address Line	Signature
A_0	UUUU
A_1	5555
A_2	CCCC
A_3	7F7F
A_4	5H21
A_5	OAFA
A_6	UPFH
A_7	52F8
A_8	HC89
A_9	2H70
A_{10}	HPP0
A_{11}	1293
A_{12}	HAP7
A_{13}	3C96
A_{14}	3827
A_{15}	755U

Unique code for each line

Self-Test Mode

In the self-test mode, a ROM with a "self-test" sequence exercises the processor, RAM and I/O circuits while a signature analyzer displays signal codes on the interconnecting buses. Any discrepancy from known patterns are used to isolate the error.

The next step in systems that have been designed to be tested with signature analyzers is to energize the "self-test" ROM and power-up the processor with the data bus reconnected. In the free-running operation, the ROM outputs were isolated or the RAM and I/O enables were inactive. In the self-test mode these devices have to be reconnected to the system under test. Since the processor and ROMs are known to be working, the processor is not to be used to execute subprograms that will generate a start or stop pulse. Also, it should not be used to generate known address or data bus sequences between the start and stop events. Then, by writing a series of 1 and 0 test codes to RAM and reading them back with the signature analyzer connected to a given RAM or I/O line, the operation of that portion of RAM or I/O subsystem can be verified. Again, the observed display digits must be the same as those listed in the repair manual for the equipment or those obtained from a working identical system. The combination of the free-running test and the self-test probing of a system with the signature analyzer allows the entire system, including all buses and devices, to be verified. If a fault occurs, it can be isolated to a given bus, component or part of a component by noting which signatures are wrong and which are correct. As an example of the types of documentation that would be provided in a system repair manual, *Figure 9-9* shows the hexadecimal display codes that might be observed for a hypothetical memory decoder of a system or output port.

Signature Analyzer Summation

The signature analyzer offers a cost-effective test instrument that can effectively troubleshoot complex digital systems and microcomputers without investing in the more expensive troubleshooting equipment which will be described later in this chapter. The signature analyzer is basically a single-probe error detector for systems that produce a long sequence of known bit streams. More expensive test equipment offers several different ways to troubleshoot a system. These include displays on CRT screens of system waveforms, storage and listing of hex codes in sequence, and automatic computer-controlled testing of certain systems. Of these more complex test instruments, the logic analyzer is the least expensive and will be considered next.

Figure 9-9.
Typical Service Manual
Listing of Correct
Signature Codes

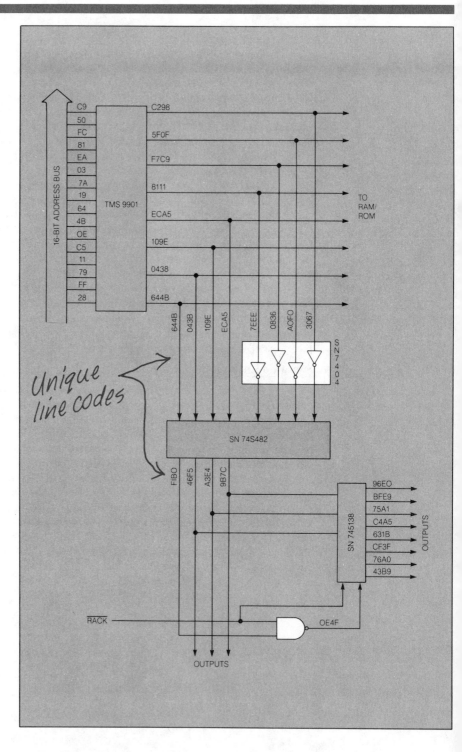

LOGIC ANALYZERS

The logic analyzer is a type of oscilloscope that can freeze observed time signals, monitor many signals simultaneously, and observe the sequence of instructions that results from a specific combination of signals.

While the multi-channel oscilloscope can be used to determine general signal activity, such as the existence of a periodic refresh cycle, on a memory of the type shown in *Figure 9-1*, it is not possible to completely freeze the memory operation or catch momentary signal errors with such an instrument. Further, in microcomputers, often there is the need to monitor many signals at the same time, possibly after some specific combination of signals has occurred in the system. Also, it may be desirable to determine the sequence of instructions that occurs after some combination of signals is observed. A multi-channel oscilloscope cannot satisfy such measurement requirements, but a special instrument known as a logic analyzer can. The general operation of a logic analyzer is relatively simple, but it is usually a fairly complex instrument. *Figure 9-10* shows a typical logic analyzer displaying timing waveforms. The block diagram of a basic logic analyzer is shown in *Figure 9-11*.

Figure 9-10.
Typical Logic Analyzer Showing Timing Waveforms
(Courtesy of Hewlett Packard Co.)

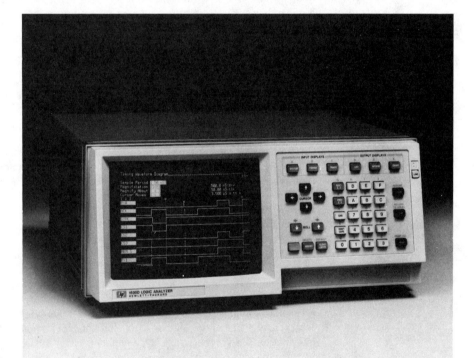

Sampling

The input section consists of a sample clock driving a sample-and-hold circuit. This circuit determines when the input digital code from each test probe is sampled and stored in the analyzer memory. For example, an analyzer might have a sample clock running at a 100 megahertz rate (100 million samples per second) which means a sample once every 10 nanoseconds (ns). Since the displayed waveform is from the sample-and-hold circuit, instead of real time as in an oscilloscope, there is some amount of delay in the displayed transition time. The amount of this delay depends upon the sampling rate; the faster the rate, the less delay, thus, the less error. The error is given by a plus and minus range around the actual transition time. Thus, the precision of the instrument using a rate of 100 megahertz has a possible error range of -10 ns to $+10$ ns. Some analyzers have a 400 megahertz sample clock to provide precision in the -2.5 to $+2.5$ ns range. This means an edge transition from a 0 to a 1 or a 1 to a 0 can be determined within 5 ns if the analyzer has a 400 megahertz clock. This is more than sufficient for most modern microprocessor-based systems.

Input Channels

Depending upon the cost of the instrument, the analyzer may provide from 16 input channels or probes as indicated in *Figure 9-11* to over 40 input channels or probes. Each channel is connected to a separate line; thus, a 16-channel input device can monitor all lines of a 16-line bus at the same time.

Memory

In order to accomplish its varied functions, a logic analyzer must have a large memory.

In order to display the waveforms of the channels on a CRT screen, the most recent samples must be stored in the analyzer memory. The product of the length of the memory multiplied by the sample clock period is the total time represented across the width of the display screen. For example, if the most recent 8,000 samples are stored in the analyzer and the analyzer is operating with a 10 ns period sample clock, the width of the screen represents a total time of 80,000 nanoseconds or 80 microseconds. To display a longer time, the sample clock frequency would be decreased. Again using the same 8,000 sample memory (for each channel being monitored), but with a 10 megahertz clock, the total display screen width would represent 8,000 times 100 ns (0.1 microsecond) or 800 microseconds. This might represent the time to perform 100 memory refreshes or 400 microprocessor instruction cycles. If the analyzer is capable of monitoring 16 channels and saving 4,000 samples per channel, the total analyzer memory would be 64,000 bits of information or 4,000 words of information. This is not a very large memory, but it can be very expensive because the memory must be constructed from high-speed devices to store the samples at the 100 megahertz rate.

Display

When testing memory using a logic analyzer, the user can control at what point in time or under what combination of circuit conditions the memory is to store successive signal samples.

Since an analyzer memory must, of necessity, be limited; how does one determine which 4,000 samples are being displayed? Generally, the analyzer is programmable to collect samples immediately, after a specified delay, or after some signal combination or pattern has occurred. This enables the user to specify very precisely which time period of the system operation is desired in terms of some feature of the signals being monitored. As a result, the analyzer must have signal pattern detectors and delay counters that can be programmed from front panel controls. These detector and counter circuits provide the signals that cause the memory to start storing successive samples. The display circuits provide the basic display by drawing the waveform showing the 0 and 1 levels on the face of the CRT for each channel being probed.

**Figure 9-11.
Block Diagram of 16-
Channel Logic Analyzer**

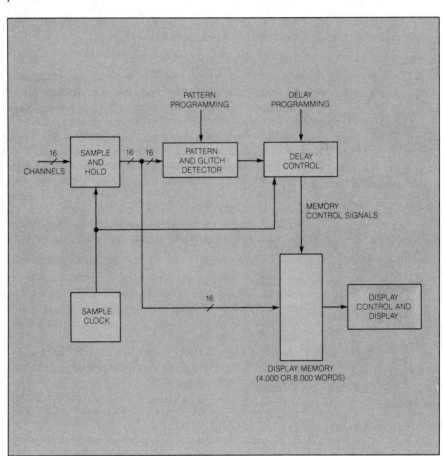

Glitch Detector

The instrument may also have glitch detectors which will pinpoint signal errors such as momentary 0's or momentary 1's that are not supposed to be present. (A glitch is an unwanted signal transition usually due to noise.) These are generally detected as a transition from 0-to-1-to-0, or a 1-to-0-to-1, that occurs within a specified small period of time (such as two or more successive samples). For example, if normal signal changes should not occur but once every 100 nanoseconds, the instrument could be programmed to mark as glitches any transitions from 0-to-1-to-0, or 1-to-0-to-1, that occur in less than 40 nanoseconds.

The ability to program instructions and store and display a large number of system waveforms give the logic analyzer many powerful features which the multi-channel oscilloscope doesn't have. Further, the logic analyzer's ability to detect and display asynchronous signal events makes it more versatile than the oscilloscope, which is best at displaying repetitive or synchronous events.

LOGIC ANALYZER EXAMPLE

Figure 9-12 shows a waveform display as it might be observed on a logic analyzer. Only a few channels are shown for simplicity. This display assumes that the analyzer is connected to measure the refresh signals provided by a refresh controller of the type discussed previously. The system processor has been electrically removed or disabled from the memory by applying voltage to pull its HOLD line to its active state. The HOLD line is activated by a monostable multivibrator and switch combination in the logic analyzer to provide a hold condition on the processor throughout the active display time. This causes the processor to set the three-state buffers on all of its address, data, and memory control signals to the high resistance or disabled state and prevents the processor from attempting a memory access. Thus, all memory activity will be controlled only by the refresh controller.

Instrument Setup

The programmability of the logic analyzer allows the user to select the signals to be analyzed and the initial levels at which they are to start.

The sample frequency is set at 100 megahertz to provide a sample period of 10 nanoseconds and a total display time of about 40 microseconds for a 4,000 word analyzer memory. This allows the analyzer to display the occurrence of about five refresh cycles. The signals chosen for display are $\overline{RAS}$, $\overline{CAS}$ (which should remain high for refresh activity), RFSH CLK (the clock that triggers the refresh cycle when it makes a low-to-high transition once every eight microseconds), and the least significant three address lines for the row address.

The storage and display of information captured by the analyzer is programmed to start when all of the following conditions are true:
1. HOLD is active
2. the three least significant address lines are at zero, and
3. the clock makes a low-to-high transition.

This programming capability permits the user to tell the analyzer which signals to use and what level they should be when the display is to start. Thus, the analyzer displays only signal patterns that are of interest.

Since the system signals are sampled only at the sample clock times of the analyzer, the display indicates changes in signal levels at only the sampled times even though the actual system signal may have changed sometime between the previous sample clock pulse and the one showing the change. (Refer to the discussion regarding sampling error.) The analyzer determines whether a signal is a 0 or a 1 at a sample time by comparing to see if it is above or below a certain voltage level programmed by the user into the analyzer. For TTL circuits, the user normally would program in a threshold voltage of 1.4 volts. Other logic families may require a different threshold; for example, ECL circuits would require a threshold of 0 volts. (Refer to Chapter 1 for the discussion on logic families.)

Display Meaning

Once the relationship between the actual and the display signal waveforms is understood, it is possible to determine what the display waveform is telling about the system operation.

Figure 9-12.
Logic Analyzer Display -
Refresh Controller
Example

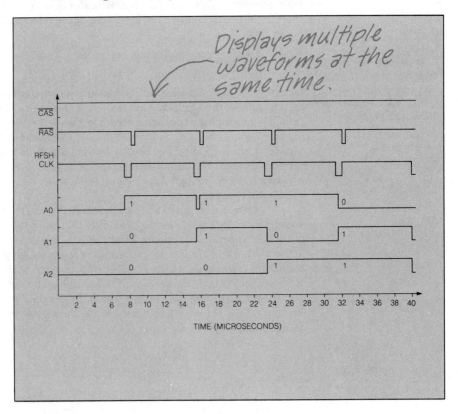

Checking $\overline{RAS}$ and $\overline{CAS}$

The first signals to be checked are the $\overline{RAS}$ and $\overline{CAS}$ waveforms. The $\overline{CAS}$ signal should remain at the 1 level throughout the display as it does in *Figure 9-11*. Since it does stay high, there is no fault which is erroneously pulling $\overline{CAS}$ low. This is important because if $\overline{CAS}$ goes low during this time, it would cause one or more circuits on a given data line to apply voltage levels to that data line. This voltage might cause a failure in one or more of the circuits connected to that data line.

By understanding the interrelationships between signals in the dynamic memory, cause and effect relationships become apparent.

The $\overline{RAS}$ line should pulse low once every eight microseconds for about 250 nanoseconds, which it does in *Figure 9-12*. If the $\overline{RAS}$ line is stuck at either 0 or 1, or if pulsing does not occur at the 125 kilohertz rate (every 8 microseconds), the entire memory would fail to operate properly. For this case, the fault would have to be in the line from the controller $\overline{RAS}$ output to the memory bank, or the circuit generating $\overline{RAS}$ must be faulty. If a refresh controller is used like that in *Figure 6-9* but with the timing shown in *Figure 6-8*, the $\overline{RAS}$ signal is generated by a monostable multivibrator that outputs a 250 nanosecond low pulse. The multivibrator is triggered by the rising edge (low-to-high transition) of the 125 kilohertz refresh timing clock. If $\overline{RAS}$ from the controller is stuck at a 1, the multivibrator is faulty, or there is an open or short in the multivibrator clock input line, or the refresh timing clock is inoperative.

Checking Addressing and Timing

Observing address signals and timing signals can verify that major subsystems are working properly.

Since in *Figure 9-12* the $\overline{RAS}$ and $\overline{CAS}$ signals are operating normally, the next signals to be checked are the counter outputs A_0, A_1, and A_2 and the refresh timing clock. First, the clock should be a 125 kilohertz pulse train if it is to produce the timing shown in *Figure 6-8*. The signal should be high for 7.5 microseconds and low for 0.5 microsecond. During the return to a high level, the $\overline{RAS}$ should go low for a period of 0.25 microsecond. The three-state buffer should be output enabled to allow the counter generating refresh row addresses A_0 through A_7 to connect its signals to the row address lines of memory in *Figure 9-1*.

Observation of the address signals A_0, A_1 and A_2, and the timing clock waveforms in *Figure 9-12* seems to indicate that this part of the refresh controller is operating normally. The timing clock is generating a repetitive active low pulse of about 0.5 microsecond once every eight microseconds and the address signals from the controller are active during this period and the $\overline{RAS}$ low time of 0.25 microsecond. The low-to-high transition on the clock waveform seems to coincide properly with the generation of the $\overline{RAS}$ active low pulse, thus, the clock generator and the three-state buffer control seem to be operating properly.

Thus, the refresh controller seems to be operating normally which
would indicate the reason for the memory fault must be in another part of the
system. However, before deciding that the controller is operating properly, the
address signals need to be examined more carefully. The address code (only the
least significant 3 bits are displayed in *Figure 9-12*) should increment by one in
binary code from 000 for each $\overline{RAS}$ pulse just prior to the $\overline{RAS}$ active edge
(refer to the timing in *Figure 6-8*). Therefore, the address code ($A_2A_1A_0$)
should advance to 001 just before the first $\overline{RAS}$ as shown in *Figure 9-12*. It
should advance to 010 just before the second $\overline{RAS}$. However, examining the
address code just before the second $\overline{RAS}$ shows the address code advancing
first to 010 and then to 011 during the low period of the refresh timing clock
before the second $\overline{RAS}$ occurs. Thus, row 010 is skipped. Next the address
code advances from 011 to 101 for the third $\overline{RAS}$ pulse, skipping row 100. It
advances to 110 during the fourth $\overline{RAS}$ pulse as it should, but then advances to
000 for the fifth $\overline{RAS}$ pulse, skipping row 111.

Some type of circuit error is causing an incorrect advancement of the
row address count during the refresh intervals. This causes some row
addresses to be skipped and, without refresh, those rows lose their data.

Checking for Glitches

Such an occurrence would account for the failure of the entire memory
even though the refresh circuit would seem to be operating properly. To
determine what is causing the problem (a glitch or system noise should be
suspected), the analyzer display can be expanded to show two $\overline{RAS}$ pulses with
the glitch detector enabled. Glitches are displayed as vertical bars. Each glitch
contains a high-to-low transition which, if the glitch pulse is wide enough,
causes the counter to advance and skip one or more row addresses.

Figure 9-13 shows such an expanded display with the occurrence of a
glitch just before the first $\overline{RAS}$ pulse which causes the extra incrementing of
the address code from 010 to 011. The glitch could be caused by noise, a faulty
contact in the wiring from the clock generator to the counter clock input, or a
faulty refresh clock generator.

Using a logic analyzer would be the only practical way to detect such a
problem in a complex system. Even if the expanded scale display had not
shown a glitch, repeated displays eventually would indicate the error. Further,
if glitches are suspected, the analyzer can be programmed to start sampling
and displaying when the first glitch is detected by the glitch detector.

Other Logic Analyzer Capabilities

The logic analyzer has even more capabilities to make the
troubleshooter's job easier. It usually offers at least two more display options or
analysis modes.

Figure 9-13.
Expanded Analyzer
Display - Refresh
Controller

Figure 9-13.
Expanded Analyzer
Display - Refresh
Controller

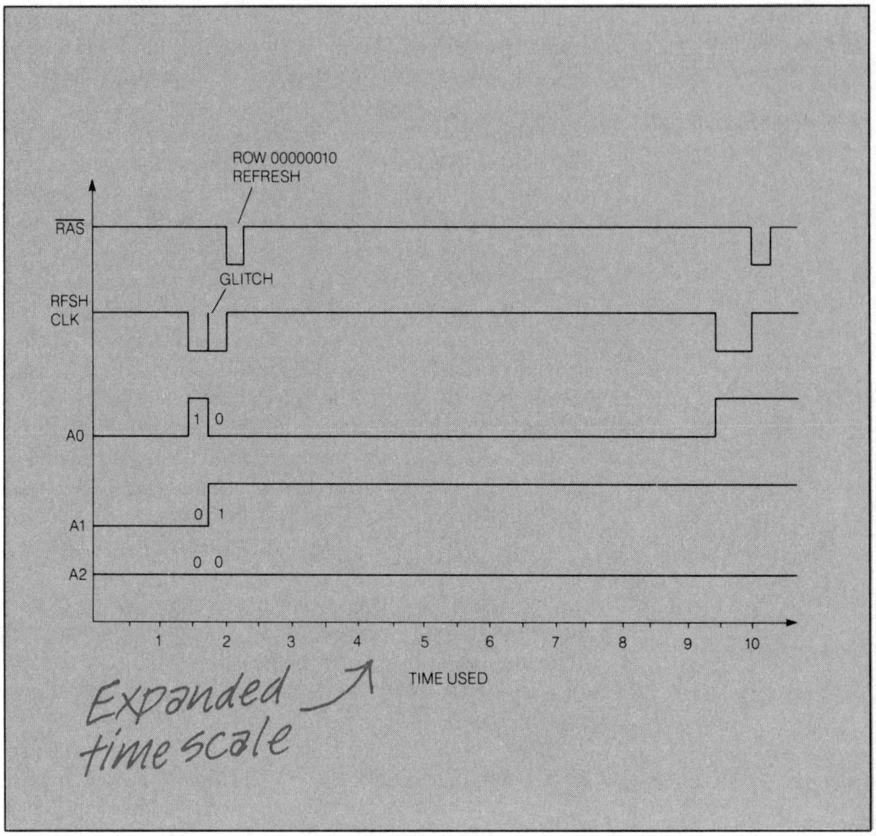

Dual Threshold Display

The level threshold display allows one to measure the time required for a signal to change between two threshold levels.

One of these is to display waveforms using single or dual threshold input circuits. These are useful for observing time relations; for example, the time it takes a signal to change from a 0 to a 1 or vice versa. In *Figure 9-14a*, a slowly varying signal is shown along with its single threshold mode display. The slow rise time is not evident with the single threshold of 1.4 volts. By using dual thresholds of 1.0 and 2.0 volts with the same signal and by using a three-level analyzer display, the display waveform of *Figure 9-14b* results. The stairstep display indicates how long the varying signal is taking to make the 0-to-1 transition.

**Figure 9-14.
Alternative Analyzer
Display Thresholds**

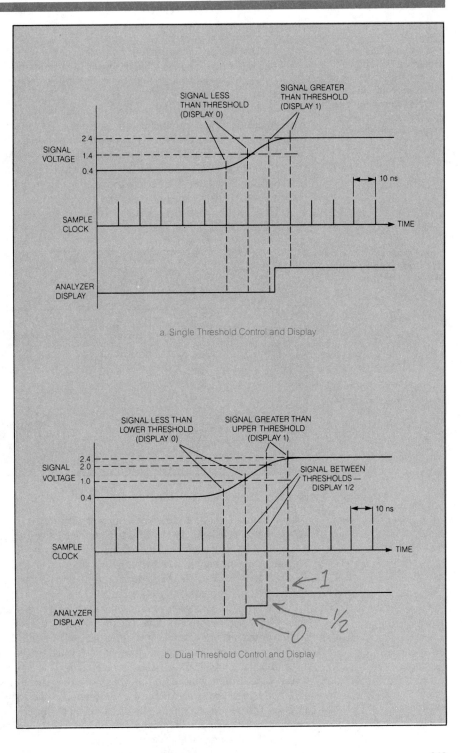

a. Single Threshold Control and Display

b. Dual Threshold Control and Display

Hex and Binary Code Display

The hex and binary code displays allow the troubleshooter to notice an unexpected change in the progression of addresses and the rate of repetition of specific refresh signals.

One display option that is very useful for quick detection of some problems is to display hex and binary codes instead of waveforms at each specified sample condition. For example, in *Figure 9-12*, if the user had programmed the analyzer to display the two 4-bit signals that represent the 8-bit row address code from the counter upon each high-to-low transition of the $\overline{RAS}$ signal, the display would have been similar to *Figure 9-15*. Since the troubleshooter knows that each hex code displayed should increase by one from top to bottom, an addressing problem is quickly detected by noting the jump in the hex code value by two during the second, third and fifth $\overline{RAS}$ pulses. The troubleshooter could then switch to the display shown in *Figure 9-13* to determine the cause of the problem. The display shown in *Figure 9-15* also allows the user to quickly check that the $\overline{RAS}$ pulses are repeating at one every eight microseconds as required.

Figure 9-15.
Hex Code Display Option
of Logic Analyzer

$\overline{RAS}$ Pulse Number	Time in Microseconds	Address Lines A_0 Through A_7
1	8.000	01
2	16.000	03
3	24.000	05
4	32.000	06
5	40.000	08
•	•	•
•	•	•

Program Analysis

Some logic analyzers are equipped with software or hardware which allow them to break down the codes to their original instruction set. This feature can be very useful in determining why new system designs are not working properly as well as for troubleshooting systems that have failed. *Figure 9-16* is an example of a logic analyzer showing the assembly language codes for a microprocessor.

With this analyzer, input probes are connected to all of the microprocessor address bus lines, the processor data bus lines, and to the processor timing and control signal lines. This allows the analyzer to track, store, and display the instructions being performed by the microprocessor in its original language (called assembly language). This is very useful when trying to determine whether or not the program in the program memory (as executed by the processor) is the correct sequence of instructions. The analyzer can be programmed to begin a trace of the program under several conditions; for example, beginning the trace at a certain memory address or the transition of a particular signal.

Figure 9-16.
Logic Analyzer Showing
Assembly Language
Code
(Courtesy of
Hewlett Packard Co.)

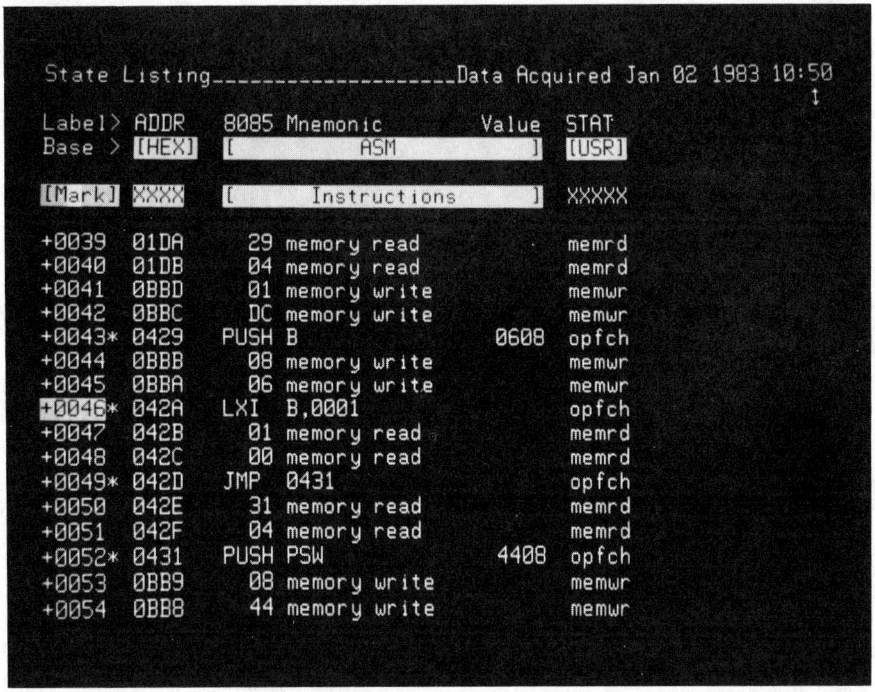

```
State Listing_____Data Acquired Jan 02 1983 10:50
                                                              ↑
Label> ADDR    8085 Mnemonic        Value  STAT
Base > [HEX]   [         ASM              ]  [USR]

[Mark] XXXX    [      Instructions       ]  XXXXX

+0039  01DA    29 memory read              memrd
+0040  01DB    04 memory read              memrd
+0041  0BBD    01 memory write             memwr
+0042  0BBC    DC memory write             memwr
+0043* 0429  PUSH B                 0608   opfch
+0044  0BBB    08 memory write             memwr
+0045  0BBA    06 memory write             memwr
+0046* 042A  LXI  B,0001                   opfch
+0047  042B    01 memory read              memrd
+0048  042C    00 memory read              memrd
+0049* 042D  JMP  0431                      opfch
+0050  042E    31 memory read              memrd
+0051  042F    04 memory read              memrd
+0052* 0431  PUSH PSW               4408   opfch
+0053  0BB9    08 memory write             memwr
+0054  0BB8    44 memory write             memwr
```

COMPUTER SYSTEM TROUBLESHOOTING

Substitution Method

The time-honored troubleshooting method used by many owners of small computer systems (such as personal computers) is to substitute known good subsystems until the system begins working again. This method also is used to get a new computer system working for the first time. For example, let's say you have just assembled a new computer system with a particular type of operating system, but it doesn't work properly. You have a friend with an identical system that works, so you borrow his/hers and begin substituting the borrowed equipment one piece at a time in your system until your system works. This method allows various pieces to be checked out individually. Since cable connections and printed circuit board connections are the most common cause of system failure, it is adviseable to try moving the cables and connectors slightly to make sure good contact is being made.

In some systems, the operating system must be modified to match the disk drive characteristics or the I/O port locations used in a specific system. Once the operating system is correct for the system under test and the fault has been isolated to a given subsystem, some of the techniques discussed in Chapters 6, 7 and 8 can be used to determine the cause of the problem. After the connection problems, the next leading cause of system failures is faulty integrated circuits. The least likely cause of system failure is discrete components such as resistors or capacitors on the circuit boards.

Computer-based Testing

The substitution method also is used in small repair shops; however, company warranty shops use more sophisticated computer-based test equipment to exercise the system and locate the fault in a home or small business computer more rapidly. This latter method also is used in factories to troubleshoot newly manufactured systems that are not operating properly.

When testing computer systems, the computer test equipment is substituted for the system's CPU (microprocessor), and takes control of the buses to perform selected sequences of tests.

The computer-based testing is much faster and more likely to find the cause of failure than the simple voltage, continuity and logic probe tests. Generally, the computer test instrument replaces the microprocessor in the system under test either physically or electrically. In the physical replacement, the microprocessor is removed from its socket and is replaced with a plug that is attached to the test instrument. In electrical replacement, the microprocessor is left in place and the test instrument generates a HOLD signal to the microprocessor to cause it to enter its idle condition. This prevents it from placing signals on the address, data, or control buses of the system under test. The test instrument then takes control of these buses to perform a prescribed sequence of tests on the system under test.

Often, before a system is tested in this manner, the microprocessor is tested by replacing it with a microprocessor which is known to be operating correctly. This approach is used only if the processor is in a socket rather than wired or soldered into a printed circuit board. Once the processor is known to be good, the fault must be either in the memory or input/output subsystems. These subsystems can consist of a large number of individual circuits, even in a relatively inexpensive personal computer. Further, the operation of input and output circuits vary considerably depending upon the function they are performing.

Memory Tests

Memory devices may be checked automatically by exercising all their locations to see if they are functioning properly. EPROMs and ROMs are checked for the accuracy of their data while RAMS are also checked for their ability to receive and store a 0 or 1 in every position.

In general, computerized memory testing involves exercising each subsystem with known conditions to determine whether or not responses are normal. Some forms of such testing have been discussed in Chapter 6 with regard to memory testing. The EPROMs and ROMs are checked by reading all locations and comparing each byte with a reference listing or table of bytes that represents the code sequence which should have occurred. By keeping track of deviations, if any, the test computer or the self-test diagnostic program within a personal computer can print out a message indicating the most likely fault in the system.

RAMs can be checked similarly by verifying their ability to store and retrieve both a 0 and a 1 in every bit position. Such software testing is feasible in small memories (less than 64,000 bytes). Larger memories may require extensive testing time, but this may not be objectionable in a repair shop since the test time is computer time, not technician labor time. As discussed previously (*Figure 9-1*), larger memories may be built so that they include automatic error detection and correction circuitry.

Video Tests

A program to check a video terminal essentially is the same as a general memory test, except that particular characters (underscores and blanks) are used to visually indicate that all circuits are operating properaly.

The checking of input and output devices such as CRT terminals, printers, and keyboards is similar to the procedures covered in Chapter 7. The CRT terminal consists of a display RAM, the video controller circuit, and a character display ROM. The entire RAM can be checked in much the same way normal data storage memory is checked. For example, a diagnostic program could be written that underscores all CRT display positions by sending the ASCII code of 5FH to each display RAM location. A screen full of underscores indicates all locations are working for that character. Then, blanks (ASCII code 20H could be written to all RAM locations. If the screen displays all black, the test is successful. This approach has the advantage of quickly testing the display RAM, display controller circuits, and character ROM all at once with a visual indication.

The codes used for the display tests (all blanks or all underscores) also have the advantage that the 0 and 1 capability of the display RAM is tested since the two codes being used to test the system are:

$$0010\ 0000 \quad \text{(blank)}$$
$$0101\ 1111 \quad \text{(underscore)}$$

Thus, each 7-bit ASCII code storage location in the display RAM is checked to see if it can store and retrieve a 0 and a 1. Any failure to store and retrieve the binary pattern would show up on the CRT screen as a character on a screen that should be all blank or as some character other than an underscore. These erroneous characters would appear, and perhaps change, if the memory failed to hold its 1 level signals. This is the most common failure of the dynamic RAM circuits that are used for display memories. Display of all wrong codes would indicate that a certain bit or memory circuit is stuck at a 0 or a 1. The defective bit could be determined by comparing the ASCII code for the characters that actually appear on the screen with the ASCII code for the desired character.

Disk Drive Tests

Other major subsystems are similarly tested. For example, disk drives can be written into with a known pattern and this pattern then read and compared with the written pattern to detect any errors. Errors in disk storage also show up as invalid error detection bytes (CRC check bytes at the end of each data record) in the recovered or read data. This error usually is indicated by an error message on the screen during routine operation.

A disk drive can fail to operate because of a faulty disk drive controller, wiring faults or connection problems in the cable connecting the controller to the disk drive and processor boards. Failures may also be caused by faulty magnetic recording and playback heads, or the disk itself. If all records are faulty, the problem is in the heads, the wiring, or the disk controller. If only a few records are bad, the problem is in the disk or in intermittent wiring. Replacing the disk can quickly and easily confirm or eliminate it as the problem. These fault possibilities can be written out on a printer or CRT screen in the test computer once a specific failure pattern has been detected.

Interface Tests

The test instrument can be set up to test input and output devices such as serial data interface circuits by providing known data input patterns. Circuit operation may be determined by checking to see if the input interface circuit has received the proper data. Since the test instrument controls both the input data and monitors the input circuit responses, it is possible for it to determine the most likely problem. Usually the test instrument is programmable and has a large number of connectors or probes that can be connected to the system under test. It will step through the input stimulus/response sequences to determine which inputs and input devices are working properly and which are faulty and why. By providing appropriate analog-to-digital converters in the test computer, analog quantities can be measured automatically as well. Such signals as clocks and power supply voltage levels under different test conditions can be monitored to determine faults in these subsystems. Generally, the more thoroughly the entire computer system is exercised with well-designed test signals and signal sequences, the better the diagnostic messages that can be generated and displayed to the troubleshooter. The troubleshooter can then concentrate on a fairly well-defined area of the computer for detailed testing with an oscilloscope or logic analyzer.

Keyboard Tests

As a final example of the computer-controlled testing of an input subsystem, the keyboard example in Chapter 7 will be considered. To test a keyboard, the computer should either cause the appropriate keys to be depressed in a known sequence through the use of a solenoid array mounted over the keyboard, or an operator should press the keys in a certain order. Probes would be connected to the rows and columns of the matrix of switches and to any output of a key scan or encoding circuit. Then, by stepping through the key switch closures in a particular sequence, the computer can compare the actual key codes, row code, and column code for the matrix to what should be observed for each key.

> A computer-based programmable instrument can completely check the input and output circuits of a system by applying known input patterns and comparing the responses to known output patterns.

If the row and column codes do not agree with their normal values, then the key code will be incorrect as well. In such a case, the test computer can print out the suspected open or faulty key with its row and column number. It can also print the ASCII character code it received along with the actual ASCII character code to help the troubleshooter determine which wires or keys are faulty. If the row and column codes are correct for all key closures, but the key code is wrong, the test computer can print out the message that the key encoder circuit or its wiring is faulty. If sufficient pattern recognition is built into the diagnostics of the test computer, it may be possible for the error messages to specify which wires or circuits are faulty and how.

If the keyboard example in Chapter 7 were tested, the computer would determine that all keys on the left side of the keyboard result in faulty ASCII codes, but the row and column codes are alright. The test program could then determine that the key matrix is working properly, but the encoding process is in error. Further, by doing a comparison between received ASCII codes and acceptable ASCII codes, the test program could decide that the D_3 line is always at 1, just as we did in analyzing the data. The advantage of the computer test is that the key test and the ASCII code analysis would be performed automatically in a very short period of time with an error message that line D_3 out of the decoder is stuck at 1. Thus, the troubleshooter would immediately check the decoder circuit and the wiring between the circuit and the processor.

Given enough input probes, the computer tester could actually determine whether the stuck at 1 condition was in the decoder circuit, in the connection to the printed circuit board, or in the wiring back to the processor through some input buffer. Then, the test computer could print the message that "the decoder circuit needs to be replaced", or "check the connection of decoder pin #___", or "there is an open in the wiring between pin #___ of the decoder circuit and pin #___ of the input buffer" and so on. The result is fast location of the system error leaving the troubleshooter only the simple task of repairing the wiring or a connection, or replacing a circuit.

GENERAL PURPOSE COMPUTER TROUBLESHOOTING EQUIPMENT

One approach that is closely related to computer testing is to use a programmable test instrument that is designed to troubleshoot computer equipment. An example of such a test instrument is the John Fluke 9010A Microsystem Troubleshooter shown in *Figure 9-17*. This instrument can be used as a signature analyzer, but is designed as a general purpose computer-based test instrument that can be used with any microcomputer (once the appropriate microprocessor probe pod is installed). It is designed to be configured to any system under test (within reasonable limits). This is different from the approach discussed in the previous section, because in that section it was assumed that a specially designed and dedicated computer test system is used to test a specific computer system.

**Figure 9-17.
Microsystem
Troubleshooter**
*(Courtesy of John Fluke
Mfg. Co.)*

With a programmable
troubleshooting
system used to trou-
bleshoot a computer sys-
tem, the troubleshooter
runs the system by replacing the computer's pro-
cessor with one in the
troubleshooting system.

The basic features of the 9010A include a microprocessor probe pod
that replaces the microprocessor in the system under test. This allows the
9010A to exercise the rest of the system. The 9010A is a programmable device
that can be programmed through an RS232 serial interface, a cassette tape, or
its own keyboard. Such programming allows the user to instruct the 9010A in
terms of which address represents what type of device (RAM, ROM, certain
types of I/O, etc.). It also allows the user to program what tests are to be made
on each of these devices and in what sequence. The instrument can be
instructed to print diagnostic or status messages and instructions to the user.
An example instruction might be to probe a certain pin or IC in the system
under test. The user can manually probe certain parts of the system while the
test instrument monitors the reaction of the system to such probing. This is a
very powerful teaming of a fast computer test instrument and a human
operator to quickly locate faults in complex systems.

The "Self-Programming" Mode

In the "self-test" mode, the troubleshooting computer system records proper system responses from a good working system. It uses these responses, stored in memory, to compare to the responses of a system under test to determine any discrepancies.

One of the most important features of an instrument like the 9010A is its ability to program itself. This can reduce the user's programming time and provide a relatively complete test procedure for any given system. The instrument enters this "self-programming" mode when the LEARN command button on the instrument console is depressed after the microprocessor pod has been connected to a known good system. The test instrument then steps through all possible memory and I/O addresses. This is done to determine if there is a component that responds to that address and how it responds. This enables the 9010A to completely profile the good system. It can determine which memory addresses are not used, which are used for program memory and what program is stored in that memory. It can also determine which locations are RAM and how each I/O address responds to a known stimuli. Once it has established the memory and I/O addresses (called mapping), and how each address responds, it is ready to exercise all of these locations. Exercising these addresses in a system under test allows the test instrument to check their responses and compare them to the correct responses. In this way, the major faults (component or bus problems) can be isolated quickly without any extensive programming efforts on the part of the user.

To check the more sophisticated I/O portions of the system, the user will want to program special test sequences to work with the test instrument in the self-programming mode. This will allow the instrument to verify operation of serial interface devices, video controllers, and disk controllers. For example, the instrument can be programmed to stop after it has tested all memory and simple I/O and bus components. Then it can instruct the operator to probe the output of a serial interface chip. Next, the instrument can output a series of ASCII character codes to that device while monitoring the serial data that results. If the serial data is correct for the codes sent, the output portion of the interface is verified. The instrument can then instruct the operator to place the probe on the input of the serial interface and send another stream of serial data. It would then monitor the codes provided by the interface at the system parallel data bus to see if the codes are received properly. Other signals such as $\overline{CTS}$ or $\overline{DTR}$ of the serial interface component could similarly be tested, as could individual lines of parallel interface circuits. These tests are somewhat slow since the operator must find the appropriate point to be probed, but they are about the only possible way of completely testing such components. Analog-to-digital or digital-to-analog converters could be similarly tested using known analog inputs and measuring analog output generated by the 9010A.

Certainly the use of such an instrument enables close to 100% fault detection in time periods ranging from fractions of hours to hours. This compares to much lower detection percentages available from a human troubleshooter armed only with an oscilloscope or voltmeter and days of effort.

FUTURE TECHNIQUES

Many of the techniques presented in this chapter point to the future of troubleshooting of digital systems. In large systems, the trend will be to include more and more self-testing error detection and fault diagnosis circuits and software. These additions will increase the cost of the system, but will make it much simpler to repair and maintain.

Separate Diagnostic System

Attempts are being made to build a parallel system into a digital system just to monitor the operation of the original system and detect and flag any misoperation. Significant progress still needs to be made in this area.

There could be two parallel digital systems within a given system: one, the actual system being used and the second, a monitoring system to check for proper operation and detect errors. The monitoring system will detect a malfunction and signal the operator as to what to do to correct it.

Of course, reliable data from the monitoring system is dependent upon proper operation of that system. Should there be a failure in the central processor, the main power supply, or the diagnostic system itself, the diagnostic software will not be able to perform its tests. Consequently, a failure could occur which may be undetected or which the diagnostic system is unable to isolate.

If the diagnostic portion of the system periodically monitors the voltages at various points in the power supply, it can detect the failure of a power supply as a rapid drop in one or more of the supply voltages. It would still have enough stored power, or it could switch to standby power provided by a battery, to print out on a printer an error message, for example:

MAIN POWER SUPPLY HAS FAILED IN THE +5 VOLT SECTION; HAVE SWITCHED TO AUXILIARY BATTERY POWER.
SUSPECTED COMPONENTS: DIODE D2 AND FILTER CAPACITOR C4.

In the case of truly critical failures such as the microprocessor suddenly failing, the system cannot provide diagnostics. One approach that can be used to prevent this type of failure is to provide back-up processors that monitor the other processors in the system. Then if one stops working properly, the other processors can vote to take that processor out of the circuit electrically and assign one of the standby processors to take over its tasks. In the meantime, a message such as:

REPLACE PROCESSOR # ____

can be printed out while the system continues to work normally.

If the system does not have such self-testing features or does not have sufficient testing capabilities to check and locate all errors, there still will be computer-based test equipment that will, to a large extent, automatically exercise the failed computer until it determines the fault. The troubleshooter still will have to possess the analyzing ability and digital testing skills to repair the suspected fault indicated by the diagnostic systems. In simple systems, there will be limited diagnostic features and the techniques presented in this text will have to be used to locate the fault the old-fashioned way through hard work.

WHAT HAVE WE LEARNED?

1. Many memory systems have automatic error detection circuitry (called a parity generator) and error correction circuitry included in the design.
2. Fault isolation may involve many different tests with different circuits and test equipment.
3. Timing relationships are more critical in systems that are more complex and require the use of multi-channel oscilloscopes or logic analyzers for fault isolation.
4. A signature analyzer can display data bit streams and circuit characteristics, but cannot show timing relationships nor identify glitches.
5. Even with computer-controlled testing, the troubleshooter is often required to perform manual tasks to help the computer isolate the fault.
6. The amount of data displayed by a logic analyzer is the product of the analyzer memory multiplied by the sample time.

Quiz for Chapter 9

1. In *Figure 9-1*, if the memory devices have 256K locations (one bit per location), how would the design change?
   a. No change would be required.
   b. The same structure would not be suitable.
   c. The refresh controller and $\overline{RAS}$ generator would have to be changed.
   d. The error correction would need to be changed.

2. Refering to question 1, how many address lines would the processor have to provide for the structure in *Figure 9-1?*
   a. 16
   b. 18
   c. 20
   d. 22

3. How large would the memory in question 1 be (in megabytes)?
   a. 0.256
   b. 2.048
   c. 4.096
   d. 8.192

4. How many address pins would each circuit have?
   a. 9
   b. 16
   c. 18
   d. 20

5. In question 1, how many of the processor address lines would be sent to the memory circuit address multiplexer? (The multiplexer is the device that interfaces between the low order address lines and the address inputs on the individual memory devices.)
   a. 9
   b. 16
   c. 18
   d. 20

6. In *Figure 9-1*, if the data code sent to a location is 93CAH, what will be the value stored into parity bits P_1 through P_6?
   a. 011110
   b. 100010
   c. 101110
   d. 010001

7. In question 6, if the parity bits are 111011, what action should be taken?
   a. Bit 11 should be corrected to a 0.
   b. Bit 11 should be corrected to a 1.
   c. Bit 4 should be corrected to a 0.
   d. Bit 4 should be corrected to a 1.

8. Again, in question 6, if the parity code read-out of the location is 111111, what action should be taken?
   a. Indicate a parity error in bit P_1.
   b. Indicate a parity error in bit P_6.
   c. Indicate parity error in both bits P_1 and P_6.
   d. Correct bit 11.

9. The purpose of the logic analyzer is to:
   a. verify the logic operation of the gates in a system.
   b. sample and display system signals.
   c. analyze the functional logic operations of a system.

10. If a logic analyzer uses a 50 megahertz clock and a storage of 4,000 words, how long a time in microseconds is represented by the horizontal width of the display?
    a. 20
    b. 40
    c. 80
    d. 800

11. In *Figure 9-12*, the signal on line A_0 indicates:
    a. a noise spike has occurred on line A_0.
    b. the row counter has been incremented twice.
    c. there is a problem with the $\overline{RAS}$ generator.
    d. there is a problem with the refresh clock generator.
    e. any of the above.
    f. b and d above.

12. A glitch of the type shown in *Figure 9-13* acts:
   a. like a second clock pulse.
   b. to cause a second $\overline{RAS}$ signal.
   c. to cause an error on the A_1 signal.
   d. to hold line A_2 at 0.

13. A glitch is a:
   a. momentary 0-to-1-to-0 signal sequence.
   b. momentary 1-to-0-to-1 signal sequence.
   c. a noise pulse.
   d. any of the above.

14. A dual threshold display in a logic analyzer provides information about:
   a. glitch occurrences.
   b. rise times.
   c. fall times.
   d. propagation delays.
   e. all of the above.
   f. b and c above.

15. If a logic analyzer is set up to display information in hexadecimal form, providing a total of 6 hex digits, how many signal probes and analyzer channels are required?
   a. 6
   b. 18
   c. 24
   d. 30

16. The signal sequence indicated in *Figure 9-15* indicates:
   a. the same basic information as the waveforms in *Figure 9-12* for address line operation.
   b. the possible presence of random glitches.
   c. the occasional double incrementing of the row counter.
   d. any of the above.

17. If the display in *Figure 9-15* had continued all 00's, the likely problem would be *(Figure 6-9)*:
   a. faulty refresh timer.
   b. faulty counter.
   c. open in RFRQ line.
   d. fault in RFGR line.
   e. any of the above.

18. If the display in *Figure 9-15* were all 00's or random hex digits on the output of the address multiplexer while the outputs of the row counter were correct (00, 01, 02, 03, etc.), the likely fault would be *(Figure 6-9)*:
   a. fault in the multiplexer or its control lines.
   b. faulty counter.
   c. faulty refresh timer.
   d. faulty RFRQ signal.
   e. any of the above.

19. Some logic analyzers can be programmed to display assembly language instructions as they are executed.
   a. True
   b. False

20. The general approach used by automated computer test equipment is:
   a. display of logic analyzer signals.
   b. replacement of suspected faulty subsystems with known good ones.
   c. providing a standard stimulus to each portion of the computer and verifying the response and repeating for all parts of the system under test.

Testing Complex Digital Devices

ABOUT THIS CHAPTER

From the beginning of the integrated circuit era, the trend has been to design and build the system with fewer and fewer circuits. This means that the circuits must be more and more complex, incorporating all or most of the system in a single circuit. It is very difficult to determine if these very complex circuits are functioning properly during a troubleshooting procedure.

One of the features of such circuits and systems designed with such circuits is that there are many thousands of functions that each circuit performs and the troubleshooter must exercise the circuit to the point that it can be said to be faulty or acceptable with a high degree of confidence. To establish the operational properties of such a circuit may require unacceptable testing times. Even if such exhaustive testing is desirable, the circuit has thousands of points within the circuit that must be examined. However, only a few of these points can be brought out of the circuit for testing purposes. The problem becomes one of how such a device can be designed to make it feasible to test it with a reasonable number of test conditions to determine whether the device is working properly or if it needs to be replaced.

Many of the techniques of the last few chapters will be difficult to apply to such circuits. This chapter deals with some of the issues of how these circuits are designed to simplify testing and how such tests can be performed.

THE DESIGN OF COMPLEX INTEGRATED CIRCUITS

Throughout this book various types of integrated circuits have been examined and testing techniques for such devices have been covered. The most complex of these devices have been the microprocessor and memory devices and the systems considered in Chapters 6, 7, and 9.

Placing a large portion of a system into a single VLSI integrated circuit increases system reliability but complicates system testing.

The designer of a modern digital system can significantly increase the reliability and performance of such a system while significantly reducing system costs by providing all or most of the system on a single integrated circuit. These very large scale devices are usually custom designs that implement a specific digital system or a major portion of such a system. Such a custom design might be used to implement the digital circuits of a personal computer on a single integrated circuit or a few (up to 15) integrated circuits instead of the hundreds of circuits needed without this approach. Such an approach might be used to place the entire display subsystem described in *Figure 7-15* in a single circuit, resulting in a considerable saving of printed circuit board space and wiring and assembly costs.

Complex systems can be placed inside a few custom integrated circuits by using gate array and standard cell integrated circuit design.

Custom integrated circuits are often called *A*pplication *S*pecific *I*ntegrated *C*ircuits or ASIC devices. There are two general techniques used in designing such circuits that will be presented in this section. One is the use of *gate arrays* and the other is the use of *standard cells* to provide a given digital system or subsystem inside a single integrated circuit. Both techniques require the use of a computer-aided design workstation and associated programs to allow the designer to wire the design using the computer and to simulate the design operation. The computer is further used to generate the masks required to fabricate the circuit, once the designer is satisfied with the operation of the circuit.

Gate arrays allow designers to implement custom VLSI integrated circuits in a minimum time and at a minimum cost.

Gate arrays are integrated circuits providing a large number of fundamental gates that can be interconnected to form any desired system or subsystem. *Figure 10-1* shows the internal structure of such an array. The device provides alternating columns of gates and interconnect channels which can be used to connect the outputs of gates to inputs of other gates or device output pins, or to connect the device input pins to the inputs of gates. By providing the proper interconnection of a large number of such basic cells, any system can be designed. This process is simplified by the computer-based approach that calls up functional unit programs that provide automatic connections to provide counters, registers, decoders, and all the other devices that have been examined in previous chapters of this book. Then, the wiring of the final circuit is similar to the wiring of individual integrated functions on a printed circuit board. The difference is that the wiring is not on an easily tested printed circuit board. Instead, it is inside the ASIC circuit where the troubleshooter cannot easily get to points to test the operation of the system. *Figure 10-2* shows an example gate array IC consisting of hundreds of gates interconnected on the integrated circuit with 40 pins for input and output to the final external circuit.

Standard cell ASIC design is similar to gate arrays in the problems it presents to the troubleshooter and in terms of how it is similar to the wiring of functional integrated circuits on a printed circuit board. The difference is that the designer is actually designing the system with counters, registers, memories, and microprocessors stored in the computer library of the design workstation. The structure of such a circuit is illustrated in *Figure 10-3*. Again, most of the system wiring and, therefore, most test points of interest are inside the integrated circuit and may be inaccessible for device testing purposes unless the designer deliberately makes these points available to the troubleshooter.

**Figure 10-1.
Gate Array Custom
Integrated Circuit
Diagram**

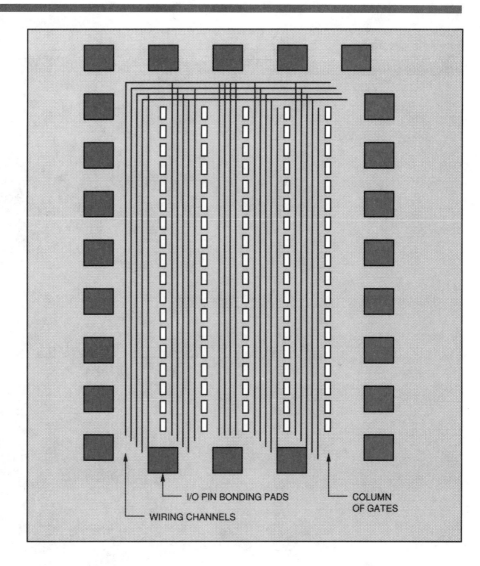

I/O PIN BONDING PADS

COLUMN
OF GATES

WIRING CHANNELS

**Figure 10-2.
Gate Array Integrated
Circuit Chip** *(Courtesy
Texas Instruments, Inc.)*

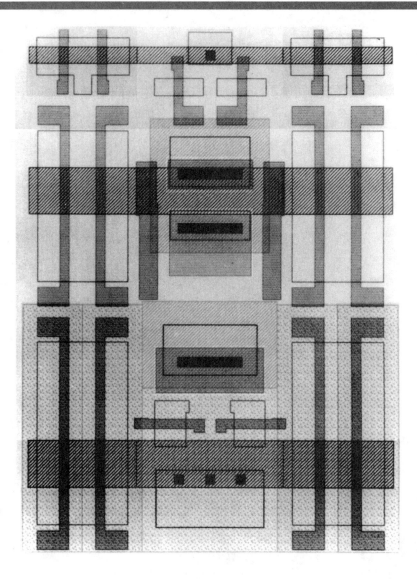

Figure 10-3.
Standard Cell Custom
Integrated Circuit

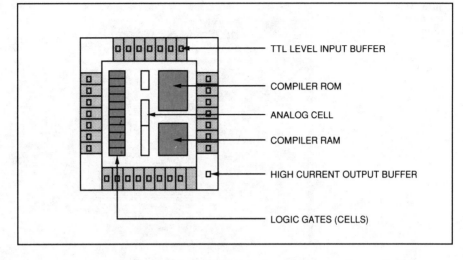

- TTL LEVEL INPUT BUFFER
- COMPILER ROM
- ANALOG CELL
- COMPILER RAM
- HIGH CURRENT OUTPUT BUFFER
- LOGIC GATES (CELLS)

Figure 10-4 shows an example standard cell IC of the same complexity of the gate array circuit shown in *Figure 10-2*. The difference in the layout structure is obvious when the two photos are compared. The gate array is a very orderly and repetitive structure with fixed interconnection areas while the standard cell design consists of many different size and shape functional areas connected by direct wiring paths. In either case, most of the test points needed to verify the detailed operation of the integrated circuit are within the integrated circuit and not available to the external world unless the designer provides access to these points in some way. The techniques that can be used to make these test points available through spare I/O pins on the integrated circuit will be examined in the next section.

PROVIDING TESTABILITY IN ASIC DESIGNS

Custom ASIC circuits of the types shown in *Figures 10-2* and *10-4* can be made testable by providing a means of injecting test signals at certain points in the system and by providing a means of monitoring important output points in the system. The process of allowing the troubleshooter to inject a signal at a certain point is known as *providing controllability* to that point in the circuit. It is key to troubleshooting a system and has been used throughout this book as early as using the pulser in Chapter 3 all the way through the techniques of Chapter 9. Allowing the troubleshooter to monitor a certain point in the system is known as *providing observability* and it, again, has been used throughout this book as early as using a logic probe in Chapter 3 through the multichannel approaches of Chapter 9.

**Figure 10-4.
Standard Cell
Integrated Circuit Chip**
*(Courtesy Texas
Instruments, Inc.)*

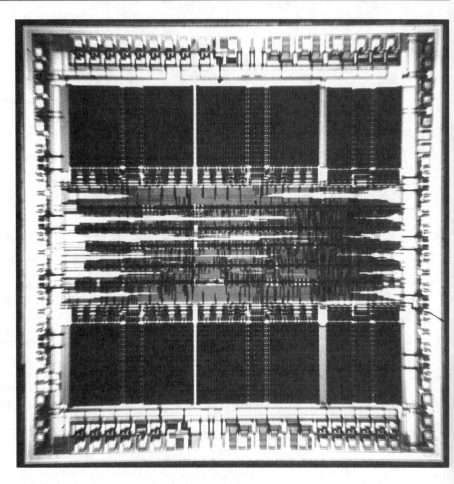

Providing Controllability in ASIC Designs

Controllability is the ability to insert test signals at desired points in a VLSI design.

     The basic approach to providing the troubleshooter the means to inject a test signal at a given point inside the integrated circuit is to use unused gates and unused pins on circuit gates as shown in *Figure 10-5*. When the circuit is operating normally in the system, the *test enable* signal is inactive and normal operating signals flow through the gates. When the circuit is to be tested, the test enable signal is active, turning off the normal flow of signals through the signal insertion point and allowing the externally applied test signal to flow to the test point and through the rest of the system under test. This approach requires two of the IC pins to be allocated to the test procedure. If there are ten such test points, 11 pins would be required (10 test signals and at least one test enable signal). This approach would rapidly use up the available integrated circuit pins if many points were to be made controllable using the approach of *Figure 10-5*. However, the basic approach of *Figure 10-5* provides the basis for more acceptable testing approaches. The approach of *Figure 10-5* can also be used with proper modifications to isolate modules for testing purposes or to split a large circuit into more manageable test modules.

Figure 10-5.
Test Signal Injection
Techniques

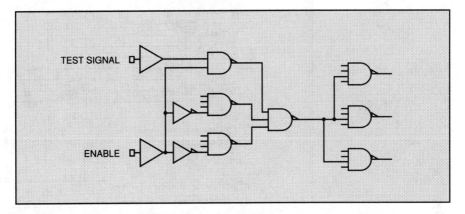

In order to provide access to a large number of signal injection points while using up just three of the integrated circuit pins, an extension of the approach of *Figure 10-5* must be used. The basic idea is to use a long shift register with one input being the input serial data to the shift register and the other input being the clock that shifts the data in. The third terminal is the test enable signal. The basic structure is shown for an 8-bit shift register in *Figure 10-6*. This arrangement allows the test control circuit to shift in a pattern of 8 zeroes and ones by applying the appropriate 0 or 1 to the input to the shift register prior to each shift pulse. Each shift pulse moves the pattern to the right one bit position, so that after 8 shift pulses, the first 0 or 1 presented to the input will be at position or signal point A, the second 0 or 1 presented to the input (during the second shift pulse) will be at position or signal point B. This continues until the last 0 or 1 presented to the input during the 8th shift pulse appears at point H. Thus, after 8 shift pulses, the signals used to test points A through H are in place inside the circuit and the test enable can be activated to cause these 0 and 1 signals to flow through the integrated circuit to generate outputs that can be analyzed to see if the circuit is working properly. In practice, far more than 8 test signals will need to be injected and more than just one pattern of such test signals needs to be generated. However, the basic strategy of *Figure 10-6* is the one used to provide test signals to all such points using only three of the integrated circuit pins to implement the test.

It is the function of the AND and OR gates in *Figure 10-6* to control the signal flow in response to the test enable signal. When test enable is active in *Figure 10-6* the row of AND gates passes the test signals from the shift register through the OR gates into the logic to be tested. During this time the normal system signals are blocked by the column of AND gates. When test enable is inactive, the test signals are blocked by the row of AND gates and the normal system signals are allowed to flow through the column of AND

Figure 10-6.
Test Signal Injection
Using Shift Registers

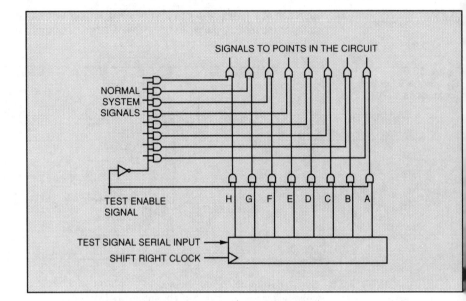

gates and then through the OR gates to the rest of the system, just as if the test circuitry was not in the system at all.

Providing Observability in ASIC Designs

Observability is the ability to monitor signals at desired points in a VLSI design.

The other aspect of building in test capability inside large scale custom integrated circuits is to provide a means of gating a test point to be monitored to an output pin of the integrated circuit. Again, a spare gate is used to perform this function as shown in *Figure 10-7*. The problem with this approach is similar to the problem with the approach of *Figure 10-5*. If 10 test points need to be brought to the outside for measurement, 10 integrated circuit pins would be used up in the process. These pins could be the same ones used for normal output if the structure of *Figure 10-8* is used. In this

Figure 10-7.
Approach to Observe or
Test an Internal Circuit

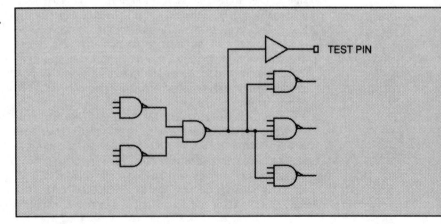

case, the test enable disables the normal signal flow to an output or an input pin and enables the flow of the test signals and the signals to be measured to these pins. In *Figure 10-8*, if test enable is inactive, the INA pin delivers the normal system input through the external pin INA to the core logic and the normal system output signal is delivered from the core logic to the normal output pin (OUTB). When the ENABLE is active the test data can be sent in through the OUTB pin to the insertion points in the core logic and the resulting output test data is sent out to the test equipment through pin INA.

**Figure 10-8.
Use of Normal I/O Pins
to Provide Test Data
Access**

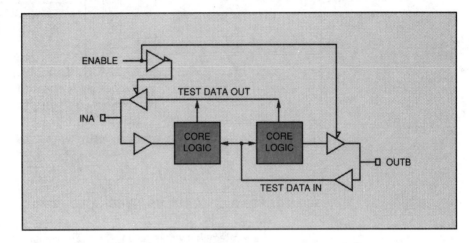

If more test points are needed than the circuit has input and output pins, the approach of *Figures 10-7* and *10-8* fails. The designer again has to resort to the shift register to provide the measurement of a large number of points. The basic approach is shown in *Figure 10-9*. This example deals with providing the means to test the operation of an 8 bit adder within the system. The test structure would have to provide 16 bits of test signals through a structure like that shown in *Figure 10-6*. Eight of these test signals would be one of the 8-bit numbers presented to the adder and the other eight bits would be the second number presented to the adder. When all of the test stimuli are in place through the use of the input structure of *Figure 10-6* a pulse is sent to load all the adder output signals to be measured into the shift register of *Figure 10-9*. Then, these test output signals can be shifted out into the test control circuit for analysis by applying shift pulses to the register of *Figure 10-9* (and to an equal length register in the test control circuit) to shift all test signals out to the control system. In the case of *Figure 10-9* eight such shift pulses would have to be applied. Then, the test control logic can compare the output of the adder with the desired output (the proper sum of the two 8-bit input test numbers) and determine if the adder is functioning properly. By using this type of approach, many internal points of a system can be examined while using just two of the integrated circuit pins (one for the load enable and one for the serial output of the test signals). These do not have to be extra IC pins since the approach of *Figure 10-8* can be employed to use the normal I/O pins for test purposes. Then, the only extra pin required for test purposes is the test enable pin.

**Figure 10-9.
Use of Shift Register to
Observe 8 Internal
Nodes**

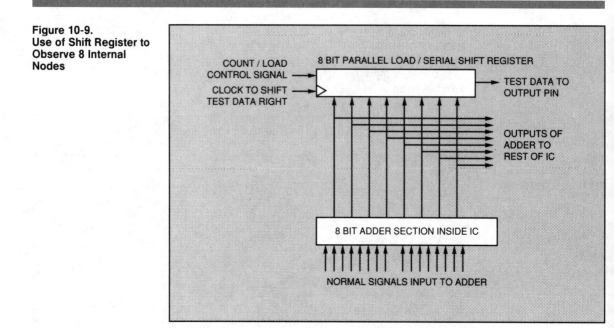

SCAN TESTING OF COMPLEX INTEGRATED CIRCUITS

Scan testing utilizes a shift register inside the normal signal path of a design to allow the insertion of test signals through a single package pin and to extract response signals from a single package pin.

The structures of *Figures 10-6, 10-8*, and *10-9* form the basis of the standard test strategy known as scan testing. The combined structures are illustrated in block diagram form in *Figure 10-10* for a specific example subsystem to be tested. In the case of *Figure 10-10*, a four bit adder within the system is to be isolated and tested through the use of the 9-bit input shift register and the 5-bit output shift register. With this structure, any or all internal points of the adder circuit can be controlled with a 0 or 1 by shifting in the appropriate 0 and 1 pattern through the Test Data In (TDI) pin into the scan path shift register to fill up the 9-bit input shift register. Then, the response of the system can be latched into the 5-bit register portion of the same scan path shift register and these five bits shifted out through the Test Data Out (TDO) pin for analysis to see if the circuit is operating properly.

By thus examining the circuit with enough different test patterns of input 0s and 1s, any faulty operation of the circuit or portion of the circuit can be detected. In this example, the test control logic would present 9 bits of test data by shifting 9 known 0s and 1s into the 9-bit serial shift register. This would allow two 4-bit numbers and a carry in (CIN) to be presented to the 4-bit adder, which is all the signal such a device can receive. Once the 9 test control bits are in place in the 9-bit register, the test enable signal is activated. This causes the adder outputs of a 4-bit sum and an output carry (COUT) to be generated. Placing the 5-bit shift register into the parallel load mode and applying a clock or shift pulse to the 5-bit register causes these five output bits to be stored in the 5-bit register. Then, the test enable signal can be deactivated. The five output bits are shifted out into the test control circuit for analysis by placing the 5-bit register into a shift mode and applying 5 shift pulses to the 5-bit register in the logic being tested and the same 5 shift pulses to an equal length shift register inside the test control circuit. Then, the test control circuit can examine the outputs (sum and carry out) and see if they are correct for the sum of the two input 4-bit numbers and the input carry. By providing enough appropriate input numbers and carry in combinations, the proper operation of the 4-bit adder section of the system can be completely verified.

**Figure 10-10.
Subsystem Testing
Using Scan Shift
Registers**

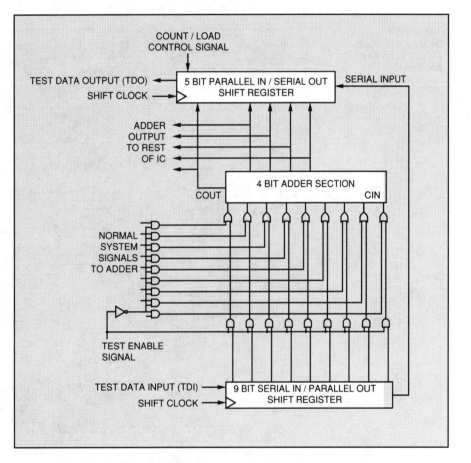

The scan testing approach is universal enough to be applied for testing either the internal structures of a given integrated circuit or a complex printed circuit board with many integrated circuits interconnected on the board. The power of the approach is that it only requires three or four extra printed circuit or integrated circuit pins to allow testing of all points within the board or integrated circuit. Further, the entire testing process can be automated by using a computer-based test controller.

The industry standard for scan testing is IEEE 1149.1

The industry has developed a standard structure for scan testing. This standard structure, known as the IEEE 1149.1 Architecture, is shown in *Figure 10-11*. It is basically a general version of that of *Figure 10-10* except the single cell of the shift register has been identified as the *boundary scan cell*. The important features of such a cell are that under test mode (TMS is active) the cell acts as one bit of a long serial shift register that allows the test controller to input bits to all signal input points of interest through successive application of the shift clock (TCK), and providing the serial bits one at a time to the serial data input (TDI). Outputs are observed by capturing them in a basic cell and shifting them out through serial output pin TDO in response to the TCK operation when TMS is active.

**Figure 10-11.
Overview of IEEE
1149.1 Scan Testing
Architecture**

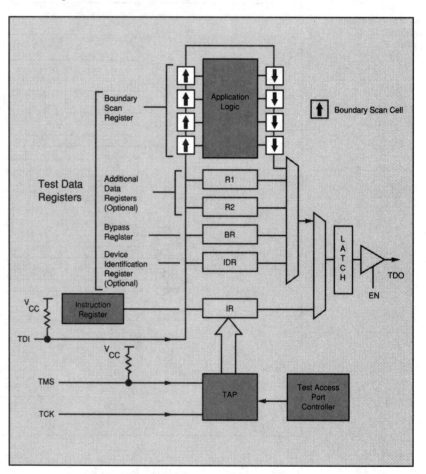

When TMS is inactive, the basic cell allows system signals to flow through the system in a normal manner so the system operates as if the basic cells were not there. The architecture allows for the additional scanning of standard identifier or other registers through TDI and TDO as well as copies of the system instruction register. Alternatively, the serial bit sequence can be simply passed out from TDI through the bypass register to TDO if the application logic of the board or integrated circuit is not to be tested. This would test the proper operation of the TDI to TDO path prior to the testing of the application logic or the instruction register.

All of the testing of the system would normally be automated through a computer controller shown in *Figure 10-11* as the *test access port controller*. The structure of *Figure 10-12* would allow such an automated test controller to serially access all ICs on a board through the control of the TDI, TDO, TMS, and TCK signals that each IC has been designed to recognize in accordance with the structure of *Figure 10-11*.

**Figure 10-12.
Boundary Scan
Diagnostic System**

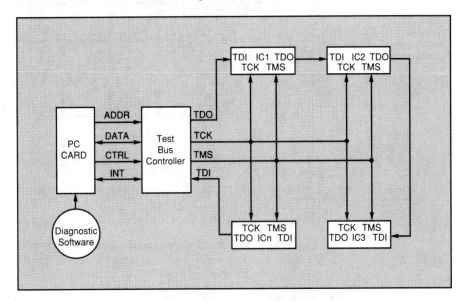

Integrated circuit manufacturers are already providing integrated circuits that can be used to perform the controller and the boundary scan register functions. For example, *Figure 10-13* shows the use of Texas Instruments, Inc., devices to provide scan testing of a computer system consisting of a processor and memory. The unidirectional octal scan cells (BCT8244) are used to gain access to address bus and timing and control signals, and the bidirectional octal scan cells (BCT8245) are used to gain access to the data bus signals. The board or integrated circuit containing these functional units must also provide 4 pins to implement the test port signals of TDI, TDO, TCK, and TMS.

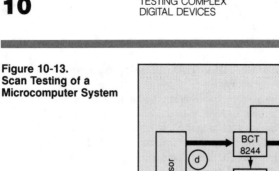

**Figure 10-13.
Scan Testing of a
Microcomputer System**

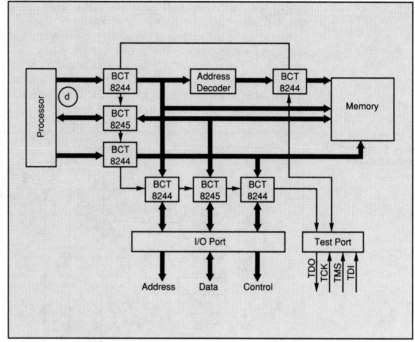

Figure 10-14 shows additional devices to provide scans of up to four submodule paths inside a module using the ACT8999 scan testing interface under the control of the ACT8990 scan testing controller integrated circuit. The host microprocessor, related program memory, and I/O, along with the ACT8990 circuit perform the automated testing controller function of the IEEE scan testing standard approach.

The troubleshooter's task in the scan testing approach becomes one of designing the scan 0 and 1 patterns and determining the expected response of a good system. Then the test controller must be programmed to exercise the system with these scan patterns. The most difficult part of this task is to design just enough different patterns to completely determine the proper operation of the system. Too few patterns will not detect all possible faults and too many patterns would make the testing too time-consuming and expensive. To understand the problems involved in the design of test patterns to be used in a scan test operation, some test patterns of the system of *Figure 10-10* will be considered. The troubleshooter is trying to determine if each section of the adder is working, and to make sure no signal path through the adder is stuck at 0 (ground) or stuck at a 1 (the power supply level). The patterns shown in *Figure 10-15* should suffice to verify these operational features of the adder. The first pattern applies 0s to all inputs, including the input carry. The proper sum and carry out under these conditions are all 0s (0 + 0 = 0) and these outputs will be observed unless some pin in the adder is stuck at a 1. The second and third patterns should similarly check to see that no path through the summing portion of the adder is stuck at a 0. By applying 1111 to one

**Figure 10-14.
Scan Test System for a
Multiple Board System**

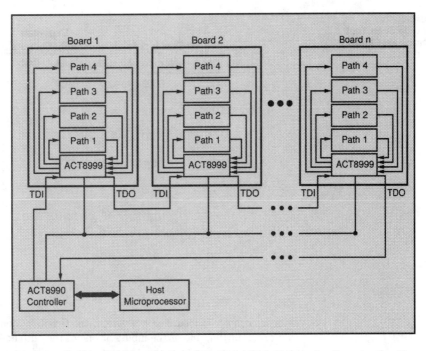

side of the adder and 0000 to the other side with a 0 carry in, the sum should be 1111 with a 0 carry out unless one of the input or output lines is stuck at a 0. The reason that both 1111 is applied to first one side of the adder and then the other side of the adder (with 0000 as the second number) is to test both sets of four inputs into the adder to determine if any of the 8 inputs are stuck at a 0.

The remaining test patterns of *Figure 10-15* exercise the addition operation of the adder to determine proper functioning of its internal logic. The patterns with 1111 on one side of the adder and 0000 on the other side with a carry in of 1 will check the carry propagation portion of the logic by checking to see if the sum is 0000 and the output carry is a 1. Finally, the addition of individual bits is checked by the last two test patterns. By adding 0101 to 0101 (with no carry in) the operation of adder bits 0 (least significant bit) and 2 is verified if the sum is 1010 (with no carry out). Similarly the operation of adder bits 1 and 3 is checked by adding 1010 to 1010 (with no carry in) to see if the logic will provide a proper sum of 0100 with a carry out of 1.

Once these test patterns and proper responses have been developed, the troubleshooter must examine them to see if some of the patterns are unnecessary (too many tests) and if any other patterns are needed (too few tests to properly verify operation of the function). Finally, these test patterns and proper responses must be programmed into the test system so the tests can be performed automatically on the structure of *Figure 10-9*. The Operational Verification comments in *Figure 10-15* can similarly be programmed into the test system as fault messages in case one of the desired

**Figure 10-15.
Example Scan Test
Patterns for Figure
10-10**

9-Bit Test Inputs			Expected 5-Bit Outputs		Operational Verification
Number 1	Number 2	CIN	SUM	COUT	
0000	0000	0	0000	0	None of the pins are stuck at 1
0000	1111	0	1111	0	None of the pins are stuck at 0
1111	0000	0	1111	0	None of the pins are stuck at 0
0000	1111	1	0000	1	Carry logic is working
1111	0000	1	0000	1	Carry logic is working
0101	0101	0	1010	0	Sum logic is working for even bits
1010	1010	0	0100	1	Sum logic is working for odd bits

responses is not obtained. For example, if the first test fails the test system could print out that one of the inputs or one of the outputs is stuck at a 1. If the carry propagation tests fail, the test system could print out messages to have the designer check the carry in and carry out paths for opens or stuck-at-0 faults. If such faults are not found the system would instruct the repair technician to replace the adder (if it is an IC on a printed circuit board) or replace the IC that the adder is a part of. Similar instructions could be included for other test failures.

SUMMARY

With properly designed test patterns and corresponding response patterns, an automated test controller can isolate which parts of the system are faulty and print out repair instructions to the troubleshooter. Thus, the approach of *Figures 10-11* and *10-12* combines all of the features of self-testing and troubleshooting that have been discussed throughout this book. Many of the techniques discussed in Chapter 9 could be applied to the testing strategies to be used in the scan testing approach, especially the concepts of signature analysis and the characterization of a known good system to provide reference outputs to be used to test suspected systems. The approaches of *Figures 10-11* and *10-12* along with automated testing should see increasing use in the digital systems of the future, all of which should make the testing and repair of complex systems a relatively straightforward process.

WHAT HAVE WE LEARNED?

1. When large portions of a system are placed in a single integrated circuit, it is difficult to verify operation of the integrated circuit.
2. Gate array and standard cell integrated circuit design techniques are two approaches that can be used to economically place large portions of a system into a single custom integrated circuit.
3. Unused gates and input/output pins can be used as connections to inject signals into test points of a system or integrated circuit, and to observe the response signals of a system or integrated circuit.
4. Shift registers and associated logic can be used to introduce a large number of test signals into an integrated circuit or system and to observe a large number of response signals in such a system while only using a few of the input/output pins.
5. Scan testing is a standard technique for implementing the approach of using shift registers and associated logic for automatically testing large scale systems and integrated circuits.

Quiz for Chapter 10

1. In order to provide observability to a point in a system, the designer must:
   a. provide a means of injecting a signal to that point.
   b. provide a means of delivering a signal from that point to external equipment.
   c. provide visual means of examining the point.
   d. all of the above.
   e. none of the above.

2. In order to provide controllability to a point in a system, the designer must:
   a. provide a means of injecting a signal to that point.
   b. provide a means of delivering a signal from that point to external equipment.
   c. provide visual means of examining the point.
   d. all of the above.
   e. none of the above.

3. In order to avoid the use of an excessive number of I/O pins to provide testability in a system, the designer must use:
   a. a gate for each point of signal injection and for each point of measurement.
   b. a shift register.
   c. multiplexed I/O pins.
   d. all of the above.
   e. none of the above.

4. Which of the following ASIC approaches involves a repetitive structure of identical devices:
   a. gate array.
   b. standard cell.
   c. PLA.
   d. all of the above.
   e. none of the above.

5. Which of the following ASIC approaches is similar to wiring up of functional devices on a printed circuit board:
   a. gate array.
   b. standard cell.
   c. PLA.
   d. all of the above.
   e. none of the above.

6. In a scan testing structure each of the test elements must provide which of the following capabilities:
   a. serial shift in and out.
   b. parallel flow through the element.
   c. test enable control gating.
   d. provision for test clock input and control.
   e. all of the above.
   f. none of the above.

7. In scan testing of the 4-bit adder section of *Figure 10-10,* the inputs are 0110 and 0110 and the carry in is 1. The output is a 1000 and a carry out of 1. What is the probable fault or faults with the carry in circuitry? (There may be more than one answer.):
   a. the carry in logic is working properly.
   b. the carry out logic is working properly.
   c. the carry in connection is stuck at 0.
   d. the carry in connection is stuck at 1.
   e. the carry in connection is open.

8. In the example of problem 7, what is the probable fault or faults with the carry out circuitry?
   a. the carry in logic is working properly.
   b. the carry out logic is working properly.
   c. the carry out connection is stuck at 0.
   d. the carry out connection is stuck at 1.
   e. the carry out connection is open.

9. In the example of problem 7, what is the probable fault or faults with the portion of the adder circuitry that generates the leftmost bit sum?
   a. it is probably working properly.
   b. it is stuck at 0.
   c. it is stuck at 1.
   d. there is an open connection out of the adder.
   e. none of the above.

10. In the example of problem 7, what is the probable fault or faults with the portion of the adder circuitry that generates the bit sum in the bit position second from the left (just to the right of the leftmost bit)?
   a. it is probably working properly.
   b. it is stuck at 0.
   c. it is stuck at 1.
   d. there is an open connection out of the adder.
   e. there is a problem in the carry input logic to the bit adder.
   f. none of the above.

Appendix

OSCILLOSCOPE OPERATION

The oscilloscope provides the display of a signal as it varies with time by plotting the amplitude of the signal under test versus time. The display is performed by a cathode ray tube (CRT) similar in many ways to the picture tube of a television set. The CRT tube consists of an electron gun, deflection plates, and a phosphor coated screen all placed in a glass tube from which all air has been removed as shown in *Figure A-1*. The electron gun forms a fine beam of electrons that is "fired" toward the face of the CRT. A spot of light is produced by the electrons hitting the phosphor on the face of the CRT. The phosphor emits light of a certain color, usually green in oscilloscopes.

The spot can be focused to a fine point by the focus control on the front panel of the oscilloscope. The astigmatism control found on some oscilloscopes adjusts the spot to a nearly perfect round shape. The brightness control varies the brightness or intensity of the spot. This control usually has a range such that the spot brightness can be varied from off to very bright.

CAUTION: The brightness should not be left at a high level when only a spot is present; it will damage the screen.

Deflecting The Beam

Signals applied to the deflection plates cause the spot of light to move up, down and across the face of the CRT. The signal that moves the spot of light across the screen, usually from left to right, is called the horizontal deflection signal. This signal has a shape as shown in *Figures A-1* and *A-2*, thus, it is called a sawtooth waveform. Its voltage amplitude is linearly proportional to time: that is, as time increases, the amplitude of the waveform increases in direct proportion.

Notice in *Figure A-1* that the left horizontal deflection plate is connected to ground and the right plate is connected to the deflection voltage. When the deflection voltage is negative, the spot is forced to the left side of the screen. As the voltage increases, the spot moves toward the right side. The spot is in the middle of the screen when the voltage is zero and at the right edge of the screen when the voltage is maximum. The speed at which the spot moves across the screen depends upon the frequency of the horizontal deflection voltage. At very low frequencies, one can actually see the spot move across the screen. However, at higher frequencies the spot moves so fast that one sees a continuous line, called the trace, across the screen. The speed of movement across the screen is referred to as the sweep rate and is measured in units of time versus distance. One or more controls allow the user to set the sweep rate.

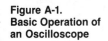

**Figure A-1.
Basic Operation of
an Oscilloscope**

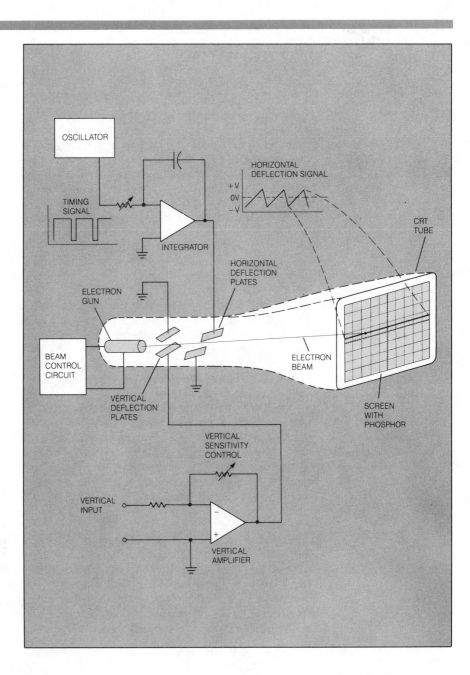

Reading The Screen

The screen of the CRT has a grid pattern on it which looks like graph paper. This grid is called the graticule. Setting the sweep rate or time/division control determines the time it takes for the spot to move across each square on the graticule. Usually each square is one centimeter by one centimeter (cm) and has five subdivisions created by four short lines. Therefore, if the timing of the sweep is calibrated in a certain amount of time per cm, the period of a waveform displayed on the screen may be accurately measured.

The signal whose waveform is to be displayed on the screen is applied to the vertical amplifier input. The amplified signal is applied to the vertical deflection plates of the CRT as indicated in *Figure A-1*. The voltage applied to this set of plates causes the spot to move up or down, therefore, the spot will follow the amplitude (voltage waveform) of the input signal. If no horizontal deflection voltage is applied when a signal is applied to the vertical amplifier, the spot moves up and down so one observes a vertical line. This is usually of no particular use, so normally the horizontal sweep is turned on.

When the sweep rate is set correctly, the waveform of the signal at the vertical input is displayed. Since the graticule also has divisions in the vertical direction, the amplitude of the signal can be measured if the vertical sensitivity control is calibrated in units of volts-per-division of the graticule. Thus, with a sweep rate calibrated in time-per-division and a vertical amplifier calibrated in volts per division, the period and amplitude of the input signal can be measured. Since frequency can be determined by $f = 1/T$, the frequency of a periodic waveform can be determined from the measured period. (Refer to Chapter 1 for a review of signal characteristics.)

The time settings are usually indicated by panel markings as 0.1 microsecond/cm, 1 microsecond/cm, and so on. In *Figure A-2*, the time control has been set to 0.1 microsecond/cm. Since there are 8 squares across the grid, the spot moves across the whole graticule in 0.8 microsecond. Since each square represents 0.1 microsecond, each of the five subdivisions in each square represents 0.02 microsecond. From this display, it is easy to determine that the period of the signal is 0.5 microsecond. Thus, the frequency of the signal is determined to be 2 megahertz. It is also easy to determine that the signal is on (at the logic 1 level) for 0.2 microsecond and at the logic 0 level for the rest of the period. The rise and fall times can be estimated to be on the order of 0.02 microsecond (20 nanoseconds) or less since the low to high and high to low transitions occur in less than one of the 0.2 divisions. To get an accurate measurement, the time/division control would have to be set at 0.01 microsecond/cm. The signal then would appear to be magnified 10 times in the horizontal direction from the display shown in *Figure A-2*.

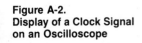

**Figure A-2.
Display of a Clock Signal
on an Oscilloscope**

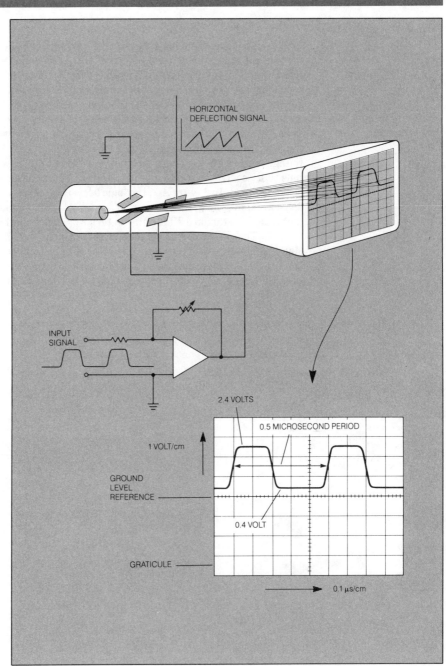

Using The Oscilloscope

The logic 0 and logic 1 levels of the signal can be determined once the vertical scale is known and a ground level (zero volt) is established. This scale is set by a vertical sensitivity control that is calibrated in volts/cm. The ground trace position can be set by connecting the vertical input to ground and moving the trace with the vertical position control to one of the vertical scale lines. In *Figure A-2*, the ground level was set to the center horizontal line. Then, by applying the test signal to the vertical input and the signal ground to the scope ground, the display of the type shown in *Figure A-2* indicates the voltage levels with respect to the known ground level. By setting the vertical sensitivity control to 1 volt/cm, the voltage at each point on the waveform can be determined. In *Figure A-2*, the logic 0 level is about 0.4 volt (two small divisions above the ground level) and the logic 1 level is about 2.4 volts. Thus, the signal is a standard TTL signal in terms of logic 0 and 1 levels.

This discussion has presented only the basic oscilloscope functions. Many oscilloscopes have several other functions and controls that make it a more versatile tool. Since these functions and the operations of the controls vary, the user should consult the manufacturer's manual for this information.

Glossary

Adder: A building block which provides a sum and a carry when adding two numbers.

Address: Usually 8 or 16 bits and is used to access a peripheral device or a location in memory.

ALU: Arithmetic Logic Unit. This is a part of the Central Processor Unit which performs all of the mathematical operations required by a computer program.

Analog: Analog circuitry, also called "linear circuitry," is circuitry that varies certain properties of electricity continuously and smoothly over a certain range.

Assembly Language: Term given to a low-level language used to program the Central Processor Unit.

Asynchronous: Refers to circuitry and operations without common clock signals.

Binary: Base 2 numbering system consisting of 0 and 1. Binary numbers are common to computer operations since most devices function in a two-state mode (1 = on, 0 = off).

Bus: A path inside the computer which is common to many devices (such as the address or data bus). When an address is placed on the address bus, it goes to every device on the bus (such as the memory or a peripheral device) at the same time, but only the device which has the address on the bus will respond.

Capacitor: A component that stores electrical charge.

Chip-Enable Input: A control input that when active permits operation of the integrated circuit and when inactive causes the integrated circuit to be inactive.

Code Converter: A name for a class of combinational building blocks that receive information in one code and transmit the same information in another code. With respect to one particular code (say, the BCD code used for numbers in a calculator), a building block that converts TO this code is called an "encoder" and a building block that converts FROM this code is called a "decoder."

Combinational Logic: Digital circuits whose outputs depend only on present inputs.

Controller: The parts (perhaps a subsystem) of a programmed system that select stored instructions, interpret them, and transmit control signals to the other parts of the system.

CPU: Central Processor Unit. This is the foundation of any processor or microprocessor. The CPU performs all processing, ALU, address generation, and timing and control functions.

Comparator: A building-block that compares two binary numbers. There are several kinds of comparison: telling when the numbers are equal, when one is greater, when one is greater-than-or-equal-to the other, and so forth.

Counter: A special kind of register made up of flip-flop circuits with one input and usually with a parallel output from each flip-flop, which counts pulses arriving at the input and stores the total count in a certain code (usually binary numbers).

CRT Terminal: Cathode-ray-tube terminal. A computer terminal with a screen similar to that of a television receiver, together with a keyboard.

Data: Information.

Data Selector: A combinational building-block that routes data from one of several inputs to a single output, according to control signals. Also called "multiplexer." Two or more such one-bit selectors operating in parallel would be called a "two-bit data selector," etc.

Decoder: A code convertor that converts from system code to another code. e.g. it "recognizes" one or more combinations of input bits and puts out a signal when these combinations are received.

Digital: Information in discrete values or levels, not continuous.

Dynamic Memory: Read/write memory that must be read or written into periodically to maintain the storage of information.

Enable: Term given to a signal which allows a circuit to output data.

Encoder: A code convertor that converts external code to a system code.

Erasable Programmable Read-Only-Memory: An EPROM is a semiconductor memory whose contents can be erased through exposure to ultra-violet light, thus allowing the device to be re-used with a new program. The largest EPROM currently available is 64K.

Flowchart: A diagram which shows the logical flow or sequence of a computer or microprocessor program.

Gate: A "logic gate" is an AND, OR, NOT, NAND, NOR or "Exclusive-OR" gate. In an MOS transistor, the "gate" is the metal plate for holding the charge to control the transistor.

Glitch: Term given to a random signal which causes data or addressing errors.

Hardware: The physical parts of any system.

Hexadecimal: Base 16 numbering system common to most of today's computers. Binary numbers are assembled in groups of four (such as 0101) and have values from 0 to 9 and A to F (for the numbers 10 through 15).

Input/Output Devices (I/O): Computer hardware by which data is entered into a digital system or by which data are recorded for immediate or future use.

Intermittent: A condition that is randomly present and then absent in a system.

Instruction: A step in a microprocessor program.

Integrated Circuit (IC): Broad term given to the solid state components common to today's digital systems. Small-scale IC's (SSI) typically have less than 100 transistors per chip. Medium-scale IC's (MSI) typically have more than 100 transistors per chip. Large-scale IC's (LSI) typically have over 1,000 transistors per chip.

Interface: Term given to the circuitry which performs I/O signal-conditioning between the processor and a peripheral device.

K: Kilo or thousand. Typically used to refer to any number ending in an even thousand (such as 2K, 4K). In memories, due to binary system, K is a reference to multiples of 1,024 (210).

Logic: Refers to the circuitry in digital systems and the functional system upon which the circuitry is based.

Logic Analyzer: An instrument that samples monitored voltages and displays the sequence of signal levels (0 or 1) on a CRT screen.

Logic Clip: A light indicating device used to monitor digital signals on the pins of an integrated circuit.

Logic Probe: A light indicating device used to monitor digital signal points in a system level 1 and 0.

Logic Pulser: A device used to inject digital pulses into a system.

Memory: Portion of a computer where data or instructions are stored until the processor is ready to use them.

Microcomputer: Term given to a system designed for a specific application, or a system which uses a microprocessor as its CPU.

Microprocessor: Name given to an LSI device which contains all of the functions necessary to a processor (CPU, ALU, address generation, and timing and control signals).

Mnemonic: Term given to an abbreviation which defines an assembly language step in a microprocessor program.

MOS Transistor: A class of transistors that operate by means of an electric field produced by a voltage on a metal plate called the "gate." The field acts through a thin layer of oxide insulation upon a semiconductor channel, controlling its depth and therefore controlling current through the channel.

Multiplexer: See "Data Selector."

n,(n): Symbol used to refer to random or unknown numbers.

Node: Term given to a physical connection point in an electronic circuit.

Noise: Any signal that isn't supposed to be there. Electrical noise may be caused by small, irregular sparks when a switch is opened or closed. Or it may be caused by radio waves or by electric or magnetic fields generated by one wire and picked up by another.

Open circuit: An unexpected high resistance path in a circuit.

Oscillation: The term given to a signal which swings above and below a given reference point.

Oscillator: A circuit that generates a repetitive or periodic signal waveform.

Oscilloscope: An instrument used to display plots of electrical signals versus time on a CRT screen.

Output Enable: A signal that when true connects the outputs of a storage cell to the output lines of the device.

Parity: The name given to a series of error-checking bits in transmissions. For even parity if a given data bit sequence has an even number of 1's, a 0 is assigned to its parity bit position. If a data bit sequence has an odd number of 1's, a 1 is assigned to its parity bit position to make it an even number.

Parallel Data Transmission: Two or more bits of a group are said to be transmitted "in parallel" when they are all transmitted at the same time (as in a group of wires) from the same source to the same destination.

Parallel Register: Two or more flip-flops (or dynamic storage units) with a common clock signal, used to store bits transmitted in parallel.

Parity Check: A check to see if the number of ones in an array of binary digits is odd or even.

Period: The time between like points of a repetitive signal.

Phase: The relationship of a signal to a given reference. Electronic signals are commonly considered to be in cycles of 360 degrees, and the clock signal is commonly considered the reference. Phase relationship is generally a comparison of any signal against the common reference.

Positive Logic: In electronic binary digital circuits, this means the decision to let the "higher," more positive of the two voltage levels represent 1 and to let the "lower," more negative level represent 0. Positive logic is always assumed in this book unless "negative logic" is specifically stated.

Processor: The portion of a computer which performs all decision-making, arithmetic, timing, control, and routing functions.

Program Counter: In a programmed system, the parts that provide a method for adding 1 to the address of the current instruction. May consist of the address register and an adder.

PROM (Programmable Read Only Memory): A program in a PROM is electronically "hard-wired", and once the program is inserted in the PROM, it cannot be altered without using a new PROM.

RAM (Random Access Memory): A memory with a number of storage locations, where words may be "written" (stored) or "read" (recovered) in any order at random.

Refresh Cycle: The cycle used in dynamic memory operation to insure reliable storage of information.

Register: Temporary storage for data coming into or out of the processor, or for data which is not completely processed.

Ringing: The tendency of a digital signal to overshoot its desired level. Ringing is usually quickly damped allowing the signal to settle at its proper level.

ROM (Read Only Memory): This is a storage device which is typically programmed at the factory by the manufacturer.

R-S Flip-Flop: Any of several kinds of flip-flops, in which a momentary 1 at the R (reset) input changes the "true" output to 0, and a momentary 1 at the S (set) input changes the "true" output to 1. Varieties include clocking and master-slave features.

Sampling: Term used to describe the random testing of a signal, circuit, or system. With a sufficient number of samples (based upon a theory of linearity), the operational status of a given signal, circuit or system can be determined.

Sequential Logic: One or more flip-flops or dynamic storage units, typically with one or more logic gates, and typically with several inputs and several outputs. The combination of bits at the outputs does not depend only on the combination at the inputs at the present moment, but on past history of a sequence of input combinations over a period of time.

Serial Digital Data: Data transfer technique in which all the data bits are transferred in succession (one after the other) along a single wire.

Short Circuit: A low resistance undesirable connection between two points in a circuit.

Signal: A word used in describing the operation of electric or electronic circuits. It means electrical voltage or current or waves carrying information, or the information itself.

Signal Tracing: A troubleshooting approach in which a known signal is injected at one point in a system and it is monitored at various points in the system to verify signal paths.

State: The "logic state" of a conductor in a digital circuit means its condition as to whether it is carrying a 1 or 0.

Static Memory: Memory that maintains information storage as long as power is on.

Synchronous: Refers to two or more things made to happen in a system at the same time, by means of a common clock signal.

Three-State Buffer: An output circuit that when disabled disconnects output voltages from output lines.

Timing: Term given to describe the clock reference and/or its relationship to other signals.

Transition: Term used to describe the action of a digital signal changing from one level to another.

Index

Answers to Quizzes

Chapter 1
1. c
2. a
3. b
4. b
5. b
6. d
7. d
8. b
9. a
10. a
11. d
12. c
13. c
14. c

Chapter 2
1. c
2. f
3. d
4. c
5. b
6. b
7. a
8. a
9. c
10. d

Chapter 3
1. c
2. c
3. a
4. d
5. b
6. a
7. c
8. c
9. d
10. c
11. a
12. c
13. c
14. b
15. c
16. d
17. c
18. c
19. d
20. e

Chapter 4
1. c
2. b
3. a
4. c
5. c
6. c
7. c
8. a
9. b
10. c

Chapter 5
1. b
2. b
3. a
4. b
5. c
6. a
7. a
8. d
9. b
10. d
11. c
12. c

Chapter 6
1. b
2. c
3. c
4. a
5. b
6. d
7. d
8. b
9. e
10. b
11. b
12. c
13. b
14. e
15. c
16. a
17. d
18. a
19. a
20. a

Chapter 7
1. c
2. b
3. d
4. e
5. d
6. a
7. d
8. a
9. b
10. e

Chapter 8
1. a
2. c
3. b
4. e
5. c
6. a
7. b
8. c
9. c
10. d

Chapter 9
1. c
2. d
3. d
4. a
5. c
6. a
7. c
8. a
9. b
10. c
11. f
12. a
13. d
14. f
15. c
16. d
17. e
18. a
19. a
20. c

Chapter 10
1. b
2. a
3. b
4. a
5. b
6. e
7. c, e
8. d
9. a
10. b, d, e